The Singapore Economy

The Singapore Economy

Gavin Peebles and Peter Wilson

Edward Elgar

Cheltenham, UK • Brookfield, US

Published by
Edward Elgar Publishing Limited
8 Lansdown Place
Cheltenham
Glos GL50 2HU
UK

Edward Elgar Publishing Company
Old Post Road
Brookfield
Vermont 05036
US

British Library Cataloguing in Publication Data
Peebles, Gavin
    Singapore Economy
    I. Title II. Wilson, Peter
    330.95957

Library of Congress Cataloguing in Publication Data
Peebles, Gavin, 1947–
        The Singapore economy / Gavin Peebles, Peter Wilson.
        Includes bibliographical references and index.
        1. Singapore—Economic conditions. 2. Singapore—Economic policy
    I. Wilson, Peter, 1951–   . II. Title.
    HC445.8. P44   1996
    330.95957—dc20   95–36676
                                                                                              CIP

ISBN   1 85898 286 3 (cased)
            1 85898 389 4 (paperback)

Printed in Great Britain at the University Press, Cambridge

Contents

Figures

Tables

Preface and acknowledgments

We have written this book with two groups of readers in mind. We hope it will be of interest to students of macroeconomics in Singapore and the region who want an introductory macroeconomics textbook that uses information from a regional economy to illustrate the theories they are taught. We also hope it will be of some help to those interested in the Singapore economy, its recent macroeconomic history and the nature of economic development in one of Asia's resourceless but resourceful and most dynamic economies.

In writing this book we have made the great commitment of faith of all applied macroeconomists of accepting the published data we have used, from whatever source, as being a reasonable reflection of what has been happening.

We would like to thank Dr G. Chris Rodrigo for providing some working papers relating to Chapter 7 and Dr Tilak Abeysinghe, Dr Ngiam Kee Jin and Mr Christopher Lee for their help in connection with the Econometric Studies Unit econometric model of the Singapore economy which we discuss in Chapter 8. In addition, our thanks go to Ms Chan Chia Lin, an Assistant Director at the Monetary Authority of Singapore (MAS) and to Ms Tan Min Lan, Senior Economist (Forecasting), Economics department, also at the MAS, for the information they kindly provided about the MAS macroeconometric model.

We would also like to thank LOIS for a few sessions of PATS; that is, the National University of Singapore 'Library On-line Information Service' (LOIS) for accessing the 'Public Access Time Series' (PATS) data bank and the Department of Economics and Statistics, National University of Singapore (NUS) for paying for these few short sessions.

We would like to add that any mistakes of fact or interpretation in this book are the results solely of our stupidity and not of any malicious intent.

GAVIN PEEBLES
PETER WILSON

The Singapore dollar

In December 1994 the value of the Singapore dollar (S$) was as follows:

S$1 = US$ 0.683
S$1 = £0.438
S$1 = A$ 0.882
S$1 = HK$ 5.280
S$1 = DM 1.073
S$1 = ¥ 68.34
S$1 = 1.749 Ringgit

1. An introduction to Singapore

In this chapter we introduce the reader to the current economic structure of Singapore and its important institutions and make some comparisons with its nature before its independence in 1965 and with the situation in some other economies.

1.1 SINGAPORE

The Republic of Singapore (hereafter Singapore) is a small independent island, city nation-state situated at the tip of peninsular Malaysia, 86 miles (137 kilometres) north of the equator and surrounded by Malaysia to the north and east and Indonesia to the west and south. A British colony until independence from Britain in 1959, it was for two years (1963–5) part of the Federation of Malaysia, before becoming a fully independent country in 1965, whereupon it joined the Commonwealth and the United Nations. In 1957 the number of people living in Singapore was about 1.45 million and by mid-1994 the total population of Singapore citizens and permanent residents was about 2 930 200 people, of whom 23 per cent were younger than 15 years of age. This population figure does not include non-Singaporeans who are not permanent residents but who live there. In 1990 about 10 per cent of those living in Singapore were foreigners, an increase over the 6 per cent ratio for 1980. This means that there were more than three million people living in Singapore in the early 1990s.

Singapore consists of one large island and a number of smaller ones which are used for such activities as oil refining and storage, but its total land area in 1993 was only about 641 square kilometres, compared to 618 square kilometres in 1981. The land area has increased since 1967 because of reclamation projects. In terms of residents, population density was 4481 persons per square kilometre in 1993, making it one of the most densely populated areas of the world.

Some commentators, perhaps exaggerating slightly, describe the economy's potential for development and the general condition of the island in the 1960s as resembling that of a 'basket case', especially after the withdrawal of British troops. It has been described as then being 'a declining entrepot garrison town of the British' (Lim and associates, 1988, p.60). A recent economic history of Singapore concludes, however, that 'in 1959 Singapore inherited a successful economy and, as Lee Kuan Yew emphasized, a stable and efficiently functioning administration' (Huff, 1994, pp.357–8). There is, perhaps, a tendency for Singaporean writers to paint a picture of an economic wreck in order to stress the difficulties inherited at the time of self-government. Most economic activity revolved around the ports, which served as an entrepot for trade with Malaya, the processing of primary exports, tourism and servicing the military bases. Its small size limits its ability to follow large-scale agricultural production or heavy industry, although government-guided industrialization had started in the 1950s and these policies were continued by the new non-colonial government after June 1959 (ibid., pp.289–90).

In words probably read by more people in more countries than those written by any economist about Singapore, it has been said that:

> After Japan, it is the most aggressively self-modernizing nation state in the Pacific, a model for Malaya, Korea, Taiwan and the Philippines. The huge international airport has turned a slum-ridden relic of British imperialism into a stop-over city with a high-rise business district, a pan-island expressway, and huge estates of regimented housing blocks. (McCrum *et al.*, 1986, p.336)

By 1992 gross national product (GNP) per capita (an indicator of per capita income earned by residents from all sources and to be defined later) was US$15 730, placing it eighteenth highest of the 132 countries for which this indicator is estimated in the World Bank's *World Development Report 1994* (Table 1). Hong Kong was ranked nineteenth in the world with a GNP per capita of US$15 360.[1] However, an alternative set of estimates using purchasing power parity criteria ranked Hong Kong fifth and Singapore sixteenth out of the same 132 countries (*World Development Report 1994*, Table 30). The *World Bank Atlas 1995* ranked Singapore ninth and Hong Kong sixth in the world in terms of GNP per capita on a purchasing power parity basis for 1994 (*The Straits Times*, 14 January 1995, p.33).

Statisticians and pedants can argue about the precise figures but it is clear that on the basis of its income per person Singapore is amongst the top 20 economies in the world, justifying its recent World Bank reclassification as a 'high-income country'. In 1986 it was classified as an 'upper-middle income country', as was Hong Kong.

For those who do not accept that a single income measure should be used for comparison of the level of development or standard of living we can refer to the results derived from using the recently devised Human Development Index (HDI) developed by the United Nations. This is a simple average of three indicators of development designed to capture three key components of human development: life expectancy at birth; adult literacy and years of schooling; and GDP per capita adjusted for diminishing marginal utility of income above a set international poverty line. In terms of the HDI, Singapore was ranked fortieth out of 160 countries in 1992 whereas Hong Kong was ranked twenty-fourth (Smith, 1993, p.95). It seemed that Singapore 'may be more advanced in terms of income than in social development' (ibid., p.97). On careful analysis it turns out that Singapore's low rank is due to a low index for 'educational attainment' and that the measure of this used was inappropriate for as rapidly a changing society as Singapore (ibid., p.105). More controversial is the Human Freedom Index included in the United Nations Human Development Report, which classifies countries according to the presence or absence of 40 basic freedoms. Singapore's rating is 11/40, placing it at the bottom of the 'medium freedom ranking' countries. This quantitative ranking appears to confirm the common view that Singapore is a more restrictive society than other high-income countries such as Japan and Hong Kong, but is not very different from the ranking of other neighbouring countries such as Malaysia, Thailand and the Philippines. Using an index of political rights Barro (1994a, Table 5; 1994b) gives Singapore a mark of 0.33 out of the possible 1.0 for highest freedom (meaning one-third of the way towards 'a full representative democracy'), placing it alongside Peru, South Africa and Hong Kong.[2] On the basis of expected changes in the level of economic development, Barro predicts that Singapore's indicator will rise to 0.61 and Hong Kong's to 0.67 by 2000.

Singapore ranks second, behind Hong Kong, out of 101 countries on the basis of an Index of Economic Freedom compiled by the independent Heritage Foundation (Holmes, 1994; *The Economist*, 11 February 1995, p.104). This index is based on rankings for ten criteria of economic freedom which include such things as trade policy, the extent of taxation, monetary policy, the nature of property rights, the amount of output bought by the government, the size of the black market and the extent of wage and price controls.[3]

This small city-nation is now probably the second busiest port in the world, and probably the world's most computerized, has a foreign exchange market with the world's fourth largest turnover, after London, New York and Tokyo, boasts of having the best airport in the world, which received 9.42 million passenger arrivals in 1993 (6.4 million of whom were tourists), had gross official international reserves towards the end of 1994 of about US$57 billion (21 per cent higher than a year earlier and equal to about 5.7 months of imports,[4] and providing the highest per capita figure in the world), a life expectancy at birth of 75 years and an adult literacy rate of about 88 per cent (*World Development Report 1994, passim*; Smith, 1993, p.102) and has recently achieved the world's highest proportion of share owners in the population.

This level of per capita output and the other indicators of development have been achieved through very high output growth rates. Over the period 1960–92 Singapore's per capita GNP grew about 6.3 per cent a year, which implies a doubling of this variable almost every 12 years. Hong Kong's grew about 6.2 per cent a year, when the average for the industrialized/high income countries was about 3.0 per cent a year. On the basis of this high growth rate, Singapore has been included with Hong Kong, Taiwan and South Korea as one of the 'four (little) tigers', 'four dragons', 'the gang of four' (depending on whom you read) or, more formally, as one of the 'newly industrialized countries' (NICs) or 'economies' (NIEs) of Asia by manifesting along with them this ability to achieve 'hyper-growth' (Chen, 1979) and illustrating the 'Asian miracle' of development.

1.2   STRUCTURE OF PRODUCTION

Singapore's size precludes large-scale agriculture and industry. In the years since independence, during which the ruling People's Action Party (PAP, which has formed the government since 1959) embarked on a development strategy relying on foreign direct investment and subsequently export-oriented policies and domestic resource mobilization for the creation of an efficient and modern infrastructure that would be conducive to foreign direct investment, there have been significant changes in the structure of the country's production. These changes differentiate it from the usual pattern of development in which agriculture declines in relative importance and industry and services increase in importance. In the early post-war years services dominated the Singapore economy, falling in relative importance as industrialization took place. Even after 1980 services continued to decline as a proportion of output as industry continued to occupy a larger and larger share of production. Table 1.1 shows the structure of production in a number of countries. We have chosen these countries for comparison to highlight the distinctive features of the Singapore economy. Included are Hong Kong, for reasons explained in the first note to this chapter; the neighbouring countries of the Association of South-east Asian Nations (ASEAN), with the exception of Brunei owing to a lack of comparative data, of which Singapore was a founder member in 1967; Japan as the largest market economy in Asia; and some English-speaking countries with which the reader might be familiar and which are usually the empirical base for many macro-economics textbooks.

The data show that, compared to 1960, Singapore has almost entirely eliminated agriculture, significantly increased its industry, especially its manufacturing industry, and reduced the share of output that comes from the services sector, although this share remains high compared with that of the more agricultural ASEAN economies. This reverses the usual trend seen during development when the services share rises. This is because in 1960 Singapore's services, in the form of the port and tourism, were already a dominant part of the economy. Its manufacturing sector share, at 28 per cent of GDP in 1992, is one of the highest in the world. Generally only the relatively rich of the former republics of the Soviet Union have higher shares. Singapore's manufacturing share exceeds that of Japan (26 per cent) and is only equalled by Thailand in ASEAN. Singapore's manufacturing sector is dominated by machinery and transport equipment: 52 per cent of total manufacturing value added in 1991, compared to 41 per cent in Germany, 40 per cent in Japan, 35 per cent in Malaysia and 31 per cent in Israel and the USA. Singapore now neither manufactures nor assembles cars as this industry disappeared in the late 1970s when the 'Second Industrial Revolution' was launched (see below). Textiles constitute only 3 per cent of Singapore's manufacturing, compared with 36 per cent for Hong Kong, and chemicals are 10 per cent in Singapore compared to Hong Kong's 2 per cent (*Word Development Report 1994*, Table 6).

Table 1.1   Structure of production (percentage of GDP): some comparisons

	Agriculture	Industry	(Manufacturing)	Services
Singapore				
1960	4	18	(12)	78
1992	0	38	(28)	62
Hong Kong	0	23	(16)	77
Indonesia	19	40	(21)	40
Malaysia				
Philippines	22	33	(24)	45
Thailand	12	39	(28)	49
Japan	2	42	(26)	56
USA	2	26	(19)	72
UK	2	33	(22)	66
Australia	3	30	(15)	67

Sources: *World Development Report 1981* and *1994*, Table 3. USA: calculated from *Survey of Current Business*, July 1993, p.32. UK: calculated from *United Kingdom National Accounts 1993*, pp. 24–5.

Let us look at this structure in more detail for 1993 and examine the structure of total employment as well. Table 1.2 shows what Singapore produces and where its 1 592 000 or so employed workforce was employed. It can be seen that in terms of their share of GDP the two sectors manufacturing, and financial and business services contribute almost equal amounts with commerce and transport and communications being important sectors also. These four activities accounted for 86 per cent of GDP in that year. Commerce and transport support the important tourist industry and transport obviously developed because of the export-oriented strategy which, in Singapore's case, requires a high level of imports. More on this shortly. Financial and business services cover the banking and insurance industries, both related to a large volume of trade and a high rate of saving and investment. In terms of employment, manufacturing activity employed 27 per cent of employed people in 1993 and all services (commerce, transport and communications, financial, business and other services) employed 65.8 per cent of people who were working: just over one million people. Important manufacturing activities are petroleum refining, paints, pharmaceuticals and other chemical products, printing and publishing, non-electrical machinery and fabricated metal products and electronics. Factories in Singapore produce about 40 per cent of the entire world supply of disk drives for computers, for example. The single industry known as 'electronic products and components' (Industrial code 384) has grown from producing 19 per cent of total manufacturing value added in 1983 and employing 24 per cent of the manufacturing workforce to producing 41 per cent of total manufacturing valued added and employing 34 per cent of the manufacturing workforce in 1993.

Table 1.2   Structure of output and employment (per cent)

	GDP	Employment
Agriculture and fishing	0.02	0.003
Quarrying	0.0005	—
Manufacturing	27.5	27.0
Utilities	1.7	0.05
Construction	7.4	6.4
Commerce	17.8	22.8
Transport and communications	12.1	10.5
Financial and business services	28.8	10.9
Other services	9.6	21.6
Less imputed bank service charges	6.2	
Add import duties	0.09	

Source: Calculated from *Yearbook of Statistics Singapore 1993*, Table 4.3 and Table 3.3.

1.3   COMPOSITION OF OUTPUT AND AND SOME COMPARISONS

We have seen which sectors of the economy produce Singapore's output. What use is made of these products in terms of who buys them? Recall basic National Income accounting, where the demand for output consists of:

C: private consumption;
G: government consumption;
I: investment, in both fixed capital and the accumulation of inventories;
X: exports.

The only two sources of supply for any economy are:

GDP: gross domestic product; and
M: imports.

So
$$C + I + G + X = GDP + M$$

or

$$GDP = C + I + G + (X - M)$$

where the term in brackets can be called net exports and labelled NX.

How does Singapore's structure of demand differ from that found in our sample of countries? Table 1.3 shows the composition of GDP according to these categories. A number of contrasts stand out clearly. In 1960 total consumption (private and government) at 103 per cent exceeded GDP and only 11 per cent of GDP was invested. This was made possible by an excess of imports over exports of 14 per cent of GDP, implying a capital account surplus that means there was borrowing from abroad to finance C, I and G. Checking the data for net borrowing from abroad in 1960 shows that it was S$297 million, 13.8 per cent of that year's GDP.

By 1992 Singapore had reduced total consumption $(C + G)$ to only 53 per cent of GDP, the lowest ratio in the world (Peebles, 1993a, p.26) and increased investment to 41 per cent of GDP, the highest in the world, although almost matched by Thailand at 40 per cent. However, Singapore's investment ratio has been consistently high at over 40 per cent since the early 1970s. Any macro-economic study of Singapore must show how it was possible to restrict consumption to such a low proportion of output and to elevate investment, and what consequences this has for the economy. The contrast with Hong Kong is instructive. Singapore and Hong Kong have similar long-run growth rates, yet Singapore's investment share is much larger and has been increased, whereas Hong Kong's share has not been increased significantly (Peebles, 1988, pp.61–3). This has led to interesting speculation about the efficiency of Singapore's investment (Young, 1992), an issue we will examine in Chapter 7. The increase in the investment ratio in Singapore has been achieved at the same time as a surplus of exports over imports of 6 per cent of GDP in 1992 according to the source used for these international comparisons. This means that it is domestic saving that has financed this huge amount of investment, not international borrowing. Singapore data suggest a lower ratio for *NX* of about 3 per cent (*Economic Survey of Singapore: First Quarter 1994*, Table A1.2). Of course net exports can fluctuate significantly from year to year for any country. In Singapore, in 1991, total consumption ($C + G$) was 54 per cent of GDP, investment was 37 per cent and net exports were about 9 per cent of GDP (*Yearbook of Statistics Singapore 1991*, p.87).

Table 1.3   Composition of GDP (per cent) and international comparisons

	C	I	G	NX
Singapore				
1960	95	11	8	−14
1992	43	41	10	6
Hong Kong	61	29	9	2
Indonesia	53	35	10	3
Malaysia	52	34	13	1
Philippines	72	23	10	−5
Thailand	55	40	10	−5
Japan	57	31	9	2
USA	67	16	18	−1
UK	64	15	22	−2
Australia	62	20	19	−1

Note: Figures have been rounded.

Sources: *World Development Report 1981* and *1994*, Tables 5 and 9.

The total volume of Singapore's trade is very large compared to its annual production. In 1993 the total volume of Singapore's exports of goods and services was about 1.85 times its GDP in that year (calculated from *Economic Survey of Singapore 1993*, pp.106,129). Hong Kong is the only other economy in the world where exports exceed annual production (Peebles, 1993b). Of course such a volume of exports requires a huge volume of imports. In Singapore's case imports of goods and services were about 1.8 times annual production in 1993 (ibid.). Singapore shares with Hong Kong a history of being an entrepot and part of its trade is still of that nature. This means that statisticians distinguish between domestic exports and re-exports for these economies. In Singapore domestic exports are defined as: exports of Singapore origin, consisting of primary commodities grown or produced in Singapore and 'goods which have been transformed, that is, manufactured, assembled or processed in Singapore including those with imported materials or parts' (*Yearbook of Statistics Singapore 1991*, p.173). Re-exports are 'all goods which are exported in the same form as they have been imported without transformation. Re-packing, splitting into lots, sorting or grading, marking, *etc.* are not considered as undergoing the process of transformation' (ibid.). Singapore still earns income from handling re-exports in terms of the income generated in the charges for unloading the goods, repackaging and relabelling them and then transporting them to the ports or airport from which they are then exported. If the goods are insured or financed in Singapore then, of course, this generates income for this sector of the economy. The entrepot trade is classified as part of the commerce sector in Singapore's national accounts (with a 31 per cent weighting) along with domestic trade (50 per cent weighting) and restaurants and hotels (19 per cent weighting) (*Economic Survey of Singapore: First Quarter 1994*, p.26).

In 1993, out of total exports of about S$119 billion, S$75 billion, or 63 per cent, were domestic exports and S$44 billion, or 37 per cent, were re-exports. Out of total domestic exports oil (all of which is imported) made up 19 per cent. The other important categories of domestic exports are electrical machinery and generators (16 per cent of domestic exports), office machinery (29 per cent), telecommunications apparatus (9 per cent), chemicals and chemical products (6 per cent), manufactured goods (3.2 per cent), miscellaneous manufactured articles (7 per cent) and food, beverages and tobacco (2 per cent) (*Economic Survey of Singapore: First Quarter 1994*, Table A4.3). We discuss Singapore's exports in more detail in Chapter 6.

Table 1.4 shows Singapore's major merchandise export markets and the sources of its imports, and the changes since 1960. The main markets for Singapore's total exports in 1993 were the USA, Japan, Malaysia and Hong Kong. Compared to the situation in 1960, the USA is a much more significant export market and Malaysia a less important one, but countries in the region, such as Japan, Hong Kong and Thailand have become more important. The OECD countries and the Asian NICs have become more important export markets, whereas ASEAN has declined in relative importance. Japan is Singapore's most important source of imports, with Malaysia and the USA also being important. For imports, OECD countries and the Asian NICs have also become more important and ASEAN less important. We examine these changes in Chapter 6.

Singapore's main imports are machinery and transport equipment (52 per cent of imports), manufactured goods (12 per cent), miscellaneous manufactured articles (10 per cent), chemical and chemical products (7 per cent), mineral fuels and bunkers (11 per cent) and food, beverages and tobacco (5 per cent) (*Economic Survey of Singapore: First Quarter 1994*, Table A4.2). This pattern reflects Singapore's comparative advantage and structure of output: hardly any agricultural production, so imports of food are necessary, its role as a refiner of imported crude oil and as a manufacturer of electronic products and machinery such as disc drives, integrated circuits, computer parts, microcomputers and electronic parts that are either finished products or are re-exported for assembly elsewhere in the region.

Table 1.4   Singapore's major export markets and sources of imports, 1960 and 1993

| | Percentage of total | | | |
| | EXPORTS | | IMPORTS | |
	1960	1993	1960	1993
OECD	36.1	43.7	28.1	52.2
USA	7.0	20.3	3.8	16.2
Japan	4.5	7.5	7.3	21.9
Germany	2.3	4.0	1.8	3.1
Netherlands	1.7	2.6	1.4	0.9
UK	8.2	3.0	8.9	2.6
Others	12.4	6.3	4.9	7.5
ASEAN	37.7	24.2	54.6	23.9
Malaysia	28.8	14.2	26.4	16.5
Indonesia	3.5	1.5	24.5	2.4
Thailand	3.1	5.7	3.6	4.1
Philippines	1.7	1.9	0.1	0.6
Brunei	0.6	0.9	n.a.	0.3
ASIAN NICs	2.6	15.4	2.7	10.4
Hong Kong	1.7	8.7	2.2	3.2
South Korea	0.7	2.8	0	3.2
Taiwan	0.2	3.9	0.5	4.0
CHINA	2.5	2.6	3.4	2.8
Others	21.1	14.1	11.2	10.7

Note: the data for Indonesia are from the IMF *Direction of Trade Statistics June 1994* and *Singapore Trade Division Annual Report 1961–66*, Appendix II.

Source: calculated from *Yearbook of Statistics Singapore*, various years.

When assessing the significance of trade for Singapore's incomes we showed net exports (*NX*) as a proportion of output (*GDP*). These are both value-added concepts and so can be compared in this way. We have, as it were, treated all imports as an intermediate input into the production of all exports. When we look at individual categories of exports we should do this as well. Final sales figures do not tell us how much those exports contributed to Singapore's income and output. Consider two categories of exports, A and B, which both record total sales of $100 million a year. Category A might be the export of some commodity produced in Singapore that requires a very high import content of, say, $80 million, whereas B requires only $30 million of imported inputs. Ignoring other inputs, we can see that export category B adds more to incomes in Singapore than does category A. Although their exports sales figures are the same, they definitely do not make the same contribution to Singapore's output and incomes. This means that, when we examine the importance of different export activities for the Singapore economy, we cannot just look at the final sales figures but will have to make an adjustment that 'takes out' the import content. We will look at this issue in Chapter 6.

Singapore's overall balance of payments has nearly always been in surplus. We explain how this is possible and what it means for the economy in Chapters 4, 5 and 6. Its merchandise trade balance (that is trade in goods) is consistently in deficit but has usually been more than offset by a surplus in services in the 1980s so that, since 1988, the current account has been in surplus. This means that, together with a capital account surplus, the overall balance of payments is in surplus.

1.4   GDP, GNP, NFIA AND IGNP

Singaporean English and life are as liberally peppered with acronyms and abbreviations as its fried rice is with chillies and its *congee* with pepper. Economic writing has a similar taste and we must tackle the definition of these variables, their relationships and why Singapore uses a particular National Income accounting concept.

The Gross Domestic Product (GDP) of a country is the total value of final goods and services produced within that country in a particular period, whoever does the producing and thus has a right to the income corresponding to that production. Here the word 'domestic' means within the domestic territory of the country. In any country part of its output will be produced by foreigners or by factors of production owned by foreigners. Similarly many citizens of a country can earn income from factors of production they own (including their own labour) that operate outside the boundaries of that country. So, for example, a Singaporean company may own a hotel in Sydney. The profits generated from that asset are part of Singapore's national product but not part of its domestic production. Conversely the profits of an American multinational corporation

(MNC) in Singapore are part of Singapore's domestic product but not part of its national product as those profits are likely to be paid to the owners, the share-holders, in the USA. There are flows of factor incomes into and out of any country. The net amount is called 'net factor income from abroad' (NFIA). This amount must be added to GDP to obtain gross national product (GNP). That is:

$$GNP = GDP + NFIA$$

where *NFIA* can be positive or negative. Table 1.5 shows the relationship between GDP and GNP in Singapore for selected years. The successive *Yearbooks* often revise data for up to the previous four years, so figures given in earlier official publications will differ from those in the latest and those in future publications will differ from the figures here.

In order to keep these absolute dollar amounts in perspective, the reader can note that in 1993 Singapore's GDP was S$89 billion (a figure that is bound to be revised, probably upwards, so round it up to 90 billion). This is approximately US$55 billion at official exchange rates, which is about 0.9 per cent of the USA's GDP, 20 per cent of Australia's, 130 per cent of New Zealand's in 1993 and 5 per cent of the UK's in 1992 (calculated from *International Financial Statistics*, April 1994). Crude as these comparisons are, they put into perspective the relative size of Singapore's annual production and provide a benchmark for gauging the dimensions of expenditures or assets expressed in Singapore dollars. For example, Singapore's official foreign reserves in 1993 were valued at S$78 billion. Its GDP was, remember, S$90 billion in 1993.

Table 1.5   GDP, GNP and NFIA, selected years (in billions of dollars)

	1960	1970	1981	1990	1991	1992	1993^p
GDP at current market prices	2.15	5.80	29.34	66.18	73.04	79.08	89.00
NFIA	0.04	0.06	−1.15	0.52	0.90	1.37	1.23
GNP at current market prices	2.19	5.86	28.19	66.70	73.94	80.46	90.23

Note: Figures have been rounded; ^{p} means preliminary.

Sources: *Economic Survey of Singapore 1992*, Table A1.8; *Yearbook of Statistics Singapore 1991*, Table 4.2; *Yearbook of Statistics Singapore 1993*, Table 4.2.

In recent years Singapore's GNP has exceeded GDP by about 1.3 per cent on average. This is not a particularly high excess when compared with Switzer-land's, where GNP exceeds GDP by about 5 per cent, Kuwait with a usual excess of about 30 per cent, Luxembourg with 35 per cent and Lesotho with a 75 per cent excess (Peebles 1993b). However, GNP has not always exceeded GDP in Singapore. The changes in the sign and amount of NFIA for Singapore are interesting. It is generally true that, if you take a large sample of countries and identify the sign of NFIA for the latest three years or so, NFIA has always been of that sign. This is true for 95 per cent of a sample of 84 countries for which there were long series of NFIA (ibid., 1993b). In Singapore, however, NFIA has changed in sign quite often, in the following way:

1968–1970	NFIA was positive, so GNP > GDP
1971–1983	NFIA was negative, so GNP < GDP
1984–1986	NFIA was positive, so GNP > GDP
1987–1988	NFIA was negative, so GNP < GDP
1989–1993	NFIA was positive, so GNP > GDP

Current government policy is to encourage local businessmen to undertake more economic activity outside Singapore because of its limited size and scope for further physical expansion. This is the policy of growing a 'second wing' for the economy. Recent political and economic changes in the region have, it is thought, given Singaporean firms great opportunities to invest in China, Laos, Cambodia, Myanmar and Vietnam, as they move away from relying on planning and autarky to entering the world trading system and accepting foreign investment, and in India. These activities will boost Singapore's future NFIA and its level of GNP compared with GDP and possibly produce a GNP growth rate higher than that of GDP. Hence future evaluations of Singapore's level of, and growth in, income should use GNP figures rather than GDP figures, a point made by business journalists in Singapore. Interestingly this is the opposite to the trend in the USA, where official emphasis has switched from using GNP figures to GDP figures as the latter more accurately reflect what is happening within the country and are more closely correlated with such things as employment and unemployment.

NFIA obviously has two components: the inflow of factor incomes from Singapore's investments and workers working abroad and the outflow of factor incomes. In assessing the incomes of Singaporeans the statisticians calculate a concept called Indigenous GNP (IGNP). They must first deduct from GDP that part which is owned by non-Singaporeans. This is the wages and salaries of foreign workers working in Singapore plus the profits of foreign firms operating there. This provides an estimate of the value of output produced by Singaporeans in Singapore. They then add the total inflow of factor incomes from abroad to obtain the incomes of Singaporeans from both within and without Singapore, hence indigenous GNP. As Table 1.6 shows, in 1993 about 33.1 per cent of Singapore's GDP was produced by, and due to, foreign workers or the owners of foreign

capital located in Singapore, making the indigenous GDP equal to 67 per cent
of total domestic production. The total factor earnings of Singaporeans from
abroad contributed an amount equal to about 13 per cent of total GDP. These
factor earnings consist of the earnings of Singapore's residents who are working
outside Singapore for less than a year, other privately owned factor incomes in
the form of dividends and interest payments from abroad plus the earnings of
government enterprises and statutory boards, as well as the interest earned on
the government's holdings of foreign reserves. This gave an indigenous GNP
of S$71.47 billion in 1993, equal to 80 per cent of GDP in that year. In other
words, the incomes due to Singaporeans were only 80 per cent of the value of
output produced in Singapore. This IGNP constituted an average of S$24 871
per person in 1993, equal to about US$15 392 at the average exchange rate of
that year (S$1.6158 = US$1). Over the period 1983–93 real IGNP per capita
(deflated by the consumer price index – CPI) grew about 5.8 per cent per year
and in the years 1991, 1992 and 1993 it grew by 4.0, 3.3 and 6.3 per cent, respectively. We return to this evidence in Chapter 9.

Table 1.6   GDP and IGNP, selected years (in billions of dollars)

	1981	1991	1992	1993[p]
GDP	29.34	73.04	79.08	89.01
minus				
Share of resident foreigners & resident foreign companies in GDP	8.16	23.94	25.96	29.46
equals				
IGDP	21.18	49.10	53.13	59.55
plus				
Factor receipts of Singaporeans from rest of the world	1.73	10.63	11.24	11.92
equals				
IGNP	22.90	59.73	64.36	71.47
IGNP per capita (current dollars)	9 854	21 620	22 839	24 871

Note: Figures have been rounded; [p] means preliminary.

Sources: *Yearbook of Statistics Singapore 1991*, Table 4.1; *Yearbook of Statistics Singapore 1993*,
Table 4.1.

1.5 LABOUR AND CAPITAL

Of Singapore's 1.64 million labour force in 1993, 60 per cent were male and 40 per cent were female. Of the 43 700 people unemployed in that year (2.7 per cent of the labour force) 58 per cent were male and 42 per cent females. The participation rate of males was 79 per cent and for females it was 51 per cent. In 1990 about 10 per cent of people living in Singapore were foreigners. This constitutes about 300 000 people. Not all of them would be workers as some would be non-working dependants of foreigners living in Singapore. In 1970 about 12 per cent of the labour force was non-Singaporean and in 1985 the ratio was 9 per cent (Lim and associates, 1988, p.143). In addition to resident foreign workers there are thousands of daily commuters from Malaysia. Commuting is made easy by the existence of a causeway link at the north of the island to Johor Baru state. Many factory workers commute by motorcycle and others by car or by a regular bus service. The Singapore government plans to build a second link that will connect peninsular Malaysia more directly with the port and factory districts of Tuas and Jurong in the west of the island. It has been estimated that by 1994 there were about 300 000 foreign workers employed in the Singapore economy (*The Straits Times*, 4 March 1995, p.34) but there are no clear official data on their employment by sector or occupation.

Among the workforce, 235 723 workers (about 14 per cent) are members of the 82 employee unions and there are 1045 members of three employer unions. The trade unions constitute the National Trade Union Congress (NTUC) which cooperates closely with the government in securing stable labour market conditions for both local and foreign employers. The Secretary-General of the NTUC is a government minister (without portfolio) and generally explains and defends government policies to his members. As has been remarked:

> The government has been able to consolidate its influence in the union movement, as represented by the NTUC. The main role of the latter is to cooperate with the government in implementing necessary policy changes and to concentrate on social, educational and recreational programmes for workers. (Lim and associates, 1988, p.443)

In return for this compliance the government has provided high levels of employment and allows the NTUC to operate commercial ventures organized as cooperatives, such as a chain of supermarkets, the biggest taxi company and an insurance company. This form of industrial relations has ensured flexibility of wages. The National Wages Council (NWC, established in 1972) exists to set non-mandatory guidelines on wage changes for both the unionized and non-unionized sectors of the economy. Wages policy is thus overseen by a triad of the government, the NWC and the NTUC. The public sector and unionized sectors follow the guidelines, as do other sectors of the economy as, it is claimed, it is in their interest to do so (Lim and associates, 1988 pp.203–4). Flexibility has also meant wage reductions in difficult times, such as in 1986 after the recession of 1985.

One factor influencing the labour market is the fact that Singapore maintains a regular army and a reserve force. The defence force (Singapore Armed Forces: SAF) consists of a standing force of about 50 000 regulars and full-time national servicemen (NSmen). National Service (NS), either in the military, in the police or the fire brigade, is compulsory for two years or for two-and-a-half years for all adult males. Singapore maintains a large reservist army of NSmen which totals about 250 000 which, with the standing force, constitutes what the government calls the 'citizens' armed force of about 300 000 regulars' (*Singapore 1994*, p.84). These NSmen 'are recalled regularly for in-camp training of up to 40 days a year' (ibid.). This means that young adults are assured of two years' training during which they can learn skills, such as driving, operating complicated machinery and obeying orders, which they might otherwise not be able to obtain, before entering the labour force. It also means that employers must expect the reservists on their staff to take time off to attend training.

The government has argued that reducing the length of national service would be bad for economic growth as, in the view of Brigadier-General (NS) Lee Hsien Loong, a 'shorter period of NS may erode confidence in Singapore and affect economic growth. This is because the reduced security resulting from this could cause the manufacturing and financial sectors to shrink as investors turn elsewhere' (Tremewan, 1994, pp.222–3).

National Service allows the government to identify future leaders and select them to receive armed forces scholarships so that they can attend good foreign universities. This is a standard way of selecting the future elite of ministers and several current government ministers are NSmen, usually at the level of brigadier-general or rear admiral. The ruling PAP also recruits members from academia and the professions and ensures that they monopolize the loyalties of those they claim to be the best of their generation. The PAP also does its best to ensure that young talented people are discouraged from joining opposition political parties.

Many workers in Singapore receive their wages in three forms: a basic wage, a bonus and deferred wages represented by their contributions to the Central Provident Fund (CPF). This latter organization is of great importance in the Singaporean system and should be outlined here. The CPF was established under the colonial administration on 1 July 1955 as a means of funding workers' pensions. The fund was based on compulsory employer and employee contributions of 5 per cent each in 1955. By 1993 the fund had 1 107 100 active contributors, 2 456 400 members and 95 831 contributing employers. It is binding for employees in most sectors of the economy, including non-exempted expatriate workers, and is open for self-employed people to join. Contributions are credited with an interest rate based on the simple average of the one-year deposits and savings rates of the four big local banks with a guaranteed minimum of 2.5 per cent per annum if that average should be less than this, as it was during early 1994. Over the years the rate of contributions has been varied, both because of rising income levels, and demographic changes and as part of macro-economic policy. By July 1994 the long-proclaimed objective of setting the contribution rates at 20 per cent for both employers and employees was established. Members of the fund are also encouraged to make additional contributions. As an illustration of the use of the contribution rate we can point out that in July 1985 the rate was 25 per cent for both employer and employee. In April 1986, as one of the policies responding to the recession of 1985, the employer's contribution was reduced to 10 per cent and the employee's remained at 25 per cent. The purpose was to reduce employers' labour costs, which is another way of saying increasing profits.

Members' contributions are paid into three accounts: the ordinary account, a special account and a medisave account. The purpose of the fund was to allow retired members to withdraw their balances at the retirement age of 55. It has now been decided that the retirement age will be raised to 60 years and then to 67 years by the year 2003. In addition, there have been liberalizations of the scheme allowing members to withdraw funds for the purchase of private or government housing in Singapore (from 1968), purchase of non-residential property such as shops, and the purchase of approved shares and unit trusts. This latter policy was extended in 1993. The fund is credited with allowing 87 per cent of Singaporean households to live in government-built Housing and Development Board flats and enabling 88 per cent of the population to own their own homes.[5]

The recent relaxation through allowing withdrawals for share purchase is part of the government's policy of encouraging widespread individual shareholding and providing funds for the purchase of shares in the companies the government plans to privatize. In October 1993 there was a big public issue of shares by Singapore Telecom which doubled the capitalization of the stock market and turned Singapore into the country with the highest proportion of citizens owning equities.[6] Furthermore, ownership of unit trusts boomed in 1993 and several new unit trusts were established. There were further liberalizations to the scheme in late 1994 which, together with changes in the investment and financing policies of government-linked companies (GLCs) and statutory boards, came to be known as Singapore's 'Big Bang'. Although in early 1994 Prime Minister Goh Chok Tong had repeated the government's view that it would be risky to allow CPF members to use their funds for investment outside Singapore, in September 1994 the Senior Minister, Lee Kuan Yew, took the opportunity offered by his speech at the tenth anniversary celebration of the Singapore International Monetary Exchange Ltd (SIMEX) to announce further liberalizations of the scheme. CPF fund holders will be allowed to withdraw funds for investment in foreign stocks traded in Singapore and then in selected local stock markets such as Hong Kong and Malaysia and others. By 1999 they will be allowed to use their funds for purchases on international markets outside the region. This was estimated to imply a potential sum of S$40 billion for share purchases through private brokers located in Singapore. (Furthermore, GLCs and statutory boards were told that they should be more active in raising funds on the local capital market rather than relying on the cosy arrangement allowing them to borrow from such public sector organizations as the Post Office Savings Bank (POSBank). They were also told to be more adventurous with their large sums of liquid assets and that, instead of merely holding them as time deposits with banks, they should put them under the management of local fund managers. This was thought to imply a further S$40 billion of funds for active management.

These liberalizations have been seen as a response to competition from other financial centres in the region and by freeing such large sums it is hoped to stimulate the local financial sector and, in the eyes of some observers, to compete fund managers away from Hong Kong. In February 1995 the Minister of Finance, Dr Richard Hu, announced that the Government of Singapore Investment Corporation (GIC) would make its investments through fund managers located in Singapore rather than through their offices in such places as New York or Tokyo. The announced purpose was to build up the fund management industry in Singapore (*The Straits Times*, 16 February 1995, p.1).

The CPF holds more than 90 per cent of its assets in government securities, thus providing the government with huge sums for it to channel to its statutory boards for development purposes, mainly in the form of public infrastructure projects such as Changi airport and public housing, both a feature of modern Singapore remarked on above, and to acquire overseas assets. In 1993 contributions to the fund totalled S$10.43 billion (about 12 per cent of that year's GDP) and withdrawals were S$10.94 billion. This was the first time withdrawals exceeded deposits in a given year and was due to higher withdrawals through the share purchase scheme. However, interest earned on assets that year covered this shortfall. In 1992, in contrast, S$9 billion were contributed and only S$5 billion were withdrawn. By 1993 outstanding balances due to members were about S$52 billion, equal to about 58 per cent of that year's GDP.

The CPF scheme has unquestionably allowed Singapore to achieve such a high investment ratio. The ratio of investment to GDP was increased to nearly 40 per cent by the early 1970s and has remained at about that ratio ever since. By July 1972 the total CPF rate was 24 per cent, by July 1973 it was 26 per cent and by July 1974 it was 30 per cent. It was increased every year after 1977, to reach 50 per cent in July 1984. In more recent years the scheme has not been without its critics. The main criticisms in the mid-1980s were that CPF rates were too high for the purpose of providing pensions for members, that the system might be a disincentive for the supply of labour for people over 55 years of age, that the scheme diverted funds from private sector borrowers and, as the scheme is a system of forced saving, it reduced both private saving and individual freedom in deciding what to do with one's own income (Lim and associates, 1988, pp.222–35). This latter criticism may have been responsible for the liberalizations of the 1990s allowing members to withdraw funds for their own limited investment purposes.

So far we have looked at indicators of average levels of income. Let us now look at the distribution of income. It is notoriously difficult, because of data problems and conceptual issues, to present an overall view of the way a country's income is distributed to the owners of different factors or to the suppliers of different skills, by different professions for example, at a given time or over time. One aspect we can get a general feel for is the distribution of income either in the form of labour income (compensation of employees) or as the residual which is the return to non-labour factors in the form of profits, interest payments and rent. Toh and Low (1994, p.9) have made estimates of the share of labour incomes in total income using the input–output tables for a number of years and they are as follows (in per cent of total income):

1973	40.08
1978	42.86
1983	49.47
1988	44.07

Tsao (1986, p.21) estimated the labour share for 1966 as 54.3 per cent and that for 1972 as only 35.0 per cent. We might conjecture that the rise in the labour share from 1973 to 1983, also shown in Tsao's estimates, was the result of the high wages policy of the late 1970s and that the subsequent decline was due to the abandonment of this policy (see below). As Toh and Low (1994, p.9) note, the labour share is lower than that found in other economies. In Hong Kong, for example, the compensation of employees was 60 per cent of total income in 1975 and 50 per cent in 1980 (*Estimates of Gross Domestic Product 1966 to 1983*, p.70). In the USA this share is about 60 per cent (Stiglitz, 1993, p.664) and was over 70 per cent in the United Kingdom in the early 1980s (Prest and Coppock, 1984, p.4).

Table 1.7 presents another way of looking at the distribution of income, where household income has been allocated to various groups of the population ranked by income level. The data are not strictly comparable but they should indicate whether Singapore stands out from the other countries in any clearly remarkable way.[7] They show the percentage of total income received by various quintiles (fifths) of households ranked by income level. So, for example, it shows that the poorest fifth of households in Singapore received 5.1 per cent of total incomes (the data are for 1982–3), compared with 5.4 per cent in Hong Kong and 8.7 per cent in Indonesia. At the lower end of the scale Singapore's poorest 20 per cent received slightly more than in the developed industrial economies, except Japan. At the top end Singapore's top 20 per cent received nearly 49 per cent of all income, compared to 47 per cent in Hong Kong and 44 per cent in the United Kingdom. Malaysia and Thailand show higher figures than Singapore. In terms of the incomes of the richest 10 per cent, Singapore's ratio of incomes, at 33.5 per cent, is second only to that of Malaysia.

Table 1.7   Household income distribution, selected countries

	Percentage of income or consumption by households					
	Lowest	Second	Third quintile	Fourth	Highest	Highest 10%
Singapore	5.1	9.9	14.6	21.4	48.9	33.5
Hong Kong	5.4	10.8	15.2	21.6	47.0	31.3
Indonesia	8.7	12.1	15.9	21.1	42.3	27.9
Malaysia	4.6	8.3	13.0	20.4	53.7	37.9
Philippines	6.5	10.1	14.4	21.2	47.8	32.1
Thailand	6.1	9.4	13.5	20.3	50.7	21.6
Japan	8.7	13.2	17.5	23.1	37.5	22.4
USA	4.7	11.0	17.4	25.0	41.9	25.0
UK	4.6	10.0	16.8	24.3	44.3	27.8
Australia	4.4	11.1	17.5	24.8	42.2	25.8

Source: *World Development Report 1994*, Table 30.

Tracing changes in income distribution over time is difficult. In a comparison of Singapore's income distribution with that of other Asian economies Medhi (1994) uses the estimates of Rao (1988, 1990, 1993) of the Gini ratio for the members of the labour force, for CPF contributors and for households.[8] Income distribution tends to be more equal when measured on a household rather than personal basis because of the high female participation rate and the large number of households with more than one working member (Huff, 1994, pp.352–3). For households in 1966 the Gini ratio stood at 0.498 for Singapore, 0.487 for Hong Kong and 0.358 for Taiwan. By 1981 the ratio had fallen to 0.443 for Singapore but was 0.481 for Hong Kong. However by 1984 it had risen to 0.474 for Singapore, indicating that 'income inequality increased moderately in the 1980s' (Tan, 1993, p.297). By 1989 the Gini ratio for employed people in Singapore had risen to 0.49. Medhi (1994, p.64 and footnote 3) concludes by saying:

> Although it may appear that income equality in Singapore has become more unequal, Rao (1990, p.155) was of the opinion that the 1966–89 experience should be viewed as a major fluctuation rather than a trend. The trend itself was one of stable inequality, perhaps, around a Gini ratio of 0.45 to 0.5. What Rao did not say was that this level of income inequality is very high by the standards of countries or economies with the same level of development. It is the highest among the Asian NIEs.

Islam and Kirkpatrick (1986) also identified the increase in income inequality during the early 1980s and argued that the policy of importing unskilled foreign workers 'has entailed segmentation of the labour market, with a higher degree of wage dispersion across sectors than would otherwise be the case' (ibid., 1986, p.116). They also showed that, in the period 1973–9, lower-paid workers, generally in the services sector and production and transport equipment operators, saw their incomes grow at a faster rate than those of the relatively high-paid workers, professionals, managers and clerical workers, but that, after 1979, their incomes grew less rapidly than those of the higher wage-earners (ibid., Table 4).

The nature of the relationship between income distribution and economic growth is not a settled matter, but the World Bank recently presented some interesting evidence on the nature of income distribution in East Asian economies and their growth rates. The bank calculated the degree of income inequality as the ratio of the share of the richest 20 per cent to the poorest 20 per cent and related it to growth. Singapore and Hong Kong had an inequality ratio of about 9 and 9.5, respectively, not much different from that of Australia. These ratios are roughly in line with those that are implied by Table 1.7. They point out that all the countries with an inequality ratio of less than 10 and per capita GDP growth over 4 per cent a year were East Asian economies (Korea, Taiwan, Singapore, Hong Kong, Japan, Indonesia and Thailand). Malaysia was also a high growth country but had an inequality ratio of just over 15 (*The East Asian Miracle*, pp. 29–32).

Finally let us look at absolute income levels. Census data provide information on income from work. For most people in Singapore this would constitute their main source of income, apart from the value of the services of their own homes. In 1990 the average monthly wage from work of working persons over the age of 15 years was S$1414, with 48 per cent of working persons earning less than S$1000 a month and 17 per cent earning more than S$2000 a month from work.[9] The average monthly income of university graduates, of whom there were 95 526 in the Census, was S$4148; the average for the 101 119 people with no formal education was S$875 a month, a ratio of 4.7 to one.

The government has always prided itself on ensuring that the basic needs of the poor are met through its provision of housing, education and medical care and pensions through the CPF scheme. There are no beggars on the streets. Most poor people do not pay income tax and the introduction of indirect taxes in 1994 was accompanied by measures to reduce the adverse impact on them. At the top end of income distribution the government does not put limits on incomes, nor does it take a large share through sharply progressive income taxes. Consider the situation in 1993. Taking the average university graduate income from work in 1990 of S$4148, we assume that this income rose 20 per cent over the years, to about $5000 in 1993. Singapore probably also shares the trend found in many developed countries by which the distribution of income within professions becomes more unequal: a few lawyers or doctors make huge salaries, much higher than the average for their profession. Within the professional and technical occupations the highest paid in terms of gross wages (including bonuses and income in kind) per month are: economists (S$7629 average and S$5408 median); general physicians (S$6646 average and S$6000 median);[10] general surgeons (S$11 184 average and S$9819 median); specialized surgeons (S$13 760 average and S$12 077 median), commercial airline pilots (S$14 879 average and S$14 724 median) and flying instructors (S$15 743 average and S$17 032 median).

These figures help us to put into context the information that gave rise to an interesting debate in Singapore in late 1993 and early 1994. An academic economist turned journalist chose as the theme of one of his first columns the large difference between the salaries of government ministers and those of other Singaporeans. He was quickly put in his place with heavy sarcasm during the parliamentary debate on the President's speech. The salaries he was talking about were S$96 000 a month for the Prime Minister and S$64 000 a month for ministers. These figures are gross salaries which include all wage supplements and variable bonuses and a car allowance for the prime minister. About one-third of the Prime Minister's salary is not automatic and his base pay is only S$45 867 a month (*Parliamentary Debates Singapore: Official Report*, Vol. 63, No. 2, 14 January 1994, col. 168). The Senior Minister noted in his speech that real estate agents get 2 per cent on each transaction, so:

> If I were a young man again and I was choosing my options, I would consider coming into politics if you would pay me 0.002% of the GDP to be Prime Minister. Then I will take it on. So have a sense of proportion.[11]

High salaries for ministers are defended by invoking comparisons with the highest private sector earnings and the necessity of removing any temptation to being corrupt. In October 1994 the government published a White Paper (*Competitive Salaries for Competent & Honest Government*) in which it proposed to establish a system under which public sector pay levels would be formally linked with a time lag to those of top earners in the private sector identified from their tax returns. It was argued that this would remove the need for continuing debate on the level of salaries. The formula would be that ministers would receive two-thirds of the average principal income of the top four people in six professions: banking, accountancy, engineering, law, managing local manufacturing companies and managing multinational corporations. On the basis of 1992 figures this would give ministers a salary of S$811 333 a year. Many people felt that, by picking just the top four people in each profession and ignoring other benefits of ministerial positions and the enhanced 'marketability' of such people when they leave the public sector for the private sector, the benchmarks were being set too high (*The Straits Times*, 26 October 1994). The White Paper's proposals were voted into law in about one month. As often happens in meritocratic Singapore, pay rises are such that the higher the salary the larger the percentage increase one receives. For example, when the new salary scales for ministers and civil servants are implemented in July 1995 those receiving about S$28 000 a month will receive a 12.6 per cent increase, whereas those earning about S$9300 will receive only a 6.6 per cent increase (*Business Times*, 9 March 1995, p.2).

Current trends seem likely to maintain the large gap between the many low-paid and the few very highly paid. Lower-paid workers face competition from even cheaper foreign workers from elsewhere in the region. Potential emigration by professionals ensures that Singapore salaries must follow international levels. The government controls the extent of employment of foreign workers through quotas and levies. For example, the quota on foreign workers in the construction industry was increased after November 1992 as that sector was booming, but there is still a quota. It was increased again in late 1994. There are heavy penalties for those found employing illegal workers and for those who overstay their visas. Foreign maids attracted a higher monthly levy of S$300 after April 1992, increased again in 1994. Salaries for such maids are about S$300, so some people see the levy as a 50 per cent tax rate on such maids, as the employers are willing and able to pay S$600 a month, of which the government is getting half. A recent government statement is that there are more than 300 000 foreign workers in Singapore making up 18 per cent of the workforce (*The Straits Times*, 30 November 1994, p.1). A private study in 1993 estimated that the foreign workforce would have to grow at 11 per cent a year if Singapore wanted to achieve real GDP growth of 6 per cent a year (*Business Times*, 3–4 July 1993, p.2). This implies an income elasticity of demand for foreign labour of nearly two and 33 000 extra workers a year.

Some low-paid jobs in Singapore are disappearing as local enterprises relocate some of their activities abroad. For example, computerization has allowed a company like Singapore Airlines to relocate some computer processing to Peking and software development and the checking of its ticketing to India. This leads to the government's continuing insistence that workers in their 20s, 30s and early 40s 'learn to upgrade themselves' by taking night and weekend classes or vocational classes.[12]

1.6   FINANCING INVESTMENT

We have seen that a clear distinguishing feature of the Singapore economy is its very high investment rate. Let us look at how this investment rate has been financed at different periods in Singapore's history. Table 1.3 showed us that in 1960 Singapore was consuming more than it produced and hence had to have a surplus of imports over exports; that is, it borrowed from abroad to make this possible.

We can identify the sources of saving for investment as either domestic or foreign. Table 1.8 summarizes some key variables. Gross domestic saving (GDS) has been estimated as GDP at market prices minus government and private consumption and adjusted by the statistical discrepancy (SD). We then add to this the difference between NFIA and net transfer to abroad (NTA). If NFIA exceeds NTA then this makes funds available so that gross national saving (GNS) can exceed gross domestic saving. GNS is used either for investment in the domestic economy in the form of gross capital formation (GCF) or for lending abroad. Lending abroad (LA) is shown as a negative item as it is subtracted from GNS to determined GCF. Borrowing from abroad augments GNS and is thus shown as a positive figure that should be added to GNS to obtain GCF.

We have already seen that in 1960 Singapore was consuming more than it produced. This is reflected in the data of Table 1.8 as a negative amount of domestic saving (GDS) and borrowing from abroad. GNS was negative so this borrowing was necessary in order for there to be a positive amount of investment (GCF) which amounted to only 11 per cent of GDP in that year. In 1965 domestic saving was positive, as was national saving, and this was again supplemented by borrowing from abroad which allowed investment to be 22 per cent of GDP. Nearly half of GCF was financed by foreign borrowing as GNS provided only 53 per cent of it. By 1970 domestic saving was significantly positive, as was national saving, and this was supplemented by an almost equal amount of foreign borrowing which allowed investment to equal 39 per cent of GDP. 1993 shares with all the years since 1988 the feature of having lending abroad; that is, Singapore's national savings exceeded the amount of domestic investment and so there were investments abroad. In 1993 investment equalled nearly 44 per cent of that year's output.

What are the sources of domestic saving? Quite clearly, the CPF scheme, being a form of forced saving, depresses individual spending so that the private consumption rate (C/GDP) in Singapore is the lowest in the world. As the scheme provides a pension for members, allows them to buy a flat and provides basic

Table 1.8   Sources of saving for investment, selected years (amounts in billion dollars)

	1960	1965	1970	1975	1993ᴾ
GDP	2.150	2.956	5.805	13.443	89.007
minus					
Consumption					
(C + G)	2.083	2.648	4.612	9.544	46.383
SD	–0.123	–0.016	–0.127	0.055	–0.449
equals					
GDS	–0.056	0.291	1.065	3.954	45.175
plus					
NFIA	0.039	0.096	0.056	0.124	1.226
minus					
NTA	0.035	0.047	0.008	0.092	1.126
equals					
GNS	–0.052	0.341	1.130	3.985	42.274
plus					
LA (+ means					
borrowing,	+0.297	+0.307	+1.115	+1.385	–3.293
– lending)					
equals					
GCF	0.245	0.649	2.245	5.370	38.981
GCF/GDP(%)	11.3	22.0	38.7	40.0	43.8

Note: Figures have been rounded; ᴾ means preliminary.

Sources: Yearbook of Statistics Singapore 1993, Table 4.2; *Economic Survey of Singapore, 1991,* Table A1.8; PATS.

medical coverage, and as education is provided by the government at low cost, the motives for high rates of voluntary saving are reduced significantly. In 1984, for example, about 64 per cent of GNS was public saving, 30 per cent was in the form of the compulsory saving through the CPF scheme and only 6 per cent was voluntary saving (Lim and associates, 1988, p.217). The public sector saves in the form of the government budget surplus and the operating surpluses of the main government statutory boards.[13] Since 1988 the statutory boards have been required to hand over 20 per cent of their operating surpluses to the government as a form of income tax and this is now an item of government general revenue (*Yearbook of Statistics Singapore 1993*, Table 13.2). These amounts have been declining in size since their first payment in 1988, probably because the statutory boards are now expected to make smaller surpluses as a result of instructions to lower their prices and charges. However it was conjectured that the policy of statutory boards handing funds to the government would not reduce the total amount of public sector saving as both the statutory boards and the government make up the public sector (Lim and associates, 1998, p.231). The economists referred to here find more to criticize than that Singapore's saving rate in the mid-1980s was too high: 'Moreover, oversaving is coupled with mis-allocation of resources into the construction sector rather than into more productive manufacturing and allied sectors' (ibid., p.37).

The view that Singapore's saving is excessive and its resources are misallo-cated has been challenged by the government. The main argument offered was that the CPF was not causing a shortage of funds and this was clear from high stock prices, historically low interest rates and the difficulty of banks in lending to good borrowers (*The Straits Times*, 26 August 1992, p.1).

Where, then, do Singapore's savings go? In financial terms public sector savings accrue to the government and the statutory boards. The CPF funds are used to buy government securities or are given to the Monetary Authority of Singapore (MAS) for the subsequent purchase of government securities. These latter flows to the MAS are called 'advance deposits'. In 1990 nearly 97 per of CPF funds were held in Singapore government securities or advance deposits. As a result of this an additional problem identified by Singaporean economists is that:

> as some of this public sector savings is deposited with the Monetary Authority of Singapore, rather than with commercial banks, significant amounts of money are withdrawn from the income stream which in turn affects the banking sector. (Lim and associates, 1988, p.228)

Luckett *et al.* (1994, p.155–6) even argue: 'Such a form of national compulsory savings causes the money supply to fall.' Here the authors are viewing this flow as more than just an ordinary 'withdrawal' from the circular flow of income represented by S in the national income accounting identity

$$S + T + M = I + G + X$$

The above saving flow, S, has no effect on the money supply in this simple familiar model of the circular flow of income.

Whether the CPF saving scheme reduces voluntary saving is an issue for which there has been no definite answer in Singapore. On the basis of a review of the literature from other countries, the estimates of Wong (1986) for the period 1974–83 and their own econometric estimates, Lim and associates (1988, pp.221–2) concluded that the CPF scheme did decrease voluntary saving. On the basis of an abstract model intended to throw light on the Singapore case, Hoon and Teo (1992) concluded that if, in their model, there was a wage income tax then a compulsory saving scheme would increase private saving but if there was a capital income tax the opposite effect could be derived. Further extending the model to include a productive role for government spending and allowing for a balanced budget policy, higher CPF rates would reduce total saving.

Individual voluntary financial savings go into commercial bank deposits or deposits in POSBank (the new name of the Post Office Savings Bank; more on these institutions in Section 1.8) or into equities and unit trusts. 1993 was a record year for private sector accumulation through unit trusts, inspired by the marked rise in regional share prices and the freeing of CPF funds to be used to buy a wider range of financial assets (*Business Times*, 22 July 1994, p.1). This contributed to the financial services sector being the fastest growing sector of the economy in late 1993 and early 1994.

What forms of physical capital are these financial flows turned into and by whom? Let us look at gross fixed capital formation. As we have seen, this accounts for about 40 per cent of GDP. In 1993, 18 per cent was carried out by the public sector (constituting 7.5 per cent of GDP) and 82 per cent by the private sector. Most of public sector investment was in the form of residential buildings (47 per cent of total), non-residential buildings (18 per cent of total) and other construction works (21 per cent). These correspond to public housing; building of factories and government offices and schools; roads and other such infrastructure. Private investment was mainly in the form of machinery and equipment (46 per cent) and non-residential buildings (18 per cent) and residential buildings (15 per cent) with this latter amount exceeding the total amount of public residential building in that year. Residential construction has always been a significant part of Singapore's GDP, averaging 8 per cent of GDP over the period 1965–79 and rising to as much as 16.6 per cent of GDP in 1984 as a result of the housing boom of the early 1980s (calculated from Sandilands, 1992, p.128).

1.7 FINANCING THE GOVERNMENT AND ITS EXPENDITURE

The fiscal year in Singapore runs from 1 April to 31 March of the following year. We can get a feel for the significance of government revenue raising and spending in the economy by looking at the contrast between these flows for fiscal year 1993 (that is, 1993–4 and designated FY93 hereafter) and that of FY94 as there have been some significant tax reforms in this latter budget.

In FY93 total government revenue, at S$31 billion, was as much as 37.2 per cent of GDP whereas total expenditure was 22.7 per cent of GDP. This puts the overall budget balance at a surplus equal to 14.5 per cent of GDP (Asher, 1994, p.35). If we define government saving as its total revenue minus operating expenditure and debt servicing then this produces a figure of 24 per cent of GDP being saved by the government. It is forecast that in FY94 revenue will fall to 31.1 per cent of GDP and expenditures rise to 23.4 per cent, producing a lower surplus of 7.7 per cent of GDP. However it is the general experience that the government tends to underestimate revenue and overestimate expenditure in its forecasts, so it is likely that its surplus for FY94 will be higher than this figure (ibid., p.35). We can see that the Singapore government takes a large part of the country's GDP in each year and uses it to maintain a large budget surplus.

Tax revenue makes up just less than half of all government revenue. Taxation policy has always aimed at keeping direct tax rates low in order to attract foreign capital and, most recently, to encourage Singaporean businesses to venture abroad. Foreign multinationals that locate their regional headquarters in Singapore, for example, are given very attractive tax breaks, as are certain financial institutions. In 1994 the corporate tax rate was 27 per cent (reduced from 30 per cent in 1993) and the intention is to reduce this to 25 per cent so as to remain an attractive location for foreign capital. Personal income tax rates are progressive and range from 5 per cent to a maximum rate of 30 per cent. This top rate was 33 per cent before 1994. A major policy change in the FY94 budget was the introduction of a broad-based value-added tax known as the Goods and Services Tax (GST). This was introduced on 1 April 1994 at a rate of 3 per cent and it was announced that this rate would not be changed for at least five years. In compensation, tax rebates were increased and direct tax rates were reduced, as noted above. This reflects a general trend in many economies of moving away from taxing incomes to taxing expenditures. The experiences of New Zealand with a GST were frequently cited by the government during the long education campaign to explain to people what the GST would mean for them. This policy shift has implications for the conduct of macroeconomic policy, particularly exchange rate policy that we will return to later.

The aim of policy has been to keep direct tax rates low and to keep Singapore an open port. There are, however, significant duties on certain products. Alcohol is quite heavily taxed, making it expensive in Singapore, cigarettes are taxed, creating lucrative and widespread smuggling activity, and motor vehicle taxes are extensive. Import duties on motor vehicles and a system of supplementary licences introduced in 1990 and known as Certificates of Entitlement (COE) are used to restrain car population growth to about 3 per cent a year. These COEs are auctioned by the government every month and in late 1994 reached S$100 000 for a ten-year licence for a large car, making private cars in Singapore probably the most expensive in the world. The government plans to introduce an electronic road pricing system in certain areas to enable it to charge motorists for road use. In 1993 taxes and charges on vehicles totalled S$3.4 billion – and Singapore's annual GDP is S$90 billion. Including all charges and taxes means that about a quarter of total tax revenue comes from motor vehicle taxes (Asher, 1994, p.39). This is one means by which income taxes (personal and corporate) can be kept low, so they only constitute about 49 per cent of total government operating revenues. Another is the fact that the state owns much land which is available for the government to sell to private developers.

In FY94 the main forms of government expenditure were security (26 per cent of total expenditure), education (16 per cent), health (5 per cent), economic and infrastructure development (15 per cent), debt servicing (7 per cent) and net lending (13 per cent). As we have seen, the Singapore government runs a large budget surplus yet has to service its debt. The total of government debt at the end of 1993 was about $70 billion, 99.98 per cent of which is domestic debt (*Yearbook of Statistics Singapore 1993*, Table 13.5). Why does the government have so much debt? This debt is almost entirely government securities sold to the CPF. The government is not selling debt to finance its expenditure but to provide assets for the CPF to hold and thus obtain an interest return. The government thus obtains these CPF funds for making investments, not current expenditures (Asher, 1994, pp.36–7).

Unlike Hong Kong, Singapore has the burden of maintaining a defence force, as pointed out above. Hence security expenditures are a significant part of government expenditure. A recent survey of various independent estimates of the proportion of GDP spent on defence by various countries produced an average figure of 6 per cent of GDP for Singapore in the mid-1980s (Soesastro, 1994, p.30). This is consistent with estimates that can be made using Singapore data. This ratio is significant when compared with the figure of only about 2.9 per cent of GDP for Australia, 4 per cent for Malaysia and 2.6 per cent for Indonesia.

1.8   OWNERSHIP

How an economy responds to shifts in demand and is able to implement macro-economic stabilization policies will depend on the nature of ownership of its productive units. Two aspects of ownership are of interest: the balance between foreign and domestic ownership and the balance between government and private ownership.

We have already seen that foreigners own about one-third of Singapore's annual production. The relative importance of foreign firms has probably not changed much recently, so we can refer to the findings of the Department of Statistics relating to the corporate sector in the 1980s, reported in *Singapore's Corporate Sector: Size, Composition and Financial Structure* that was published in 1992. A foreign-controlled company is defined as one in which 50 per cent or more of the equity is owned by foreigners. In addition to such firms there will be joint ventures in which foreign capital plays an important role also. In 1989 the total number of active companies was 34 653, up from 19 438 in 1980, of which 7914 were foreign-controlled. Although this only constituted 23 per cent of the number of companies, foreign-controlled firms owned 73 per cent of assets. Many of the foreign-owned companies are banks with large assets, so if we exclude them we see that foreign-controlled firms owned 45 per cent of all corporate assets outside the financial sector. Foreign-controlled firms were most common in the financial sector (30 per cent of all companies) and in insurance, real estate and business services, as well as in manufacturing and transport and storage. Foreign-controlled firms tend to be bigger than local firms with, for example, the average assets of a foreign firm in manufacturing being seven times the size of the assets of a local firm.

The cumulative amount of foreign equity investment in the entire economy by the end of 1991 was S$63 billion. The largest single source was Japan (19 per cent of the total) followed closely by the USA (17 per cent), the UK (13 per cent), the Netherlands (7 per cent), Hong Kong (7 per cent), ASEAN as a whole (7 per cent) and Australia (5 per cent) (*Yearbook of Statistics Singapore 1993*, Table 4.11). Most of this was concentrated in financial and business services (44 per cent of the total), the manufacturing sector (36 per cent of the total) and in commerce (15 per cent of the total). In the manufacturing sector in 1992, 57 per cent of the manufacturing workforce was employed in foreign-owned establishments in the sense that foreign ownership was at least 50 per cent of equity. The importance of MNCs and the fact that local firms tend to be small means that large firms have become very important in the manufacturing sector. Although establishments employing more than 100 workers constituted only 18 per cent of the number of establishments in 1992, they employed 75 per cent of the manufacturing workforce and produced 75 per cent of value added (*Report on the Census of Industrial Production 1992*, Tables 3 and 8). Large manufacturing firms have been behind Singapore's economic growth, not small local enterprises.

We can indicate the importance of the foreign sector in generating capital in Singapore by looking at the sources of net investment commitments in the manufacturing sector. If we take 1993 as an example, about S$3.9 billion was committed to new investment and of this total only 19 per cent was defined as local, with the rest being foreign. Of the foreign commitments the USA was by far the largest investor, with 37 per cent of total net investment, Japan (20 per cent), the UK (9 per cent), Germany (5 per cent) and France (3 per cent) being other important sources of new capital (*Yearbook of Statistics Singapore 1993*, Table 6.12). Of these investment commitments in manufacturing most were intended for the electronic products and components sector (32 per cent of total), industrial chemicals (20 per cent of total), other chemical products (9 per cent of total), non-electrical machinery (9 per cent of total) and transport equipment (9 per cent of total). On the basis of these commitments these are the sectors of manufacturing that are likely to remain an important part of Singapore's man- ufacturing sector. The government has repeatedly said that Singapore's manufacturing sector will not be allowed to decline as a proportion of GDP.

Because of its small size, Singapore's largest companies are those that tend to serve the international market. By far the largest company in Singapore in terms of sales, profits or assets is the government company, Singapore Airlines Ltd, which operates the national airline, SIA. In terms of net income, this company ranks 182nd largest in the world and in terms of market value it is 337th. DBSBank, also largely government-owned, is ranked 596th in the world in terms of market value but the Overseas Chinese Bank is 559th (*Singapore 1,000 1993: Industrial*, pp.20–22). In 1989 the largest companies in terms of assets in the financial services, manufacturing, construction and commerce sectors were all foreign firms (*Singapore's Corporate Sector 1992*, p.14).

Government involvement has been aimed at helping small local companies compete in international markets by providing them with research facilities and access to new technology that it thinks they could not obtain for themselves. A good example of this is the establishment in 1994 of the Singapore Digital Media Consortium, formed by the National Computer Board and the National Science and Technology Board. It involves three local computer firms and it is expected that other firms will join in the future. The aim is for the consortium to collab- orate with international research laboratories in the field of digital media technology and pass the fruits to the local companies which are expected partly to finance the consortium. Two of these local companies, Creative Technology Ltd and Aztech Systems Ltd, already supply about 75 per cent of the world's sound cards used in the multimedia aspects of many personal computers. The government is continuing to try to 'pick winners' and encourage the expansion of certain areas of advanced technology. Apart from electronic and computing linked sectors the government is actively encouraging the aerospace and biotech- nology industries. The MNCs, of course, brought with them the international links and marketing ability the lack of which is a severe constraint on devel- opment in many export-oriented economies. This local deficiency has been recognized by the government as a feature of Singapore (Huff, 1994, p.320).

It is difficult to pin down exactly the extent of government ownership and to summarize the position succinctly, though this ownership is very extensive. Such government ownership and control exists through the statutory boards and GLCs. Formerly the terms 'government-owned' or 'government-backed' companies were commonly used, but as they were thought to be too vague (as often the government did not have a full equity stake in some companies) the term 'government-linked company' was proposed and is the standard term nowadays.

Statutory boards are established through an act of parliament and are respon- sible to the ministry that established them and which oversees their work. Many have important commercial operations such as the Port of Singapore Authority (PSA), the Public Utilities Board (PUB), the Civil Aviation Authority of Singapore (CAAS), Commercial and Industrial Security Corporation (CISCO) and the Singapore Broadcasting Corporation (SBC; until 1 October 1994, when it was reorganized). Seah (1983, p.154) identified 72 in the early 1980s and the official *Singapore 1994* (pp.282–7) lists over 50, big and small. The statutory boards are monopolies or near-monopolies, have the force of law behind them when they set fees and charges, are protected and financed by the government when necessary and those with commercial activities are normally profitable. Lim and associates (1988, pp.70, 217–18) pointed out that they are not immune from criticism for increasing the operating costs of the private sector. An important statutory board is the Economic Development Board, established in 1961 under the Ministry of Finance to oversee Singapore's development, of which Low *et al.* (1993) provide a history.

In the 1980s there were about 600 GLCs in which the government had an equity stake. At times this ranged from complete ownership in such firms as the Urban Development and Management Co (Pte) and the very important Government of Singapore Investment Corporation (Pte) Ltd (GIC: more on this institution later) and Singapore National Printers, to a 60 per cent stake in Parkland Golf Driving Range (Pte) Ltd and 68 per cent in Neptune Orient Lines (Deluty and Wood, 1986, pp.28–30). Government ownership in the mid-1980s was mainly through three large holding companies: Temasek Holdings (under the Ministry of Finance), MND Holdings Pte Ltd (also under the Ministry of Finance) and Sheng-Li Holding Company Pte Ltd. Temasek Holdings remains the government's dominant owner of capital in Singapore. Through the ownership of shares in other companies by companies in which the government has substantial holdings, government ownership, and to varying extent control, goes down to so-called seventh-tier companies. Government involvement in the economy has ranged over many activities, from farming to banking and financial services, ship repairing, retail trade, consultancy services, real estate and development, housing, utilities, aviation, oil trading, gaming (the national lottery), printing and publishing, warehousing, salvaging, taxis, insurance, broadcasting and telecommunications. By 1991 there were 419 GLCs and statutory boards (Low, 1991, pp.94–102).

It has been estimated that in the mid-1980s as much as 45 per cent of Singapore's GDP was produced by government-owned companies and the public utilities (Clad, 1989, p.143). A rough rule of thumb used by the United States Embassy in its reports on Singapore is that about 60 per cent of the economy is represented by the public sector, 25 per cent by MNCs and so only 15 per cent by private businesses (*Business Times*, 27 January 1994, p.2).

The major GLCs or statutory boards are directed by senior government bureaucrats who tend to have more than one job. For example, in the mid-1980s the chairman of the largest commercial bank (which is mainly government-owned) was also chairman of the state airline and was a permanent secretary in the Ministry of Finance. Singapore's top decision makers who constitute a small group have been described as:

> highly skilled generalists with multiple job responsibilities – having charge of one or more ministries, statutory boards, and/or state companies. They are trouble shooters, who exchange posts readily as the situation requires, rather than bureaucratic specialists. (Deluty and Wood, 1986, pp.33–4)

A commonly heard description of Singapore is Singapore Inc. (Incorporated) by which the speaker wishes to liken the whole society to one giant firm with everyone committed to its profitability, which is generally identified with the rate of real growth. From this perspective it is natural for the government to see itself as the board of directors and the ministers and the top civil servants as department managers and thus natural for them to link their pay to the performance of the 'firm'. Citizens are thus seen as workers but more and more as shareholders, however small, in the 'firm'.

One sector in which the government is important is banking. In 1994 there were 132 commercial banks (13 of them local banks) and 76 merchant banks operating in Singapore. Commercial banking is dominated by the 'big four', consisting of the United Overseas Bank (UOB), the Overseas-Chinese Banking Corporation (OCBC), the Overseas Union Bank (OUB) and the DBSBank. This latter commercial bank was established as the Development Bank of Singapore in 1968 as a development bank for channelling funds into government-approved development projects in place of the Economic Development Board (Tan Chwee Huat,1992, p.365). Since then it has been transformed into a commercial bank operating on commercial principles and is the largest commercial bank in Singapore. It is owned by the government which, through various entities, in particular Temasek Holdings, has held over 50 per cent of its shares at times. DBSBank was exempted from certain restrictions on other commercial banks in Singapore and it was one of only two banks that were allowed to pay interest on current accounts. Its assets have grown tremendously and it held about 37 per cent of all non-bank deposits in Singapore in 1991 (Luckett *et al.*, 1994, p.17). It has been able to borrow from other government organizations such as the Post Office Savings Bank. It has provided finance for government projects such as Changi airport. It is also a major investment banker and stockbroker. In addition, it has many subsidiaries, particularly in property development, where there are 14 (Tan Chwee Huat, 1992, p.371). DBS Land is a major property developer. DBSBank is also an extremely profitable bank, thus providing more funds for the government as its majority shareholder.

In addition to DBSBank there is the POSBank, the new name for the Post Office Savings Bank, which was first established in July 1877 and became a statutory board in 1972. Owing to its exemption from certain regulations in the Banking Act and because interest on deposits is tax-free and deposits are guaranteed by the government, it has been able to secure the major share of savings deposits in Singapore (Schulze, 1990, pp.27–40). As has been pointed out many times, the number of savings accounts with POSBank, at 4 980 999 in December 1994, for example, far exceeds the total population: men, women, children, babies and all.

By having to hold the bulk of its assets in the form of government securities, and owing to the fact that it holds shares in GLCs and lends to statutory boards, the POSBank is another means by which savings are channelled to the government and the public sector. Furthermore, POSBank is very profitable and so further contributes funds to the government, as statutory boards are required to do. POSBank has a number of subsidiaries, such as Credit POSB Pte Ltd which provides loans for housing and commercial properties, and POSB Investment Pte Ltd, a wholly-owned investment holding company, with interests in certain financial services (Tan Chwee Huat, 1992, p.359). In 1993 the 'surplus' of POSBank was 34 per cent higher than in 1992, indicating its high profitability.

An important wholly-owned government financial organization is the Government of Singapore Investment Corporation (GIC) established in 1981 when it took over the task of managing the government's long-term investments from the MAS when the latter body was extensively reorganized. Neither the holdings of GIC nor its returns are published and it operates in confidence, although some of its investments are often identified from company records in other countries and are reported in the press. The commonly heard comment from a GIC official spokesman at the time of reports of GIC activity is: 'It is not our policy to confirm or deny specific investments' (*The Straits Times*, 12 March 1994, p.48). Its investments are not limited to government securities or foreign currencies and it often takes an equity stake in foreign companies, as in early 1994 when it bought shares of two Taiwanese companies, or establishes joint ventures with foreign partners.

Because of its size, the existence of a significant computer manufacturing and development sector and the government's desire to control many aspects of people's lives Singapore aims to become the 'intelligent island' by extensively applying the latest computer technology. This has already had a major impact on banking and transactions. Since 1986 there has been an island-wide electronic funds transfer at point of sale system (EFTPOS) known as NETS. This allows direct debit from one's bank account using one's bank card at many shops and restaurants. Furthermore the major banks and POSBank have many automatic teller machines (ATM) throughout the island from which one can withdraw cash using one's bank card. In addition, many transactions such as train and bus rides can be paid for using stored value cards instead of cash. These can be topped up using the direct debit system. One can also apply for and pay for shares and COEs through ATM machines and it is planned that fines will be able to be paid this way also. This electronic funds transfer system will further reduce the need to use cash in Singapore, and hence the demand for currency and the need for bank clerks, while increasing the need for computer programmers and systems creators.

1.9   DEVELOPMENT STRATEGY

There is no secret or miracle in the nature of Singapore's development. It has relied on foreign capital and direct investment and export-led growth. The crucial Singaporean contribution has been to mobilize what domestic resources there were in the 1960s to drain the land, provide an efficient infrastructure, provide an educational and housing system and compliant labour relations that would provide a workforce attractive to foreign investors. Tax incentives and an incorrupt government have ensured that the returns to foreign investors are sufficient to prevent them from relocating to neighbouring countries and to continue reinvesting in Singapore. For example, the most profitable firm in Singapore in 1991/2 was the British firm Glaxo Far East (Pte) Ltd, which had a profit margin of 93.7 per cent. Glaxochem Pte Ltd had a profit margin of 81.2 per cent. At that time nearly all of the most profitable firms in Singapore were in pharmaceuticals, the petrochemical industry or in electronics and most were foreign firms. The most profitable sector was the disc drive sector which includes foreign firms. The second most profitable firm in terms of total net profits was Hewlett-Packard (S) Pte Ltd (*Singapore 1,000 1993: Industrial*, pp.38–9). Foreign firms secure high returns in Singapore. For example, the return on equity of foreign firms during the recession of 1985–6 was 4.5 and 10.9 per cent in each year while the return for local firms was minus 1.1 and plus 1.9 per cent in these two years. In 1992 the net rate of return on capital in the electronics and components sector was 56 per cent, down from 70 per cent in 1991, and for all manufacturing it was 29 per cent (*Report on the Census of Industrial Production 1992*, p.vi). During the 1980s local companies tended to be more profitable than foreign ones only in the financial sector, whereas in the non-financial sector, and particularly in manufacturing, foreign firms were much more profitable. The average rate of return on total assets for foreign firms in manufacturing was 14.7 per cent, compared to 7.3 per cent for local firms (*Singapore's Corporate Sector*, pp.27–8).

Singapore is not unique in turning a small, resource-poor territory into a developed economy. Hong Kong can be cited as another example, as can Denmark, which makes an interesting comparison for both Singapore and Hong

Kong (Youngson, 1982, pp.139–40). It is not to belittle Singapore's development policies to say that it followed a simple formula: simple formulae are not easy to arrive at, or to accept if they are currently unfashionable; nor is it easy to mobilize the population. As the *Asian Wall Street Journal* recently remarked:

> Copying the formula it used to help build thriving shipping, tourism and banking industries here, the Singapore government detailed plans for a big new performing arts center.
>
> That simple formula – build the best possible infrastructure, provide trained workers and salt liberally with tax breaks – along with an unbeatable location astride Asia's main sea route made this tiny city-state rich. (*AWSJ*, 22 July 1994, p.1)

Some economic historians see Singapore's experiences as a good example of the 'first law of development': 'To those who have shall be given' (Huff, 1994, p.2), stressing the great initial advantages it had in terms of location, its port and its free trade history.

We must remember the size of Singapore. It might be more appropriate to compare its growth and development to that of other cities, many of which have a larger population, or to a county or a state or similar administrative region of another country. It might be objected that Singapore is an independent nation, which indeed it is, with its own army, government, currency and independent economic policy. It might be objected that these other cities or regions grew because they were able to attract investors from outside the territory, induce people to come and live and work there and obtain development funds from their central government. But Singapore is a city and much of its development is similar to that of other cities: it attracted capital and expertise from outside and it has been able to draw on neighbouring countries for labour in forms ranging from the thousands of foreign domestic maids, who allow trained women to undertake higher productivity jobs, to part of the construction industry labour force, to managers of MNCs and academics and so on. It even has its thousands of daily commuters from outside its boundaries (Malaysia and Indonesia in this case) just as any flourishing city does. We might inquire into the past growth rate of IGNP of the inhabitants of Tokyo, New York or Massachusetts or the future growth rate of Shanghai, a city with a population more than four times that of Singapore and which has recently adopted a similar development strategy. Data are hard to come by for a large number of subnational areas but it is with such entities that we should really compare Singapore's growth rates, not with those of nation states the size of Japan, Malaysia or the USA.

An early vision of Singapore's development path saw it just as a city. Lee Kuan Yew has been quoted as saying in 1963 that he looked forward to turning Singapore into the 'New York of Malaysia, the industrial base of an affluent and just society' (Turnbull, 1989, p.278). Singapore was not able to stay in Malaysia and it appears to have drawn its inspiration for making itself useful to the world from the specialities of many cities and areas and not to have limited itself to industry. Its inspiration comes partly from New York, London and Chicago (thriving foreign exchange market and SIMEX which has links with Chicago); partly from Rotterdam (flourishing port for a large hinterland); partly from Hong Kong (centre for foreign banking and financial services and source of capital for China and Asia, as well as a shopping and food centre for the tourists); partly from Hollywood (government encouragement for developing local film producing facilities and plans for becoming a communications centre for Asia); from New York again (an Asian centre for performing arts and theatre); from Silicon Valley (computer and software development, but here based in the government-supported Science Parks) and, some have said, partly from Disneyland.

Although Singapore's overall development strategy has not fundamentally changed since the policy of export-led growth was adopted in the late 1960s, there have been some changes in certain areas. The first occurred in the late 1970s. It was felt that the successes of the 1970s were mainly based on creating jobs and absorbing the domestic labour force and attracting foreign workers into labour-intensive low-productivity sectors such as textiles. In about 1979 the government adopted policies aimed at creating a 'second industrial revolution' by inducing employers to move into higher value-added activities and to increase investment in automation, computerization and research and development (Wong, 1989, pp.183–8; Rodan, 1989, chap. 5). This was to be done in part by forcing up wages through a high wages policy, or a 'wage correction policy' as it was later officially termed (Wong, 1989, p.187) and by investment in education and industrial training. This high wages policy was abandoned in the mid-1980s as another policy shift took place then.

There were a number of reasons for the changes in policy observed in the 1980s. First, the economy experienced a recession in 1985 when real output fell nearly 2 per cent, prices fell and unemployment rose to 6.5 per cent in 1986. This indicated to many people that the government might not be infallible and perhaps could not guarantee the high rates of growth that had previously been achieved.

The second reason was the uncertainty about, and dissatisfaction with, the regulation of the securities industry. During a period when most share prices were falling, a large listed company, Pan-Electric Industries, and associated companies went into liquidation in November 1985. The stock market was closed for three days in early December and banks were instructed to finance stock-brokers who were facing bankruptcy. This 'débâcle', as it was called at the time, led to calls for better regulation of the stock market and a new Securities Industry Act was enacted in August 1986 aimed at strengthening regulation of the securities industry. Subsequently there have been complaints that this sector is now overregulated compared to other financial centres in the region which are thought to have better prospects than Singapore. In 1992 there were complaints from foreign bankers of arrogance and complacency by the Singapore authorities ('City state loses its glitter', *Euromoney*, January 1993). These complaints were, no doubt, restrained in the share market boom of 1993 when activity, prices and staff bonuses reached high levels.

Another change in the mid-1980s was the result of continuing complaints by small businesses of unfair advantages received by GLCs and foreign businesses. The government noted these complaints and consolidated all previous schemes to help small local businesses, then totalling about 65 000, into the Small and Medium Enterprises Master Plan (SME) and established the Enterprise Promotion Centre (EPC) in 1988 (Toh and Low, 1990b, pp.254–5). One later aspect of this form of government assistance was to encourage and help local entrepreneurs to invest abroad through tax concessions (Asher, 1994). Singapore's direct investment abroad did increase in the 1980s and Singapore has become an important investor in China, Myanmar and Vietnam. In 1976 the accumulated value of Singapore's total investments abroad, not including those of financial organizations, was equal to about 7 per cent of that year's GNP. By 1984 the proportion had fallen to 5.9 per cent, but by the end of 1993 it had increased to 14.5 per cent with most of the increase happening after 1988. This was based on the policies of about 3200 Singaporean companies which set up overseas operations, mostly in Asia (48 per cent of total investment was there, with 26.4 per cent of the total in ASEAN: *Lianhe Zaobao*, 31 August 1994, p.21). By late 1994, a Department of Statistics survey was claiming that the total value of Singaporean firms' investment abroad had reached S$28 billion, standing at 31.2 per cent of GNP (*Business Times*, 17 October 1994).

Another response to the complaints from small local businesses was the government's decision to consider the privatization of its enterprises; a report recommending privatization of some GLCs was published in February 1987. Between 1985 and 1990 the government sold off shares in 36 GLCs, sometimes selling its complete stake but retaining large holdings in such companies as Singapore Airlines Ltd, Singapore Aerospace, Sembawang Shipyard Ltd, Singapore Shipbuilding and Engineering and Singapore National Printers (Low, 1991, pp.194–5). A further result of the privatization programme was the government's decision to float 11 per cent of the shares of Singapore Telecom in October 1993. On becoming a publicly listed company, Singapore Telecom was subsequently ranked as the world's 25th largest such company in terms of market value. Further government divestments from this company are expected. Shares were available for purchase through the CPF scheme (with about 1.45 million people obtaining shares) and there was a tranche reserved for foreigners, but there were complaints that there was bias against foreign subscribers. The shares raised about S$4.2 billion, with about S$2.18 billion of this coming from CPF savings (Metzger, 1994, p.77). We will use this important event as a small case study in subsequent chapters, showing how it affected the banking system, monetary sector and the exchange rate. It has been announced that the Public Utilities Board's gas and electricity departments will be corporatized by September 1995, with its power generation aspects allocated to two separate companies, and they will be publicly listed in mid-1996.

Singapore's development has undoubtedly been helped by the uninterrupted rule of the PAP since 1959. With severely limited prospects of a change in government, long-term policies announced by the government are backed by a high degree of credibility, thus encouraging foreign investment in Singapore. As has been noted, businessmen do not like the uncertainties about future economic policy that the possibility of a radical change in government brings with it (Kalecki, 1943, p.141).

The aims of Singapore's development strategy have been variously summarized as to transform it into the 'Switzerland of Asia',[14] into an 'intelligent island' (meaning a society planned and coordinated with the universal use of computer networks), turning it into 'Singapore Unlimited' and creating a 'caring nation'. These aims are still for the future. Let us now turn back and look at the macroeconomic history of Singapore, which we do in the following chapter.

SUGGESTIONS FOR FURTHER READING

For a history of modern Singapore we recommend Turnbull (1989, chaps 8 and 9) and Turnbull (1969) and for some entertainment Theroux (1976). Huff (1994) is the only modern economic history.

For reviews of Singapore's early economic development: Goh (1969), the studies in Chen (1983) and the economic essays in Sandhu and Wheatley (1989) which cover the more recent period. For a useful review of the literature on this topic, see Chia (1986a). For a study of the role of the Economic Development Board in Singapore's development and other topics, Low *et al.* (1993) is very useful.

Krause *et al.* (1987) usefully reviews many aspects of the economy and Lim and associates (1988) reviews problems of the economy and provides policy options from the viewpoint of the mid-1980s.

For information on companies in Singapore: *Singapore 1,000 1993: Industrial* and *Singapore 1,000 1993: Services* and *Times Directory of Foreign Business in Singapore 1988/1989*; for a government review of recent developments see *Singapore 1994* and earlier issues or *Singapore: Facts and Pictures 1994* or earlier issues.

NOTES

1. Comparisons between Singapore and Hong Kong are inevitable and such comparisons have featured prominently in the literature on Asian development. The two economies share many features. Both were small, resource-poor (both have to import much of their water, for example) island entrepots under the British Empire that subsequently industrialized but now

have significant financial sectors. Both are dominantly Chinese: Singapore's population is 78 per cent Chinese, 14 per cent Malay, 7 per cent Indian and about 1 per cent 'other'; Hong Kong's population is about 98 per cent Chinese. The 'Tale of two cities' title or a close variant has been commonly used for articles on their economic development (Geiger and Geiger 1973; Young, 1992). One theme of these 'tales' is, of course, that Singapore's development has been government-directed, whereas that of Hong Kong has relied on a policy of 'positive non-interventionalism', although the government's role there is not insignificant (Youngson, 1982).

More recently the World Bank has studied the nature of development in eight east Asian countries and, drawing on the experiences of the 'four tigers' and Japan, Taiwan, Indonesia, Malaysia and Thailand, has coined a new term: HPAEs – high-performing Asian economies. See *The East Asian Miracle: Economic Growth and Public Policy* (1993).

2. It is obvious that this indicator is based on formal institutions of democracy, of which there are only a few in Hong Kong, but most people would, we believe, argue that Hong Kong is a much freer society than the authoritarian Singapore. Recently, for example, the Prime Minister of Singapore has laid down rules that Singaporean citizens are not allowed to debate political issues (by writing opinion pieces in newspapers, for example) unless they have a platform indicated by their membership of a political party, in which case the Prime Minister will 'have to take you on' as the Senior Minister, Lee Kuan Yew, put it (*The New Paper*, 2 February 1995, pp.6–7). Members of opposition parties in Singapore are not generally considered as members of a 'loyal opposition' as they are in most Westminster-type democracies. For the way such politicians have been treated, see Tremewan (1994, chaps 6 and 7).

3. Bahrain was ranked third, the United States fourth, Japan fifth and Taiwan sixth ahead of the UK. Those seven were described as 'free'. Cuba and North Korea were in the last two places out of the 101 countries (Holmes, 1994).

4. America's reserves are 2.3 months of imports, the UK's 1.4 months, Japan's 2.4 months, Switzerland's 6.7 months and Taiwan's 11.5 months (*World Development Report 1994*, Table 17).

5. 'Ownership' is in the form of a 99-year lease, not freehold, and the flat will revert to the Housing and Development Board (the owner) at the end of the lease. There are many regulations over the ways one may use one's own home and who may live in it (Tremewan, 1994, pp.57–8).

6. Since the public issue in October 1993 the share price had fallen about 34 per cent by the end of 1994 and then had a price–earnings ratio of 31 compared to the market average of 19.8. Less than 1 per cent of the shares was held by institutional investors (*The Straits Times*, 4 January 1995, p.40). Singaporeans who had bought at the discounted special price would also have received loyalty bonus issues and so would have made a capital gain even at this lower share price.

7. For some countries incomes are ranked by household and for others by persons. The years of coverage are not the same: Singapore's figures are for 1982–3, Hong Kong's for 1980 and the other countries for later in the 1980s. Singapore's data are not strictly comparable with those of Indonesia, Malaysia and Thailand, whose figures are for persons, not households, but are comparable with those of the developed economies.

8. The Gini ratio is a measure of the dispersion of income. Its value can lie between zero and unity, with a value of zero indicating that all households had the same income. The higher the ratio the greater the degree of dispersion of incomes.

9. We can keep in mind that average IGNP for 1990 was about S$1670 per month. The 1990 Census data cover 1 537 011 workers. All data in this paragraph are from *Singapore Census of Population 1990: Economic Characteristics*.

10. The median is the 'middle' or 'average' salary in the sense that half of the people surveyed earned less than this amount and half earned more than this amount. All data in this paragraph are from *Report on Wages in Singapore 1993*, Table 1.1. The survey only covered the private sector.

11. *Parliamentary Debates Singapore: Official Report*, vol. 63, no. 2, 14 January 1994, col. 170; 0.002 per cent of our S$90 billion in 1993 is S$1.8 million, making a required monthly salary of S$150 000.

12. Lee Kuan Yew, in *Parliamentary Debates Singapore: Official Report*, vol. 63, no. 2, 14 January 1994, col. 177.

13. These include the Housing and Development Board (HDB), Public Utilities Board (PUB), Jurong Town Corporation (JTC), Port of Singapore Authority (PSA), Urban Redevelopment Authority (URA), Sentosa Development Corporation (SDC), Economic Development Board (EDB), Civil Aviation Authority of Singapore (CAAS), both universities and all four polytechnics and other educational institutions. See *Singapore 1994*, pp. 282–7, for a recent list of over 50 statutory boards.
14. This new slogan could be regarded as another policy shift, as in its early days of development Singapore considered a number of small countries as a possible model for emulation, with Israel, Finland and Switzerland being three possibilities. In the late 1960s and 1970s Israel was the chosen model. It has now been dropped from this place. We will include Switzerland in some future assessments of Singapore's position, especially relating to growth and money.

2. Macroeconomic history

In this chapter we look at the broad trends in the main macroeconomic variables
in Singapore in the form of real output, employment, unemployment, prices and
interest rates. Our approach will be descriptive and we will offer very little theory
for the observations here.

2.1 OUTPUT GROWTH AND FLUCTUATIONS

Table 2.1 shows the annual growth rates of the two main output series GNP
and GDP as well as GDP in constant 1985 market prices for the period since
1960 as well as the total labour force, its growth rate and the growth rate of
employment, and the unemployment rate. The output data thus go back to
before 1965.

Table 2.2 presents a summary of average annual growth of both GDP and
GNP for various periods. It has become a commonplace observation that the
rate of economic growth in most developed countries was lower after 1973 than
the rate achieved before this date. We thus calculate the growth rates for before
and after 1973. Similarly we are interested in the growth rates before and after
1980, roughly when the policy of the 'second industrial revolution' was
introduced. All growth rates were calculated by using log-linear regressions against
a time trend so they are not dependent on just the initial and end observations.
All other average annual growth rates are calculated the same way unless
otherwise indicated.

The growth rates show that the long-run trend in both output variables has
been about 8.5 per cent per annum for the periods 1960 to 1993 and 1965 to
1993. There have been no periods when the growth rates of the two variables
were significantly different from each other, but the trend is that after 1980 GNP
has been growing slightly faster than GDP. This is a possible reflection of the
policy of encouraging investment abroad and the retention of foreigners'
earnings in Singapore, remarked upon in Chapter 1.

The calculations also show that there was a fall in growth rates of both
variables after 1973. After 1973 GDP, for example, was growing at a rate equal
only to 56 per cent of its rate before 1973 (7.3/13.0). The early days of independence produced very high growth rates. The growth rates after 1980 are also
lower than those achieved before 1980. The long-run trend is for the growth

Table 2.1   Main macroeconomic series, 1960–93

	GNP growth rate (% p.a.)	GDP $ million	GDP growth (% p.a.)	Labour force (000s)	Labour force growth (% p.a.)	Employment growth (% p.a.)	Unemployment (%)
1960		5058.5					
1961	8.6	5490.4	8.5				
1962	7.1	5878.1	7.1				
1963	11.0	6493.3	10.5				
1964	−3.6	6213.7	−4.3				
1965	6.7	6626.8	6.6				
1966	10.8	7328.3	10.6				8.9
1967	12.0	8283.1	13.0				8.1
1968	13.7	9464.3	14.3	626			7.3
1969	13.0	10730.0	13.4	654	4.5	5.2	6.7
1970	12.6	12172.4	13.4	693	6.0	6.7	6.0
1971	11.3	13698.8	12.5	726	4.8	6.1	4.8
1972	13.2	15526.2	13.3	761	4.8	4.9	4.7
1973	9.1	17273.6	11.3	_818_	7.5	7.7	4.5
1974	6.1	18441.2	6.3	858.4	n.a.	2.8	4.0
1975	7.9	19171.4	4.0	873.0	1.7	_1.2_	4.5
1976	5.6	20548.5	7.2	910.9	4.3	4.4	4.4
1977	7.1	22143.3	7.8	940.8	3.3	3.8	3.9
1978	9.6	24046.0	8.6	994.7	5.7	6.1	3.6
1979	9.2	26284.7	9.3	1056.3	6.2	6.5	3.3
1980	6.2	28832.5	9.7	1112.1	5.3	5.5	3.5
1981	9.2	31603.1	9.6	1188.0	6.8	n.a.	2.9
1982	8.2	33772.3	6.9	1253.2	5.5	5.6	2.6
1983	10.7	36537.2	8.2	1292.8	3.2	2.5	3.2
1984	10.9	39527.5	8.3	1304.4	0.9	1.4	2.7
1985	0	38923.5	−1.6	1287.8	−1.3	−2.7	4.1
1986	0.7	39641.4	1.8	1298.5	0.8	−1.6	6.5
1987	5.7	43371.8	9.4	1329.3	2.4	4.3	4.7
1988	11.9	48203.4	11.1	1377.7	3.6	5.1	3.3
1989	10.4	52657.4	9.2	1424.7	3.4	4.7	2.2
1990	8.7	57271.9	8.8	1562.8	9.6	10.3	1.7
1991	7.1	61081.0	6.6	1554.3	−0.5	−0.8	1.9
1992	6.6	64771.0	6.0	1619.6	4.2	3.4	2.7
1993	9.6	71211.9	9.9	1635.7	1.0	1.0	2.7

Note: Labour force until 1973 refers to persons aged 15–64 and for subsequent years it refers to those over 15 years of age. Employment growth for 1975 and after is based on the number of people over 15 years of age employed. Before that it is for people aged 15–64. A change in the series for employment in 1981 means we cannot compute the growth in the labour force for that year.

Sources: *Economic and Social Statistics Singapore 1960-1982*; *Yearbook of Statistics Singapore*, various years; PATS.

rates to fall, yet they remain high when compared with those of large national economies. Singapore's population growth rate after 1980, at 1.8 per cent per annum, was lower than the rate before then, at 2.0 per cent, and so the per capita real output growth rate did not fall as much as the growth rate of total GDP.

Table 2.2   Output growth rates (per cent per annum)

	1960–93	1965–93	1965–73	1973–93	1965–80	1980–93
GDP	8.5	8.5	13.0	7.3	10.2	6.9
GNP	8.5	8.4	12.3	7.4	9.9	7.2

Source: Calculated from data in Table 2.1 and its sources.

These period averages give no indication of the extent to which annual growth rates varied at different times. Before looking at the extent of these fluctuations, let us review the main international and domestic events that might be assumed to have an effect on the short-run performance of a small, export-oriented economy dependent on imported oil.

In the late 1960s we might expect to see the impact of the political turbulence associated with Singapore's joining the Federation of Malaysia and then withdrawing in 1965 and the confrontation with Indonesia during the period from 1963 to 1966. Furthermore, in July 1967, the British government announced the withdrawal of its troops by 1971, but in 1968 these plans were brought forward. However there were a number of fortuitous events that improved Singapore's growth prospects at this time. To compensate for the earlier withdrawal of troops the new British Conservative government agreed to 'hand over valuable assets, retrain redundant employees, help create an air defence system and give a £50 million soft loan which was virtually a gift' (Turnbull, 1989, p.294). Furthermore the 1967 Seven Days' War led to the closing of the Suez canal but increased the demand for Singapore's ship repairing services just at the time when the American build-up for the Vietnam War was increasing the demand for Singapore's services as a supply centre. After June 1966 conditions for trade with Indonesia improved (Turnbull, ibid., pp.293–4).

In the early 1970s all oil-importing countries were affected by OPEC quadrupling the price of oil in the last quarter of 1973. Singapore's main export markets went into recession but experienced high rates of inflation and the demand for oil fell. The term 'stagflation' was born. In 1979 oil prices again increased significantly. In the USA a tight monetary policy was initiated in late 1979. With an expansionary fiscal policy in the early 1980s, real interest rates rose dramatically and the American economy went into a recession which was particularly deep in 1982. The American dollar appreciated significantly over the years up to 1985, leading to an appreciation of the Hong Kong dollar, which could be thought of as one of Singapore's export competitors, as the Hong Kong dollar was linked to the American dollar in October 1983.

In the mid-1980s oil prices continued their steady fall, from their peak in 1982 thus reducing oil exploration activities, and this might be expected to affect the demand for Singapore's ship repairing services. In August 1990 Iraq invaded Kuwait and in early 1991 several industrialized countries united to attack Iraq, thus launching the Gulf War. Oil prices rose again and tourism was disrupted for many countries in Asia.

Figure 2.1 shows the extent of fluctuations in the annual growth rate of GDP compared to its long-run growth trend of 8.5 per cent per annum. The only years in which real GDP fell were 1964 and 1985, when output fell 4.3 and 1.6 per cent, respectively. The lowest positive growth rates were the 4.0 per cent of 1975 and the 1.8 of 1986. The period of especially high growth was from 1966 to 1973.

The composition of Singapore's GDP series has some interesting features. Figures 2.2 and 2.3 show the developments of the main components of GDP since 1960. In both 1983 and 1984 gross fixed capital formation (GFCF) exceeded private consumption expenditures in real terms. We wonder if any other country in modern history has ever experienced this phenomenon. Through the CPF scheme the government is able to control both the overall extent of

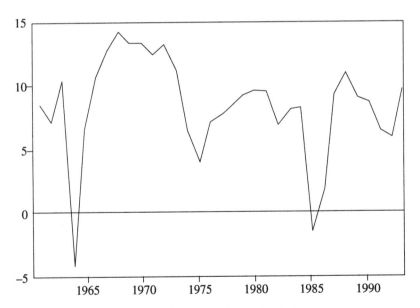

Figure 2.1 Annual percentage GDP growth rate, 1961–93

private consumption and, through the regulations governing the use of CPF funds, the way savings are spent.

The component of output known as increase in stocks has always been positive when taken on an annual basis, except for 1964. Only in 18 separate quarters since March 1975 has the increase in stocks been negative. Businesses have increased their stocks in every year since 1965. If increase in stocks becomes negative it means, of course, that demand can be met with a level of production (GDP) lower than the total of demand. Negative stock accumulation has been a contributory factor to recession in some western developed countries. During the recession of 1985 the increase in stocks was negative only in the first and fourth quarters.

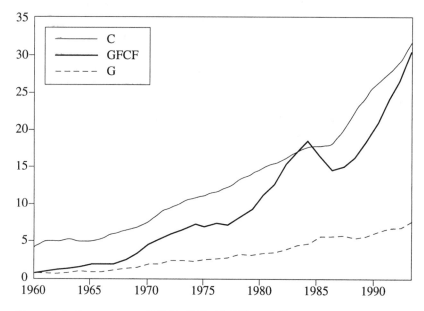

Figure 2.2 Components of GDP, 1960–93, billion dollars (1985 prices)

In Singapore, net exports were negative until 1986 when they became a positive item of GDP and have stayed a positive and large component since. In 1989, for example, net exports equalled S$5.7 billion, 9.9 per cent of that year's GDP. The early *Statistical Yearbooks* called this item net imports in which case, as it was positive, it had to be deducted from the other items of expenditure to obtain GDP.

Net exports have been the most unstable component of GDP in Singapore. We take up this issue again in Chapter 6. Fixed investment has been relatively stable, unlike the case in developed economies where investment can show large

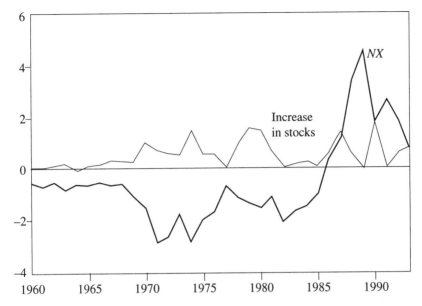

Figure 2.3 Components of GDP, 1960–93, billion dollars (1985 market prices)

annual fluctuations. The relative stability of the components of GDP can be seen in their coefficients of variation over the period 1965 to 1993:[1]

GDP	0.6138
C	0.5042
G	0.5743
GFCF	0.6794
Change in stocks	0.8238
Net exports	4.0017

2.2 EMPLOYMENT AND UNEMPLOYMENT

Table 2.1 shows the total labour force over the period 1968–93, its annual growth rate, the annual growth of the number of people in employment and the unemployment rate. The labour force and employment figures are not strictly consistent over time as their coverage has been changed slightly, but they do give a general picture of trends in the labour force and employment after 1968.

We can see a continued fall in unemployment after 1966 until 1974. In each of these years the growth in employment exceeded the growth in the labour force. Whenever the growth in employment was less than the growth in the labour force the unemployment rate rose, such as in 1975, 1983, 1985, 1986 and 1992. Only in 1985, 1986 and 1991 did the number of people in employment actually fall. In other years the rise in unemployment was accompanied by a rise in employment that was smaller than the increase in the labour force. In Singapore the unemployment rate is clearly very cyclical with unemployment being at its highest in the second quarter of each year and at its lowest in the first quarter. The differences can be quite large. In 1993, for example, the unemployment rate in the first quarter was about 1.4 per cent but in the second quarter it had risen to about 2.7 per cent. In the other two quarters it was below 2 per cent (*Economic Survey of Singapore: Third Quarter 1994*, p.12). We have not seen a clear explanation for the unemployment rate rising so much in the second quarter of each year. There does not seem to be any seasonal pattern of higher job losses in the second quarter of each year.

There are two theoretical approaches to explaining the link between labour force growth and unemployment growth. One, which we can call the modern classical 'unemployment is voluntary' paradigm, sees the change in employment as the residual effect of a rise in the labour force, together with a decision by some of these people not to take a job on offer as they think they can find a better job after a period of search. Unemployment is chosen, meaning that the increase in employment is the residual. This view is that there are always jobs there for people entering the labour market, but that some people do not choose to take them in some years. The other approach, which we can call Keynesian, views the change in unemployment as the residual, given that, at times, the number of new jobs is not sufficient for the number of people entering the labour force. Both these views will be examined in the next chapter.

Over the period 1968–93 employment increased by 993 800 people, that is at an average of 39 752 new jobs per year. Remarkably the averages of different periods are not much different from this long-run figure. Over the five years from 1968 to 1973, when we might expect employment expansion to be quite rapid, the average increase was 40 200 per year; from 1973 to 1980, which includes the recession of the early 1970s, the average was 39 100 a year and from 1980 to 1993, which includes the recession of 1885 and 1986, the average was 41 330 a year. This indicates that job creation has been quite steady over the long period but these averages conceal some large year-to-year differences. Let us look at a few years in the 1980s to get a feel for what happened.

The years 1985 and 1986 are interesting as these saw Singapore's most serious recession. In addition, 1990 saw the largest increase in employment for a long time. Table 2.3 shows what was happening in these years. The arithmetic of the table is simple: change in employment equals change in labour force minus change in unemployment (that is, minus increase in unemployment or plus reduction in unemployment). No item was calculated as a residual.

In 1990, for example, the population of people over 15 years of age increased by 47 000 but the labour force increased by 138 000. This high figure may be due to more accurate measurement in 1990, as this figure is based on the Census of that year. This would imply a large increase in the participation rate, which is the ratio of economically active persons to the total population of working age. The participation rate for men rose marginally from 78.6 to 79.0 per cent from 1989 to 1990 and that for women much more, from 48.4 to 53.0 per cent. This led to a greater increase in employment as unemployment fell by 4900 people. This was associated with a high, but not particularly high, rate of growth of GDP.

Table 2.3   Employment and unemployment in selected years

	Increase over previous year in (thousands)				
	Population over 15 years	Labour force	Employment	Unemployment	GDP (%)
1985	37.3	–16.6	–34.5	+18.0	–1.6
1986	39.2	10.7	–20.2	+30.8	1.8
1987	40.2	30.8	52.5	–21.5	9.4
1988	43.7	48.4	64.7	–16.3	11.1
1989	40.3	47.0	62.4	–15.5	9.2
1990	47.2	138.1	143.0	–4.9	8.8

Note: Figures have been rounded.

Sources: Calculated from data in *Yearbook of Statistics Singapore*, various years, Tables 2.3, 3.1, 3.3.

The contrast with the mid-1980s is interesting. In 1985 the population of over 15-year olds rose by 37 000, but nearly 17 000 people dropped out of the labour force which, together with an 18 000 rise in the number of people unemployed, meant total employment fell nearly 35 000. One interpretation is to say that 35 000 people lost their jobs: 17 000 of them dropped out of the labour force and the other 18 000 became registered as unemployed but available for work. This is the Keynesian view: the number of jobs fell (because the level of output fell for reasons exogenous to the labour market) and so the number of people unemployed and no longer economically active rose. The modern classical view would say that 35 000 people decided not to work in that year: 17 000 of them gave up being part of the workforce and 18 000 stayed actively looking for better jobs but were counted as unemployed. As employment fell, so did output. The employment decision caused output to fall, not the other way around.

In 1986 the labour force rose by only 11 000 but as unemployment rose by nearly 31 000 employment fell 20 000. Despite the increase in GDP in 1986, unemployment continued to rise and reached its highest rate in the 1980s of 6.5 per cent. This lag of employment recovery behind changes in output is common in developed economies: even though the economy is recovering, unemployment continues to increase. In the recovery after 1986 employment grew more rapidly than the labour force, so unemployment fell. This was associated with high rates of growth and those of 1987–90 were above the long-run average of 8.5 per cent.

Which sectors had falling employment during this recession? Table 2.4 indicates what happened to employment in different sectors, with those showing greatest changes at the top. We can see that manufacturing and transport and communications experienced the largest falls in 1985 and manufacturing and commerce in 1986, but manufacturing recovered rapidly after 1986. Employment in the construction sector fell over the period 1986 to 1988. Commerce experienced a fall in employment only in 1986 but recovered strongly in 1987.

Even before the recession set in, in 1984 almost 40 000 foreign workers, about 26 per cent of the estimated 150 000 foreign workers in Singapore, had 'been sent home'. One interpretation of this is that 'foreign workers acted as the buffer and lessened the adjustment problem' (Lim and associates, 1988, p.30).

Table 2.4   Changes in employment, selected years (thousands)

	1985	1986	1987	1988	1989	1990
Manufacturing	−33.9	−7.6	32.1	40.4	24.6	43.7
Transport and communications	−7.1	−4.5	7.9	7.0	8.5	8.9
Construction	2.2	−4.8	−8.0	−7.6	2.6	29.9
Commerce	4.2	−9.3	16.0	8.2	13.2	19.4
Finance and business services	−1.3	−2.1	6.7	15.2	9.7	30.0
Utilities	−1.7	0	−0.6	0.8	−0.9	−0.8
Other services	3.9	8.4	−1.4	11.7	4.8	14.4
Agriculture, fishing and quarrying	−0.3	0.2	0.1	5.9	0.5	−1.3

Source: Calculated from *Yearbook of Statistics Singapore 1993*, Table 3.3.

2.3   INFLATION

Let us now turn to the price and monetary variables in order to investigate Singapore's inflation record during its history of rapid economic growth and transformation. Table 2.5 presents some relevant series in the form of the annual increases in the consumer price index (CPI) and the GDP deflator which can be thought of as a price index of everything that makes up GDP. We have also included the annual growth rate of M2, a broad measure of the money supply which will be discussed in more detail in Chapter 5. The table also includes banks' prime lending rate (an average of the rates quoted by the ten leading banks) which indicates the average of the lowest rate at which one could borrow from them. The rate offered on savings deposits was on average 3.2 percentage points lower than this prime rate throughout the 1980s and into the 1990s. We also include an index of all shares quoted on the Singapore Stock Exchange.

We use the changes in the consumer price index to indicate the extent of inflation in Singapore. Before doing this we must remark that this index was recently subject to scrutiny by a government-appointed review committee of economists and others as the index had been criticized for understating the true extent of inflation in Singapore. The committee's views are contained in the *Report of the Cost Review Committee* published in 1993, in which they concluded that the CPI did reflect the change in the cost of living of most Singaporeans, but recommended the compilation of separate indexes for different income groups (p.1). A new index, with three separate indexes for different income groups, using the 1992/93 household expenditure survey as its base, will be published from July 1995. In many neighbouring countries the CPI indexes have been criticized for being a poor reflection of the true rate of inflation (*Asian Wall Street Journal*, 24 January 1994, pp.1 and 5). One obvious reason is that just one number cannot capture the experiences of many people of different income levels and consumption patterns and who might live in different parts of a large country. For example, the national CPI index in Malaysia, just an average for the whole country, cannot capture the different experiences of different regions and the differences between the countryside and the town, in which the inflation rate tends to be higher. Thailand has recently announced adjustments to the way it measures inflation through its CPI. Singapore is so small that the collection of price data is likely to be easy and accurate. The contentious issues are over what should be included in the index and what weights should be given to different items.[2]

We can summarize Singapore's inflation experiences by referring to the data of Table 2.6. The long-run inflation rate has been 4 per cent per annum, low by international standards, but implying a doubling of prices nearly every 18 years. Singapore's consumer price index in 1993 was 2.8 times its 1965 level. The inflation rate was highest during the period 1965 to 1980 which included the effects of both periods of oil price increases. Since 1980 the rate of consumer price inflation has fallen considerably as this period includes very moderate price increases in 1985 and 1987 and a fall in prices in 1986. Figure 2.4 shows the variation in the inflation rate and clearly indicates by how much the annual inflation rate increased in the years 1973–4 and 1980–81.

The Singapore economy

Table 2.5   Price increases and monetary series

	CPI	GDP deflator	M2 growth rate	Interest rate	Stock exchange 1 Jan. 1970 = 100
	(% increase)		(% p.a.)	(% p.a.)	
1960					
1961	0.3	−0.2			
1962	0.5	0.8			
1963	2.2	0.5	9.3		
1964	1.6	1.7	4.8		
1965	0.3	2.1	7.2		
1966	2.0	1.6	13.6		
1967	3.3	−0.2	16.9		
1968	0.7	0.8	24.3	8.00	
1969	−0.3	2.6	19.0	8.00	
1970	0.4	1.9	16.3	8.00	100.4
1971	1.8	4.7	11.2	8.00	125.6
1972	2.2	5.7	25.6	7.50	260.0
1973	19.6	12.5	15.6	9.00	380.4
1974	22.3	15.2	13.5	10.25	215.4
1975	2.6	2.6	17.9	7.08	209.8
1976	−1.9	1.7	12.7	6.78	237.2
1977	3.2	1.6	6.6	7.02	226.2
1978	4.8	2.4	10.8	7.65	300.6
1979	4.0	5.3	18.8	9.48	346.8
1980	8.5	11.5	24.5	13.60	489.6
1981	8.2	6.7	22.4	11.83	737.1
1982	3.9	4.2	15.9	9.33	553.7
1983	1.2	3.9	11.9	8.98	725.5
1984	2.6	0.7	6.2	9.40	704.3
1985	0.5	−1.2	3.8	7.20	579.7
1986	−1.4	−2.5	9.9	6.10	509.0
1987	0.5	0.8	19.8	6.10	693.4
1988	1.5	5.5	13.5	6.13	595.3
1989	2.4	5.2	22.5	6.25	722.3
1990	3.4	5.9	20.0	7.73	815.9
1991	3.4	3.5	12.4	7.10	810.7
1992	2.3	2.1	8.9	5.55	810.2
1993	2.4	2.4	8.5	5.34	1000.1

Sources: *Economic and Social Statistics Singapore 1960–1982; Yearbook of Statistics Singapore*, various issues.

Table 2.6 Inflation rates (per cent per annum)

	1960–93	1965–93	1965–73	1973–93	1965–80	1980–93
CPI	3.8	4.0	2.4	3.0	5.2	1.8
GDP deflator	3.9	4.1	3.1	3.4	4.9	2.5

Note: We had to chain-link two CPI series with different base years to obtain a complete series in order to calculate these growth rates.

Source: Calculated from data in the sources for Table 2.5.

As Figure 2.4 shows, the rate of consumer price inflation was about 20 per cent in both 1973 and 1974. Interestingly the item of consumer prices that rose most rapidly in these years was food, rising by 33 and 26 per cent, respectively. The category 'rice, other cereals' which rose 89 and 39 per cent, respectively, and 'meat and poultry' (34 and 22 per cent price increases) were the food items that rose most in price. The price of rice and other cereals fell significantly in the three years 1975–7 only to rise again in 1978. These items are largely imported. In 1973 there were negligible increases in the cost of transport but in 1974 the cost of private road transport rose by 38 per cent, public road

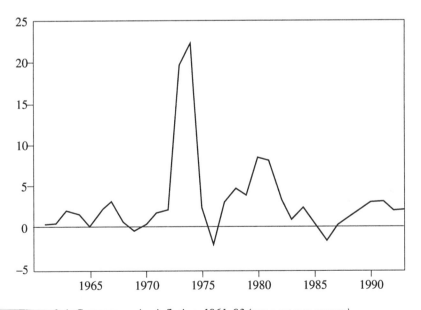

Figure 2.4 Consumer price inflation, 1961–93 (per cent per annum)

transport by 29 per cent and other travel and transport by 46 per cent. These costs would be related to the higher price of imported oil, illustrating why the Singapore government is sensitive to the possibility of imported inflation. This is reflected in the statisticians' now decomposing consumer price inflation into its domestic and imported components. See any issue of the annual *Economic Survey of Singapore* for this treatment of the data.

The next period of high consumer price inflation was in the years 1980 and 1981, when the index rose by 8.5 and 8.2 per cent, respectively. Most prices rose at similar rates and food price rises were not much different from the increases in the overall index. In 1980 transport costs rose about 15 per cent, however. Consumer prices have fallen compared to those of the previous year only in 1969, 1976 and 1986. There are few countries in the world that have recorded falls in consumer prices in recent years. The effects of inflation on Singapore's macroeconomic policies and its exchange rate will be discussed in Chapter 6.

The combination of high growth and low inflation in Singapore has attracted attention (Parkin, 1993, p.1025). We can indicate the extent to which inflation and growth are related by referring to the scatter diagram shown in Figure 2.5. The diagram shows the relationship between average annual inflation and growth rates for a large number of countries whose annual inflation rates did not exceed 100 per cent per annum, over the period 1980 to 1992. The general view about the nature of the likely relationship between inflation and growth has changed over the years since the Second World War. In the early post-war years, under the influence of Keynesian economics, it was felt that moderate inflation could contribute to growth. It was felt that inflation would increase profit margins as wage increases lagged behind price increases, thus encouraging more investment. In the Keynesian paradigm, saving was not a limit to investment as increases in investment would cause incomes to rise and thus provide the saving out of the higher level of income. In the early 1970s there was a revival of earlier classical views that argued that high inflation produced negative real interest rates and this reduced the incentive to save, thus reducing investment. This is a classical view as it sees investment being limited by the need for a prior act of saving. Further ideas developed in the late 1970s argued that high and variable inflation rates reduce the incentive to save and invest and would thus probably produce low growth rates of output. The scatter of observations in Figure 2.5 shows that, if anything, there is a slight inverse relationship between inflation and growth: high inflation countries tend to have lower growth rates. No economy with an annual inflation rate over 20 per cent grew faster than 5 per cent per annum. All those that grew faster than 5 per cent per annum had annual inflation rates less than 13 per cent. Turkey stands out as a high inflation country (46 per cent per annum) and a high growth one (4.9 per cent per annum). Turkey's recent economic performance has not been so good, however. There is great variation in the growth experience of countries that have

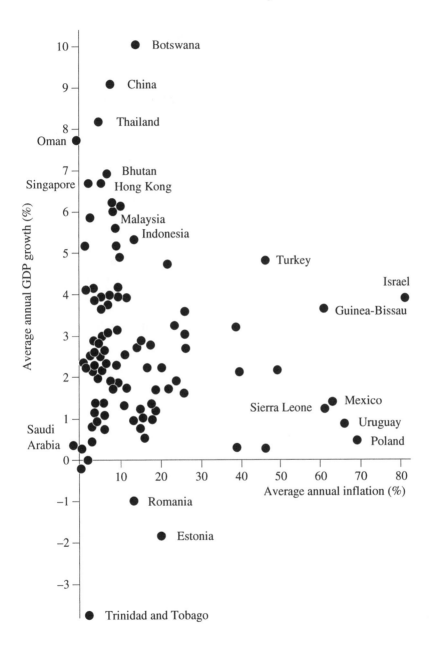

Figure 2.5 Growth rates and inflation, 1980–92

experienced annual inflation rates in the range 0 to 10 per cent. Singapore stands out as a low inflation-high growth economy as do Malaysia, Thailand and Hong Kong.

Figure 2.6 is a scatter diagram of Singapore and world inflation rates measured by the consumer price index over the period 1963–92, allowing us to see the extent to which Singapore's inflation rate differed from the world rate and when. We can see that, with the exception of just two years, 1973 and 1974, Singapore's consumer price inflation has always been lower than that in the rest of the world. The only years when Singapore's inflation approached the world rate were 1967, 1978, 1980 and 1981. This world rate is likely to be misleading if we take it as an indicator of what was happening to prices in Singapore's main trading partners. This world rate is an average of inflation rates and has become very sensitive to high inflation in some countries. For example, it is claimed that in 1993 the world rate of inflation was 19.9 per cent, but in the industrial countries it was only 2.8 per cent (*International Financial Statistics Yearbook 1994*, p.64). This was due to very high inflation in the developing countries (2000 per cent per annum in Zaire and Brazil, for example) and in former planned economies (with 255 per cent in Romania). In fact Singapore's inflation rate of 2.4 per cent in 1993 was higher than that in such countries as Canada (1.8), Australia (1.8), Japan (1.3), New Zealand (1.3) and the UK (1.6) and others. In 1994 Singapore's inflation rate was 3.6 per cent.

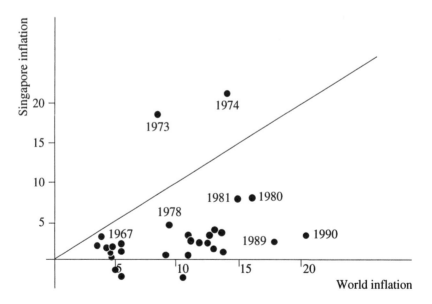

Figure 2.6 Singapore and world inflation, 1963–92 (per cent per annum)

2.4   INTEREST RATES

Table 2.5 shows that interest rates in Singapore have been quite low recently and falling. The rate given in that table is the average of the banks' prime lending rate. Deposit rates are lower than this rate, of course. Since 1984, when the banks' saving deposit rate was 6.53 per cent per annum, the rate has never exceeded this; by 1992 it was 1.79 per cent and in 1993 it was 1.59 per cent. In these latter years inflation was at least 2 per cent per annum. Singapore is an economy with low real interest rates, an observation we will have to explain later.

Despite these figures, the World Bank has argued that real deposit rates in Singapore have been high. Its general argument is that high real rates of interest are good for growth as they encourage saving and hence investment, although they do recognize that public sector saving has been an important factor based on 'mandatory provident fund contributions' (*The East Asian Miracle*: *Summary*, p.22). The bank argues that negative real deposit rates and a high variability in real rates due to variable inflation rates are bad for economic development, and that the real interest rate on deposits in Singapore has averaged 2.48 per cent over the period 1977–91 and had a standard deviation of only 1.71 per cent. Japan's real deposit rate averaged minus 1.12 (standard deviation 3.89) and Hong Kong's minus 1.81 (standard deviation 3.16)[3] (*The East Asian Miracle*, p.206) so these economies, at least, do not seem to have suffered from having negative and fluctuating real interest rates and they do not have compulsory saving schemes either.

The change in Singapore's interest rates at times of great variation in the inflation rate are interesting. During the first oil shock of 1973–5 the inflation rate rose from 2.2 per cent in 1972 to about 20 per cent in both 1973 and 1974. The prime lending rate increased by, at most, three percentage points, producing large negative real interest rates in these years. In 1980 the inflation rate increased by 4.5 percentage points and the prime lending rate rose by nearly the same amount. In the early 1980s the increase in inflation rates did not produce negative real lending rates. In 1980 the deposit rate averaged 9.52 per cent and the inflation rate was 8.5 per cent, probably preserving positive real rates on deposits too. The explanation of these different patterns is probably that before 1975 Singapore banks were allowed to operate a cartel that controlled interest rates. Only after the banking deregulation of 1975 were interest rates market-determined.

2.5   LATEST DEVELOPMENTS

At the time of writing provisional data for 1994 have just been released in Singapore, so it might be worthwhile reviewing the figures to see if any of the above trends have changed. Table 2.7 summarizes the important variables we have been discussing in this chapter. We can see that GNP was less than GDP, meaning that net factor income from abroad was negative to the extent of S$434 million. This reverses the pattern of the previous five years when GNP exceeded GDP (see Chapter 1). IGNP was 80.5 per cent of GNP compared to a ratio of 81.5 in 1993.

Table 2.7   Provisional data for 1994

	Billion dollars	Percentage increase over previous year
Gross National Product	104.8796	12.7
IGNP	84.4483	11.3
IGNP per capita (dollars)	28 820	9.2
Gross Domestic Product (Current prices)	105.3132	14.0
Gross Domestic Product (1985 market prices)	78.7654	10.1
Private consumption	33.2093	4.3
Government consumption	7.8585	0.8
GFCF	29.5909	7.6
Increase in stocks	−1.2049	−221.8
Net exports	12.2760	201.3
Statistical discrepancy	−2.9644	
Unemployment rate (%, June)	2.6	
CPI inflation rate (%)		3.6
GDP deflator (%)		3.6
Minimum lending rate (%)	6.49	

Source: *Economic Survey of Singapore 1994, passim*; authors' calculation from there.

Real GDP growth has been put at 10.1 per cent for 1994, the same as the revised growth rate for 1993, the first time two consecutive years have seen double-digit growth since the early 1970s. This GDP growth rate was associated with a huge increase in external demand of 21.1 per cent compared to a 2.0 increase in total domestic demand. We can see this reflected in the components of GDP. Private consumption rose by 4.3 per cent and government consumption by 0.8 per cent. GFCF rose 7.6 per cent. Net exports rose from S$4.08 billion in 1993 to S$12.28 billion (in 1985 prices) in 1994 to be more than three times higher! This huge surge in net exports reflects the growth in foreign demand and shows up in the fact that the current account surplus rose from S$8.36 billion in 1993 to S$18.25 in 1994. A new occurrence in 1994 was the fact that the increase in stocks was negative, the first time this item has ever been negative on an annual basis since 1964. This item fell from being S$989 million in 1993 to minus S$1.205 billion (in 1985 market prices), a decline of S$2.2 billion, about 3 per cent of 1993's GDP. In many economies such a fall in demand would be associated with a decline in or slowdown in the growth of GDP, but in Singapore, with external demand growing so rapidly, it just changed a 5.3 per cent increase in final domestic demand to a 2.0 per cent increase in total domestic demand.

Despite these high growth rates in the aggregate variables, nominal IGNP per capita rose 9.2 per cent. When we take into account the reported 3.6 per cent consumer price inflation, real IGNP per capita rose about 5.6 per cent. Manufacturing output grew 12.9 per cent and construction by 15.7 per cent. Transport and communications grew 11.2 per cent and Financial and business services grew only 1.4 per cent compared to its 9.9 per cent growth in 1993.

2.6 CONCLUSIONS

From the above review we can see that Singapore is a high-growth, low-inflation country. The growth rate has been quite stable, with GDP falling only in 1964 and 1985. Growth was low in 1975, prompting some people to make an easy generalization that Singapore's growth rate has been subject to a ten-year cycle. We will examine this view in Chapter 7. Unemployment rates have fallen steadily from the early days of independence, a trend contrary to the long-run increase in unemployment rates in several European countries. Interest rates and rates on bank deposits are very low. An interesting feature of recent macroeconomic history has been the increase in the total amount of investment and the marked increase in net exports after 1986.

In the next two chapters we present a review of macroeconomic concepts and theories to give us a framework for understanding the nature of the relationships between these main macroeconomic variables and to help us understand the ideas underlying some of the research that has been done on the Singapore economy. In subsequent chapters we apply these ideas to look at such issues as the nature of the monetary system, the role of international trade in the economy, the exchange rate and the policy towards it, the nature of growth in Singapore and cycles in the economy. We also look at the way economists and statisticians have attempted to model formally the simple macroeconomic relationships we have discussed, such as the consumption function and the income multiplier.

SUGGESTIONS FOR FURTHER READING

Economic Survey of Singapore: both annual and quarterly issues are very useful reviews of the progress of the economy and the main statistical source is the annual *Yearbook of Statistics Singapore*. For historical data, see *Economic and Social Statistics Singapore 1960–1982*.

NOTES

1. The coefficient of variation is calculated as the standard deviation expressed as a proportion of the mean of the series. The coefficients were calculated from the series in constant 1985 prices.
2. Some private organizations produce their own Consumer Price Indexes based on expatriates' expenditure patterns, in which items such as school fees, private transport, travel and entertainment are more significant than for Singaporeans. For details of the coverage and weighting of the CPI see *Monthly Digest of Statistics*, any issue, and the *Report of the Cost Review Committee*, pp. 137–50.
3. Hong Kong's deposit rates are low as the government has allowed a cartel arrangement among the commercial banks to set deposit rates quite low to maintain the spread between their borrowing and lending rates and this contributes to the high profitability of banks in Hong Kong. Consumer interest organizations there are trying to have the arrangement abolished.

3. Macroeconomic thinking and concepts

When reading about the Singapore economy the reader may come across references to such things as 'a monetarist small econometric model for Singapore' (Toida, 1985) or to a comment that 'the model is very Keynesian in nature' (Toh and Ramstetter, 1994, p.361) or to a test of 'the rational expectations– permanent income hypothesis for Singapore' (Thornton, 1993). You may read that a model contains a Phillips curve and there has been an attempt to identify the 'natural rate' of unemployment (Low, 1994, p.25). We need, therefore, to understand what these different terms mean, to appreciate the nature of different approaches to understanding the working of the macroeconomy and the role of government, the disagreements about the direction of causation between major variables, what the important variables are, and so on. We also need to be aware that the macro-economic models presented in many leading textbooks used in Singapore are based on assumptions that are not relevant to the understanding of the Singapore macroeconomy.

In this chapter we review the evolution of macroeconomic thinking from the pre-Keynesian era to today. In a limited space we can only indicate the main differences in approaches taken by various influential macroeconomists and the resulting so-called 'schools' of economists and the new emerging theories each offer to support a particular theoretical position.

We start with pre-Keynesian economics, which is usually called the classical economic model. This pre-Keynesian way of looking at macroeconomic rela-tionships never really died out and has been revived and adapted in various forms as a challenge to Keynesian economics. It is important to understand the logic of this model as subsequent developments were either a refutation of its logic and relevance to the real world, by John Maynard Keynes (1883–1946) and his followers, of course, or a basis for modifications aimed at challenging the Keynesian ascendancy of the 1950s and 1960s, by Milton Friedman, Robert E. Lucas Jr. and Robert J. Barro, amongst others. We then indicate Keynes's reasons for rejecting the classical approach. We then show how the classical model was revived and discuss the new concepts and theories that were integrated into its basic framework, then indicate the reaction to this revival of classical ways of thinking.

3.1 PRE-KEYNESIAN OR CLASSICAL ECONOMICS

The macroeconomic model outlined here is an *ex post* rationalization of the basic beliefs of important economists who lived in the eighteenth and nineteenth centuries, the most important of whom were David Hume (1711–76), Adam Smith (1723–90), David Ricardo (1772–1823), John Stuart Mill (1806–73) and those who lived into the twentieth century, such as the now influential American Irving Fisher (1867–1947) and the University of Cambridge economists Alfred Marshall (1842–1924) and A.C. Pigou (1877–1959) who taught Keynes. Younger economists, especially those in the USA, who have been called New Classical economists, want to resurrect the method of Marshall to study economic fluctuations and abandon the approach of his pupil, John Maynard Keynes (Lucas, 1987, pp.107–8).

We first look at the determination of output in the short run in the classical model. We assume that there are two factors of production, capital, K, and labour, N. The capital stock is constant in the short run. Output is measured in real terms so we can think of it as units of some food crop. It is a function of the amount of labour performed. Diminishing returns to labour are assumed and so the aggregate production function linking total output, Y per time period, to the quantity of labour is shown in the upper part of Figure 3.1. The marginal physical product of labour (MPN) is the increase in total output brought about by employing one more worker. As there are diminishing returns this is an inverse function of N and is shown in the lower part of Figure 3.1. MPN is measured in units of Y. The figure shows that when N_1 workers are employed their MPN is 5 units of Y. Think of employers hiring workers and paying them a real wage measured in units of Y. Employers will hire workers up to the point where MPN is just equal to the real wage. If the real wage were 5 units of Y then N_1 workers would be hired. This is because profit maximization implies that all workers whose MPN exceeds their cost to the employer are worth hiring, hence the MPN schedule is a demand for labour schedule in the short run: the lower the real wage, the greater the volume of employment and the greater the volume of employment, the greater is the economy's total output.

It was obviously unrealistic to think of the real wage as being paid out in terms of units of Y, so the model was adapted to allow for money payments by employers and purchases using money by people. The real wage can then be thought of as the money wage, W, deflated by the price of a unit of output, P, so the real wage is W/P. If the money or nominal wage were $5 dollars and the price of a unit of Y were $1 then the real wage would be 5. Think of the employers selling output in a competitive market: they would push output to the point where price equals marginal cost, MC. Here, MC is equal to the money wage divided by MPN:

$$P = MC = W/MPN$$

Rearranging gives

$$W/P = MPN,$$

so $W/P = MPN$ is the consequence of profit maximizing under competition. This is the same result as above: employment is pushed to the point where the real wage equals the MPN. Given the production function and the price of output at \$1 a unit, if the money wage is \$5 the employers will hire N_1 workers such that the MPN is 5.

The extent of employment will depend on the willingness of workers to work at different real wages. We assume that the supply of labour is a positive function of the real wage offered. This result can be derived from the theory of household behaviour and has become a standard assumption for the macro-economics of labour supply. See Abel and Bernanke (1995, pp.276–81) for a modern treatment. Most writers are willing to assume that the substitution effect of a change in wages dominates the income effects over the existing range of wages so that labour supply is taken to be a positive function of the real wage.[1]

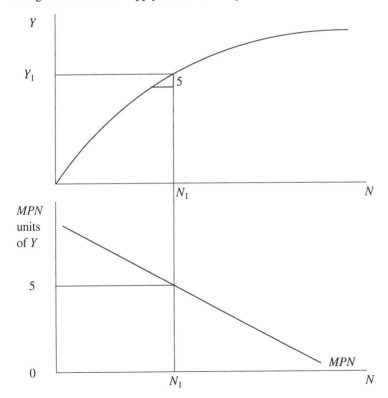

Figure 3.1 The production function and the marginal product of labour

We also assume that the labour market is competitive. If we believe the labour market sets the market-clearing real wage then equilibrium employment is shown in the upper part of Figure 3.2. N^* workers are employed and Y^* units of output are produced. The real wage is just equal to the marginal disutility of labour and every worker who wants to work at the existing market wage has a job. The economy's output is determined by the nature of the production function, the stock of capital and the willingness of workers to work.

The lower part of Figure 3.2 shows a different way of presenting this equilibrium which is very important. We plot the demand and supply curves for labour against the money wage. The employer would compare the money value of the marginal product (*MPN.P*), that is *MPN* times the price level, with the money wage. There is thus a different demand curve for labour for every price level. At price level P_1 of $1, N^* workers would be employed at the money wage of $5. We have seen that at this real wage ($5/1) N^* workers would be willing to

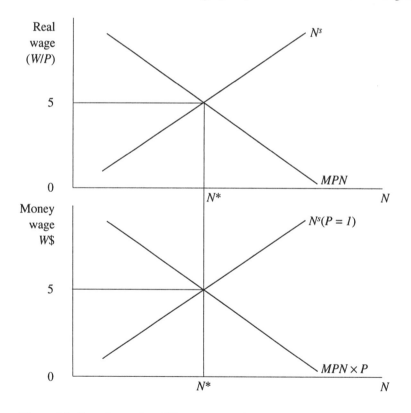

Figure 3.2 Two views of equilibrium in the classical labour market

work, so the economy is in equilibrium at a money wage of $5 when the price level is $1. Corresponding to N^*, output would be Y^*.

Now consider what would happen if the price level doubled to $2 per unit. This is shown in Figure 3.3. The value of the marginal product (*MPN* times P_2) would double at every N and thus shift upwards to be twice as high as before. If the money wage remained at $5 then employers would wish to employ more workers, as prices are higher and so the real wage is lower at any money wage. Workers were willing to supply N^* units of labour when the real wage was 5 ($5/1). With the price level having doubled they would only supply this amount at a money wage of $10 (twice as much) as this would provide them with the same real wage as before (10/2 = 5/1). In other words, in a competitive labour market on classical assumptions an increase in the price level would bring about a similar increase in the money wage, the real wage would remain the same and so employment and output would remain unchanged. The change in a nominal variable like the price level cannot produce an increase in output. How could it? Merely increasing the price level does not make workers want to do more work, does not increase the capital stock they have to work with, does not enhance the productivity of the workforce. How could output change? In other words, if we were to think of an aggregate supply schedule (*AS*) for the economy relating Y to P it would be perfectly inelastic with respect to the price level.

What determines the price level in this model? Take the simple equation of exchange, an identity that is true in all models. The money stock is M and V represents the income velocity of circulation of money. V is defined as PY/M, which we can think of as the number of times a unit of money is used to purchase final output in a given time. Thus M times V is the amount of nominal

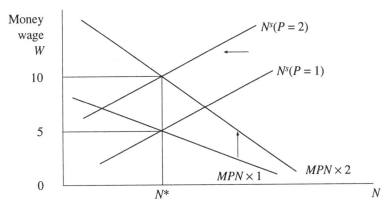

Figure 3.3   The effect of a change in the price level in the classical labour market

expenditure in any period. PY is the nominal value of output sold in a given period, hence

$$MV \equiv PY \text{ is always true.}$$

The classical model turns this equation of exchange into a theory (the Quantity Theory of Money) by assuming that the money stock is exogenous to the rest of the economy; that is, we can assume it to be determined by the monetary authorities and not to respond to changes in any variables in the economy. V is assumed to be constant in the short run, or at least not affected by changes in M. Output is already determined at the level Y^* and so

$$MV = PY^*$$

On the basis of the above assumptions this produces the proposition that any change in M will bring about a proportional change in the price level, P.

Another way to see the implication of this is to write

$$M = (1/V)PY \text{ or } M/P = (1/V)Y$$

If V is 4 then $1/V$ is 0.25; that is, people wish to hold an amount of real money (M/P) equal to one-quarter of a year's flow of income. If the exogenous money stock is to be voluntarily held by the public then, at a given level of Y, the price level must take on the required value. The demand for real money (M/P) is proportional to the level of real output, Y. This reflects the basic belief of quantity theorists that, although the monetary authority can determine the nominal money supply, it cannot determine the real money supply as this is determined by people's desires to hold real money as manifested through this simple demand for money function. If Y remains constant in the short run when M rises (which it must in this theory) then there must be a proportional increase in P to keep the real money supply at the appropriate level for it to remain equal to the amount demanded at the constant level of Y.

Figure 3.4 shows this equilibrium. If Y^* is 100 units and M is \$25 and $V = 4$ then nominal expenditure in the economy is \$100 and as this must equal PY^* the price level is 1. The labour market is in equilibrium where the real wage is 5 so the money wage is \$5. If the nominal money supply were to be doubled to 50 dollars then nominal spending would double and, given the fixed level of Y, prices would double. As the real wage remains the same the nominal wage would double to \$10 and the real wage remains the same at 5 (10/2). The nominal money wage is 'just another price' that moves in tandem with any change in the price level to keep the real wage at the equilibrium level. Changes in M only change nominal variables. This is the famous 'neutrality of money' proposition: money is neutral with respect to real variables in the economy causing only changes in nominal variables. In the classical model this is true in both the short and long run. Classical economists knew that this proposition was not always true in the short run, but it has been elevated almost to the position of an axiom by modern classical economists.

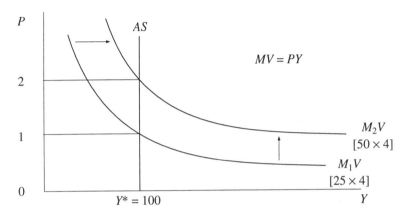

Figure 3.4   The determination of the aggregate price level in the classical model

We can complete the model by considering the determination of the rate of interest. Households receive money incomes either as wages or as profits. They decide how much to spend on consumer goods and how much not to spend, that is to save. It was not reasonable to assume that households would just accumulate unspent money balances, as there would be no return on them. They would wish to hold an interest-bearing financial asset. There are two types of financial asset in this model: corporate (company) bonds and government bonds. Companies issue bonds to obtain funds for their investment projects and the government issues bonds to cover its budget deficit. We assume for simplicity that the bonds issued by the government or by companies are perpetuities that are never redeemed by their issuer. This means that if you buy a bond you will be guaranteed a fixed coupon payment, let us say $5 a year for ever, for each $100 nominal valued bond you might buy. As long as you own the bond you get $5 each year. These are not shares where the dividend you get depends on the profitability and policy of the company but a guaranteed sum. If you no longer wish to hold the bond you can sell it through the bond market. The price you would get for your bond is determined by the demand and supply of bonds at the time you decide to sell it. Let us assume that you bought a $100 bond for $100 and it pays $5 a year. In that case you would be receiving a 5 per cent annual rate of interest for as long as you hold the bond. If, however, at the time you bought the bond, the supply of bonds had been particularly high then sellers might have had to sell them for, say, $90, in which case you would get a 5.6 per cent annual rate of interest (5/90). In other words, the interest rate you receive is inversely related to the price you pay for a bond, and this price is determined by the demand and supply of bonds. The demand for bonds depends on how much households are trying to save and the supply is determined by the investment plans of firms and the government budget deficit. If business-men have plans for a large amount of investment they will have to sell a lot of bonds, depressing the price of bonds and thus pushing up the rate of interest.

We can represent the determination of the rate of interest by using what has been called the classical loanable funds theory of the rate of interest. In Figure 3.5 we put the amount of planned investment, the government budget deficit and the amount of saving on the horizontal axis and the rate of interest on the vertical axis. The supply of saving out of the predetermined level of income Y^* is shown as $S(Y^*)$. It is an upward-sloping function as households are assumed to be willing to save more, that is consume less, out of their incomes the higher the interest rate. The rate of interest was regarded as the 'reward for saving' in the classical view. Investment is assumed to be an inverse function of the rate of interest, an assumption which Keynes fully accepted. The lower the rate of interest the more investment projects will be profitable and so the more investment there will be and the greater the supply of bonds on the market. Assume that government expenditures on goods and services, G, are all financed out of taxes, T, so there is no budget deficit at the moment and so the government does not have to sell bonds. The sole 'demand for loanable funds', or supply of bonds, is coming from the private sector. Given household saving desires, the equi-librium rate of interest will be r^* where desired saving is equated with planned investment at point A and firms are able to obtain all the funds they wish for investment purposes at the current rate of interest. Let us assume that both S and I are 40 at point A. If planned investment were to increase by, let us say, 10 units then the $I(r)$ schedule would shift to the right by this amount and the rate of interest would be pushed upwards. As the rate of interest rises, households decide to save more and the higher rate of interest induces some firms to reduce their investment plans. In Figure 3.5. we show how equilibrium is restored. At the new equilibrium rate of interest, saving has risen by 5 and the original investment plans have been cut back by 5. At the new equilibrium at point B investment is 45 and saving is also 45. As saving has risen by 5, consumption must have fallen by the same amount. In other words the realized increase in investment of 5 has reduced consumption by the same amount, so that $C + I + G$ remain the same; this must be as income is fixed at Y^* and $Y^* = C + I + G$. We are ignoring imports and exports here. In other words, the rate of interest acts as an equilibrating mechanism ensuring that total spending on final output $(C + I + G)$ remains the same when any of these items changes.

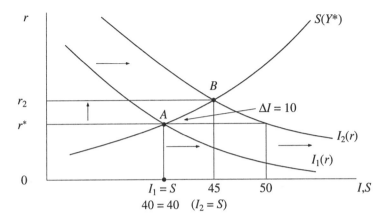

Figure 3.5 The equilibrating role of the rate of interest in the classical model

For an exercise, consider what would happen if people decided to reduce their consumption, that is to save more out of any given level of income. The saving function would shift to the right. The interest rate would fall. This would induce some households to revise their higher saving plans and save less, but it would also encourage more investment to offset the fall in consumption. Again $C + I + G$ would remain constant.

Now add the government budget deficit, as in Figure 3.6. The budget deficit is 10 as $G = 20$, but T is only 10. The total demand for loanable funds is shown as $I(r) + (G - T)$ and this produces an equilibrium rate of interest of r_1 where people are wiling to save 50. Society's saving of 50 goes partly to business-men who invest 40 and partly to the government to cover its budget deficit. What the government does with its share of society's saving is not known, but classical economists tended to think it would not be put to as good use as if it were channelled to profit-seeking businessmen.

At the equilibrium rate of interest injections equal withdrawals:

$$I + G = S + T$$
$$40 + 20 = 50 + 10$$

Income is 100, T is 10, so disposable income is 90. Out of this people choose to save 50, meaning C is 40. With I equal to 40 and G equal to 20, total spending is 100 (40 + 40 + 20).

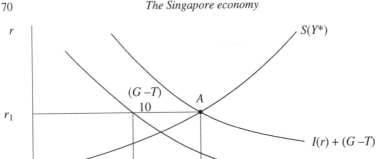

Figure 3.6 The effect of government borrowing on the rate of interest in the classical model

Now consider what will happen if the government, facing an election perhaps, increases its expenditure to 30, thus incurring a higher budget deficit of 20. The demand for loanable funds schedule shifts to the right, pushes up the rate of interest, discourages some investment but encourages households to save more. A possible equilibrium is shown as point *B* in Figure 3.7. Initially equilibrium was at point *A*, as in Figure 3.6. Assume that the functional forms are such that at the interest rate at point *B* saving rises to 55 (that is, consumption falls to 45) and investment falls to 35. Injections thus remain equal to withdrawals and total expenditures still equal 100:

$$I + G = S + T$$
$$35 + 30 = 55 + 10$$

Now the government takes more of society's saving and private businessmen get less for investment. We have assumed that people's saving behaviour does not change when the government budget deficit increases in the sense that the saving schedule does not shift. New Classical economists have an argument suggesting that people may save more when they see that the government deficit increases. We will cover this argument later.

We can see why early classical economists thought government budget deficits were a bad thing – even if they were not financed by borrowing from the central bank, which would increase the money supply and cause inflation. Such a view of the nature of the role of the rate of interest was used in the 1920s and 1930s by, amongst others, the British government, to argue that higher government expenditure aimed at reviving the economy at the time of a recession

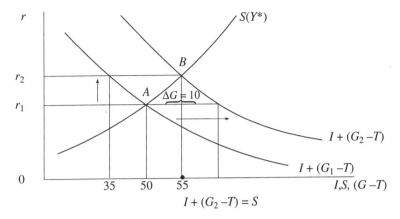

*Figure 3.7   The effect of an increase in the budget deficit in the
classical model*

would just 'crowd out' private investment, leaving total spending the same and
ensuring a lower rate of growth of the capital stock.

This ingenious theory of the rate of interest, reflected in the writings of
Alfred Marshall, among others, was an important element of the classical way
of thinking as it produces an automatic mechanism that ensures that changes
in one item of expenditure produce offsetting changes in others, leaving total
spending unchanged. A fall in consumption, for example, would induce an increase
in investment through a fall in the interest rate. A fall in consumption means
people are saving more now, that is, wanting to consume more in the future.
The fall in the rate of interest induces more investment, so society's capital stock
will be larger in the future and thus able to meet the higher consumer demand
in the future. It also implies that investment is constrained by the extent of current
saving and that saving determines investment. Keynes did not accept this view
as relevant to the 1920s and 1930s.

Let us put together the three elements of the classical model and draw out
the main implications. Output is determined in the labour market, which reaches
an equilibrium where the demand and supply of labour are equal. Whatever
quantity of output is produced can be sold. This is often referred to as 'Say's
law', as Keynes used this term to describe this proposition when he tried to
demolish it. This aspect of the model is reflected in many statements by
economists such as David Ricardo and both Mills (father James and his son John
Stuart) that aggregate output could never be excessive. If there were signs of
overproduction and unemployment these were due to the wrong composition
of output being produced, not to general overproduction or deficient demand.

The *MPN* schedule is interpreted as a demand for labour function. Changes in real spending cannot shift this function; therefore an increase in consumption demand, for example, does not increase the 'demand for labour' and increases neither wages nor the volume of employment. This aspect of the simple model above reflects the argument of John Stuart Mill that the demand for commodities does not constitute the demand for labour (Mill, 1848, pp.80–81), a proposition thought to be the characteristic of the classical approach and one which Keynes dismissed as completely erroneous.

Flexible wages and prices ensure that the labour market would be in equilibrium where everyone wishing to work at the current market wage could find a job. If anyone was counted as unemployed then this must be due to frictions in the labour market resulting from people currently being between jobs. Essentially any recorded unemployment must be voluntary as people either preferred leisure to work or are 'working' by looking for a better job.

Changes in output must be due to changes in the productivity of workers (*MPN* schedule shifts) or a change in the willingness of workers to work (labour-supply schedule shifts). We will show later how modern classical economists have proposed new theories based on both these factors to account for changes in output that are not caused by changes in demand – how could they be in this model? – but are associated with changes in some items of spending and occur even though they maintain the argument that the aggregate supply schedule is vertical. Other modern classically oriented economists have produced arguments why the aggregate supply curve might not be vertical in the short run. This opens up the possibility that demand fluctuations can produce changes in output, something that cannot happen in the simple classical model.

The rate of interest is a real variable linking and coordinating household saving decisions with the investment plans of firms. Saving is a good thing as it makes investment possible by freeing resources. What is saved is bound to generate a similar amount of investment.

Changes in the money supply change only nominal variables. The money wage is 'just another price' and the labour market need not be analysed in any way different from that used to analyse a competitive market for any commodity.

Money is neutral, having no effect on real variables. Changes in the money supply change only the price level and the money wage in the same proportion. The classical approach was to believe that important conclusions about real economies can be drawn by examining very simple models in which there is no real role for money, or for a banking system that creates credit, and then just adding money afterwards as an attempt to make it more realistic. Money was assumed to make no difference to the nature of this real economy and its equilibrium. Some modern classical economists build models in which money plays no role in determining output. These models, as we shall see, use the parable of Robinson Crusoe's existence to provide insights as to why output fluctuates, why there are recessions and so on in real economies. Keynes completely rejected this approach and tried to build a monetary theory of production. He created macroeconomics that did not generalize from propositions about the behaviour of one person (who is called a representative agent in modern economics) to propositions about the whole economy. New Classical economists are happy to make this generalization; Keynesian economists and others are not happy to do so as it involves the fallacy of composition of arguing that what is true of one individual (microeconomic propositions about individual behaviour, for example, such as how many hours' work a person would like to do each week) must also be true for all individuals when we take them as whole (macroeconomic propositions about how much work will actually be done).

3.2 THE KEYNESIAN REVOLUTION

In the UK unemployment was at least 10 per cent in nearly every year in the 1920s. In 1932 it reached 22 per cent of the labour force. In the USA real output fell by 30 per cent from 1929 to 1932 and unemployment reached nearly 25 per cent in 1932. Money wages did not fall very much and there did not seem to be a strong self-equilibrating mechanism returning the economy to its previous levels of output and employment. The Great Depression had arrived and spread to other economies. The classical model did not seem to have much to say on the causes of such severe and widespread reductions in output or to offer helpful policies. What policies were recommended by some economists, such as public works expenditure projects, could not be derived from the logic of the classical model and, in fact, would be seen to be useless in the light of that model. John Maynard Keynes rejected the classical model as being a special case whose characteristics 'happen not to be those of the economic society in which we actually live, with the result that its teaching is misleading and disastrous if we attempt to apply it to the facts of experience' (Keynes, 1936, p.3). In the late 1920s he had supported government spending polices, as did his 'classical' colleagues such as A.C. Pigou and D.H. Robertson, to boost demand and reduce unemployment but he, and they, had no theoretical basis for such policies. Economists such as Hayek opposed such polices and relied on deflation and high unemployment to 'break the rigidity of money wages' (quoted from Hutchison, 1981, p.112). Some cynics argue that Keynes just created the *General Theory of Employment, Interest and Money* (Keynes, 1936) as an elaborate theoretical justification for government spending policies at times of depression. Keynes argued that the classical model was a special case, only applicable to the case of a full-employment economy, and it seemed clear to him that in the early 1930s economies were nowhere near full employment and there seemed no strong self-equilibrating forces at work.

Keynes rejected virtually every aspect of the classical model, turning some of its propositions completely around into the opposite structure. We can briefly summarize Keynes's vision of the economy before presenting a usable version of part of his theory.

Keynes believed that the fundamental problem of human existence was that the propensity to save had always tended to exceed the inducement to invest (Keynes, 1936, pp.347–8). Saving depressed aggregate demand. This meant that total spending could be less than that required to produce full employment as Keynes reversed Say's law and argued that demand determined supply. The level of output could be at less than full employment and there were no certain strong forces tending to return it to full employment. Saving was thus seen as a bad thing at times of recession and consumption needed to be encouraged. If demand was deficient, government spending should be used to boost demand.

Some classical economists had argued that changes in the money supply could change the rate of interest but nowhere in the classical theory, according to Keynes (ibid., pp.182–3), was there a clear mechanism through which this could happen. He rejected the classical theory of interest and replaced it with a monetary theory in which the rate of interest is not the mechanism equilibrating saving and investment; that is ensured by changes in output in the Keynesian model.

Keynes did not base his argument on the assumption of rigid money wages, but argued that in times of recession falling wages would not necessarily provide the self-equilibrating mechanism accorded to them in the classical model, as there was no guarantee that falling money wages would boost demand enough to return the economy to full employment. This is a very different view of the world from that of the classical model, where there is always sufficient demand for whatever is produced. This Keynesian criticism (expounded in his chapter 19) was not really absorbed by Keynes's early interpreters, especially by those in America.

A Model of Demand

Here we present the Hicks–Hansen IS/LM model of demand derived from *The General Theory* by J.R. Hicks and Alvin H. Hansen, amongst others, and subsequently the central model of demand in hundreds of macroeconomics textbooks. We will assume that any change in demand is translated into identical changes in actual output. This is the same as assuming that the economy aggregate supply schedule is horizontal at the prevailing and constant price level, at least up to full employment. We will relax this assumption later. Consider the following equations:

$$Y = C + I + G$$

$$C = a + c(YD)$$

$$YD = Y - T$$

$$T = \bar{T}$$

$$I = \bar{I}$$

$$G = \bar{G}$$

The first just says that income is the sum of expenditures for consumption and investment purposes and government expenditure on goods and services. The second is a consumption function that says current consumption is a function of disposable income YD. The term a is autonomous consumption that can change if people decide to change the proportion of income they consume or save. The term c, the slope of this function, is the marginal propensity to consume. Keynes hypothesized that it is positive and less than unity. The third just defines YD as income minus taxes. The next says that taxes are assumed to be exogenous. We can think of them as lump-sum taxes: they are not a function of income. The next two say that both investment and government expenditures are exogenous: a bar over a variable indicates it is exogenous.

We can substitute the equations and definitions into the first equation and rearrange to solve for Y. This gives us the following expression for Y:

$$Y = \frac{a + \bar{I} + \bar{G} - c\bar{T}}{1 - c}.$$

The item on the top is the sum of autonomous and exogenous expenditures. Any change in these items will produce changes in Y equal to $1/(1-c)$ times that change. If c was 0.6, for example, an increase in $\bar{I}$ of, say, 100 would increase Y by 250 (100 times 1/0.4). This is the multiplier theory that Keynes said constituted about half of the General Theory.[2]

The multipliers for a, I and G are the same:

$$\Delta Y/\Delta a = \Delta Y/\Delta \bar{I} = \Delta Y/\Delta \bar{G} = 1/(1-c)$$

and that for a change in taxes is:

$$\Delta Y/\Delta \bar{T} = -c/(1-c).$$

That is, an increase in taxes of 100 would reduce Y by 150. Hence combining an increase in G of 100 with an increase in T of the same amount to finance it would increase Y by 100 (250 − 150). Income would increase by the amount of the increase in G. This is Samuelson's balanced budget multiplier theorem.

This interpretation of Keynes stressed the instability of I and the fact that this would produce larger fluctuations in Y, so a fall in I would cause output to fall by a larger amount and would be an explanation of a recession in the economy. In this model an obvious way of preventing Y from falling would be to increase G or reduce T by the amount required to offset the effect of the fall in I.

Now assume that I is an inverse function of the rate of interest:

$$I = \bar{I} - i(r)$$

where I is autonomous investment and the coefficient i shows us by how much lower investment would be for every one percentage point increase in the rate of interest. Now substitute this expression for I in the first equation determining Y above and solve for Y. We would get:

$$Y = \frac{a + \bar{I} + \bar{G} - c\bar{T}}{(1-c)} - \frac{(i)r}{(1-c)}$$

We can plot this function IS_1 as in Figure 3.8, showing the relationship between Y and r. When r is equal to zero, Y is determined by the first term in the above equation, its horizontal intercept on the Y axis. The slope of this function $(\Delta r/\Delta Y)$ is $-[(1-c)/i]$. The less sensitive investment is to changes in the rate of interest, the smaller will be i and thus the steeper this function will be. If investment were very sensitive to the rate of interest this would be a relatively flat schedule. This schedule is labelled IS as it shows all combinations of Y and r where injections equal withdrawals, that is, $I = S$, in the early version. The lower is r, the greater is I and thus income will be higher so that saving, which is a positive function of Y, will be higher.

Consider the IS_1 schedule of Figure 3.8. Its position is fixed by the total of autonomous and exogenous expenditures. Thus it will shift by the extent of any change in these expenditures times the simple multiplier. Hence for a given ΔG the horizontal shift in the IS curve to IS_2 would be $\Delta \bar{G}/(1-c)$. If the rate of interest were fixed at r_1, or if the government's policy were to keep it constant, the full simple Keynesian multiplier process would occur and output would rise to Y_2.

What determines the rate of interest and would it remain constant when Y changed? Here we present a very simple version of Keynes's liquidity preference theory of interest. Keynes argued that in a monetary economy the rate of interest was not the reward for saving but the reward for parting with liquidity; that is,

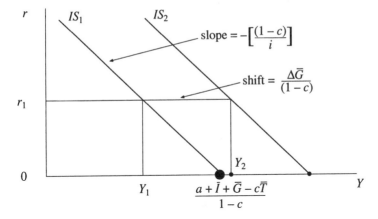

Figure 3.8 The IS curve of the Keynesian model

it is the inducement for people to hold bonds rather than non-interest-bearing liquid money balances. In this model the rate of interest equilibrates the demand for money with the exogenously determined supply of money. Keynes retained this classical assumption.

Keynes argued that the demand for money would be a positive function of the level of income and an inverse function of the rate of interest. It is a positive function of income as at higher levels of Y the amount of transactions would be larger and hence the need for money for transactions purposes would be greater. The demand for money is an inverse function of the rate of interest because at low rates of interest bond prices would be high. High bond prices would lead people to believe that bond prices were likely to fall, so holding money rather than risky bonds would be a sensible decision. At higher rates of interest bond prices are low, so people might expect bond prices to rise so they would rather hold their assets in the form of bonds rather than as money. There have been several other subsequent theories justifying the negative interest elasticity of demand for money and there is much empirical evidence that the demand for money is an inverse function of the rate of interest.

We summarize the demand for real money balances equation as follows where $(M/P)D$ is real money demand:

$$(M/P)D = m + m_1(Y) - m_2(r)$$

where m is the autonomous demand for money, m_1 is the coefficient linking money demand to the level of income and m_2 is the coefficient linking money demand to the rate of interest. If money demand is a sensitive function of the rate of interest, m_2 would be a large number as it shows by how much lower the demand for money will be (measured in million dollars) when the rate of interest rises one percentage point.

We will assume the price level is fixed, so the real money supply (M/P) is exogenously determined as the nominal money supply is exogenous. For there to be equilibrium the following must be true:

$$(M/P) = m + m_1(Y) - m_2(r).$$

If Y were to rise then the demand for money for transactions purposes would rise, but as the demand for money is an inverse function of the rate of interest an increase in r would free money for transaction purposes and people would hold the fixed money supply at a higher rate of interest. As incomes rise people sell bonds to obtain money for transactions, bond prices fall, that is, the rate of interest rises, and this equilibrates the rising demand for money with the fixed supply.

From the equation above we can obtain an expression linking the equilibrium rate of interest to the level of income. Obviously it is a positive function. Rearranging the above equation gives:

$$r = \frac{m - (M/P)}{m_2} + \frac{m_1}{m_2}(Y)$$

This is the *LM* curve (originally called *LL*) showing the combinations of r and Y where the demand for money (L for liquidity) equals the exogenously fixed supply (M for money). Figure 3.9 shows such a curve. The intercept of the *LM* curve shows us that it would shift if there were a change in m, m_2 or (M/P). An increase in m would mean people wanted to hold more money at every level of Y and r. This would increase the intercept on the r axis and shift the *LM* curve upwards, or to the left. An increase in the real money supply would reduce the size of the intercept and shift the *LM* curve downwards, or to the right. A reduction in the real money supply would shift the *LM* curve upwards, or to the left. We can see that a fall in the price level will increase the real money supply and thus shift the *LM* curve to the right, and conversely for an increase in P. At the moment we are still holding P constant. We will assume that behavioural parameters such as m_1 and m_2 (as well as c and i) are stable.

Figure 3.10 shows the full aggregate demand equilibrium where the *IS* and *LM* curves intersect. The level of output would be Y_1 and the interest rate r_1. On the *IS* curve the goods market is in equilibrium; that is, injections are just offsetting withdrawals in the circular flow and so all output produced will be bought. As we are on the *LM* curve the money market is in equilibrium; that is, the fixed money supply is being held voluntarily, as is the existing volume of bonds.

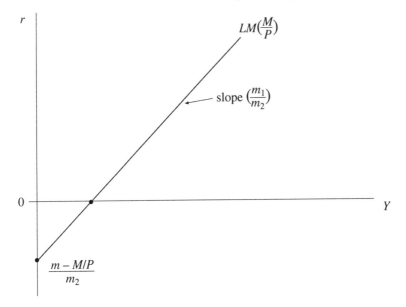

Figure 3.9 The LM curve of the Keynesian model

We can see that a great number of factors go to determine both Y and r in ways much more complicated than in the simple classical model. Let us do some simple comparative static exercises in which we will concentrate on the changes in Y that will occur. First, consider factors that will shift the IS curve. We have already seen that the horizontal shift in the IS curve is given by the simple Keynesian multiplier. If G were to increase then the IS curve would shift to the right. In the model of Figure 3.11 income rises, as does the interest rate, and we reach a new equilibrium at point B. The larger the multiplier the greater the shift in IS and so the greater the tendency of Y to rise. If the LM curve is relatively flat this will translate mostly into a change in Y, not in r. If the LM curve is steep then r will rise, reducing induced investment (that part of investment that is a function of r) and offset part of the increase in G and lead to a rather small increase in Y. In other words, even if the simple multiplier was large, there would be small fluctuations in Y if the LM curve was steep. Changes in T shift the IS curve and so would also bring about changes in equilibrium. The flatter the LM curve the greater the impact of fiscal policy changes such as changing G and T on Y.

A fall in I will shift the IS curve to the left and thus lead to a fall in output and the rate of interest. If the LM curve is steep there will not be much of a fall in Y as the fall in the rate of interest will induce a larger amount of investment which will partly offset the effects of the fall of autonomous I.[3]

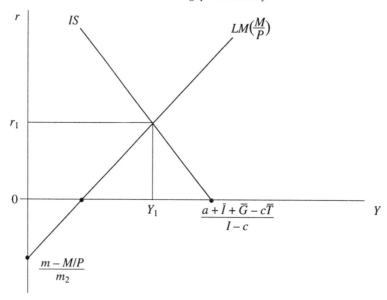

Figure 3.10 Equilibrium output and interest rate in the IS/LM *model*

Let us look at the impact of changes in the nominal money supply on equilibrium. We keep the price level constant so this change in the nominal money supply is the same as a change in the real money supply. An increase in the money supply shifts the *LM* curve to the right, the interest rate falls and so the level of income rises. This is because the fall in the interest rate induces an increase in *I* and so produces a higher level of *Y*. If the *IS* curve is relatively flat there will be a large increase in *Y*; if it is relatively steep there will be a small increase in *Y*. Hence monetary policy would be effective in changing the level of *Y* if the *IS* curve were relatively flat.

Consider what would happen if the government increased *G* but decided it did not want the rate of interest to rise. It simultaneously increases the money supply to shift the *LM* curve to the right by the appropriate amount. This is shown in Figure 3.12. There is a full multiplier impact of the increase in *G* on *Y* as the rate of interest does not rise. Note what we would observe in the real world: an increase in the money supply and an increase in government spending and then an increase in *Y*. We might attribute this increase in *Y* to the increase in the money supply alone and think that money caused income to rise. This would be wrong. We will return to this point in Chapter 5 when we look at money in Singapore.

Consider what happens when *I* increases and the money supply is kept constant. As long as the *LM* curve is not vertical the level of income rises. As *M* is constant, velocity ($V = PY/M$) has risen. In other words, the Keynesian

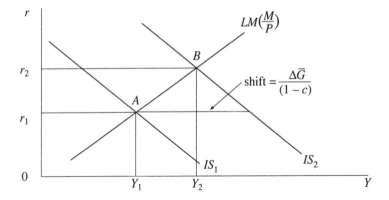

*Figure 3.11 The effect of an increase in government expenditure in the
IS/LM model*

model is a proper theory of what determines *V*. In this model there is a clear
implication that if demand fluctuations are caused by changes in *I* or shifts in
the *IS* curve then high rates of interest will be associated with a high value of
velocity; we are moving up a given *LM* curve and so *PY* is rising even though
M is constant. There is ample evidence that velocity and interest rates do move
together. See Parkin (1993, pp.775–6) for accessible evidence for the USA.

We now develop a theory of aggregate demand. This is a very different concept
from the concept of aggregate demand in Keynes (Keynes, 1936; Amadeo, 1989;
Davidson, 1994) but has become the standard textbook interpretation. We ask
how income in real terms, that is *Y*, varies as the price level varies. Consider

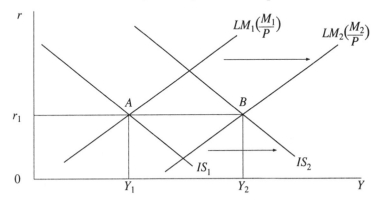

*Figure 3.12 The effect of an increase in government expenditure and money
supply in the IS/LM model*

Figure 3.13. The top panel shows the *IS/LM* equilibrium. We successively reduce the price level from P_1 to P_2 and then P_3. As the price level falls, the real money supply rises and the *LM* curves shifts to the right, producing a higher level of *Y*. The relationship between these levels of demand, *Y*, and the price level is shown in the lower panel of Figure 3.13. This is the aggregate demand curve. It shows the desired level of output at different price levels as well as the total nominal expenditures (*P* times *Y*) that are possible given a fixed nominal money supply and people's spending decisions.

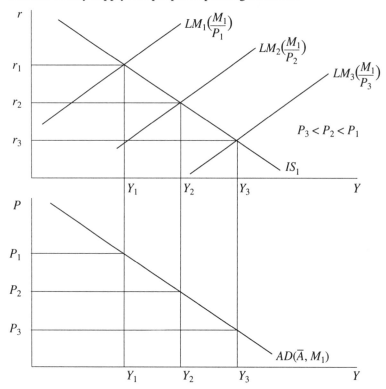

Figure 3.13 Deriving the Aggregate Demand (AD) *curve*

The position of this aggregate demand depends on the total of autonomous and exogenous expenditures (labelled *A*) that fix the position of the *IS* curve and the nominal money supply. Hence we label this aggregate demand curve $AD(\overline{A},M)$ to show the two main factors that determine its position. Changes in either of these determinants will shift the *AD* curve.

Consider shifts in the *IS* curve. As we have seen, these translate into changes in *Y* as long as the *LM* curve is not vertical. So an increase in *I*, for example, would shift the AD curve to the right; a decrease would shift it to the left. Similarly, increases in G or a or a reduction in T shift it to the right, whereas decreases in G or a or an increase in T shift it to the left. How far the AD curve shifts depends on the size of the multiplier and the slope of the LM curve: the greater the multiplier and the flatter the LM curve, the greater the shift in the AD curve and vice versa. If I is unstable, the multiplier is large and the LM curve is relatively flat then the AD curve will be unstable.

Now consider increases in the nominal money supply. For a given level of A there would be a greater level of Y at any given price level as the real money supply would be greater. This means that the AD curve would shift to the right for any increase in the nominal money supply and leftwards for any given reduction in the nominal money supply. We can say something more precise about this relationship. Consider Figure 3.14. We double the nominal money supply from M_1 to M_2. The LM curve shifts to the right and the AD curve to the right or upwards. We can identify the extent of this upward shift. At income level Y_1 the real money supply must be the same for the LM curve to be in the same position. So if M were to double the LM curve would remain in the same position if the price level were to double (because $M_2/P_2 = M_1/P_1$). That is, at money supply M_2 the price level must be P_2 at income level Y_1. In other words, the AD schedule shifts upwards to be twice as high as previously when the money supply doubles. More generally the vertical shift in any AD curve is proportional to the change in the nominal money supply.

We will now combine this aggregate demand curve with an aggregate supply curve. For the Keynesian story to make any sense this aggregate supply curve must have some elasticity with respect to the price level; that is, Y must be greater at a higher price; it cannot be vertical as in the classical model. Here we derive a possible non-vertical aggregate supply curve that is often associated with Keynesian economics. We simplify drastically. Assume that when prices fall there is no immediate corresponding fall in the money wage. This is because wages have been set by contract for a given time period and are not due for immediate renegotiation or because workers, through their trade unions, would oppose any cut in nominal wages. This means that the classical mechanism of falling nominal wages at time of recession will not operate.

Consider Figure 3.15. The original equilibrium is at point A with a money wage of \$5 and a price level of 1. The value of the marginal product schedule is $MPN \times 1$. Assume that the price level falls to 0.5. In the classical model the money wage will fall to \$2.50, the real wage will remain at 5 and the economy will remain on both the demand and supply curves for labour and employment and output will not change. If the money wage remains at \$5 then, as the price level falls to 0.5, the real wage will rise to \$10 and employers will reduce employment to N_1 at point B, and so output will fall. As employment falls disequilibrium emerges in the labour market with the supply of labour, now much

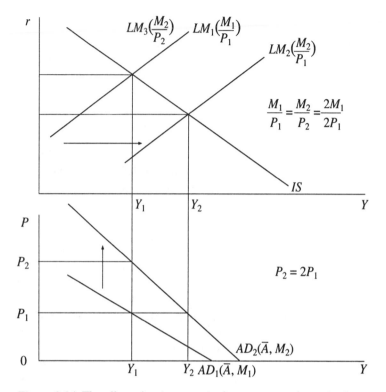

*Figure 3.14 The effect of an increase in the money supply on the Aggregate
Demand curve*

higher, exceeding the level of employment; this is involuntary unemployment
of the extent *BA*.

This means that over the range of prices up to 1 the supply of output is a positive
function of the price level. If something pushed the price level up from 0.5 towards
1 the value of the marginal product would increase towards *MPN*.1 and
employment would increase over the range from point *B* to *A* and output would
rise. Once the price level is at 1 we are back on both the demand and supply
curves for labour and no further increase in either *N* or *Y* is possible as a result
of price increases. If the price level doubled to 2 we would be back in the classical
world where the money wage would just double to $10 and employment would
remain at N^*. This means that the aggregate supply curve when the money wage
does not fall at a time of recession and is fixed at $5 is that shown in Figure
3.16. We combine it with a given *AD* schedule and we get the determination
of both output and the price level. The *IS/LM* section reminds us that the money

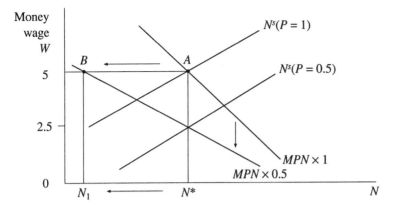

Figure 3.15 Involuntary unemployment in the Keynesian model

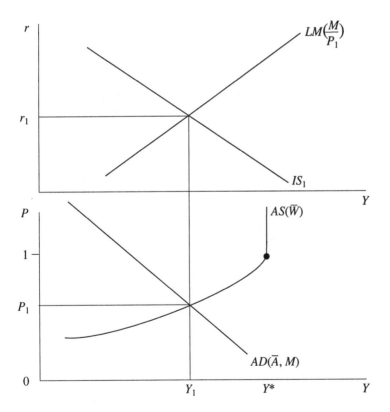

Figure 3.16 IS/LM and Aggregate Demand and Supply equilibrium

supply plays a role in determining P and r, as do the real expenditures which make up A.

If I were to increase the AD curve would shift to the right, increasing both output and prices. Employment would increase and unemployment would fall. Because this is caused by a shift in the IS curve, the interest rate would rise. We would thus observe an increase in I and Y accompanied by rising interest rates, prices and employment and a fall in unemployment. This is what we do see in expansions in business activity. We would say that these variables are procyclical: they move in the same direction as the cyclical movement of real activity, increasing when it increases and decreasing when it decreases. This model also predicts that real wages would be countercyclical: they fall as output rises. There is not much empirical support for this as real wages tend to be mildly procyclical in the USA (Abel and Bernanke, 1995, pp.300–308) and other economies. We return to this point later.

This combined IS/LM aggregate demand/supply model determines the main macroeconomic variables: the level of Y, its composition, r and, given the rigid money wage, the price level, P. A fall in I will shift the IS curve and the AD schedule left, output and prices will fall, employment falls, workers are dismissed from their jobs as the real wage rises and the money wage does not fall, involuntary unemployment emerges. This model was thought to have done a good job of explaining the reasons for fluctuations in output and employment: they are caused by fluctuations in demand. The implied policy is that, as an economy slips into a recession, the government could offset the fall in demand by increasing the money supply (to shift the LM curve to the right to keep demand at Y^*) or, if the recession was severe, it could use fiscal policy by increasing G or reducing T to shift the IS curve. This is the recent interpretation of Keynes's view by Paul Krugman (1994, pp.30–32) who stresses that monetary expansion is 'the usual and basic Keynesian answer to recessions', but we believe he has misunderstood the motives behind what he calls Keynes's whimsical policy of 'hiding bottles full of cash where enterprising boys might find them' (ibid., 1994, p.31).[4] Of course, Keynes was developing his theory over the period 1930–35, and even later, and his policy was increased government expenditure, public works projects,[5] the possible 'comprehensive socialisation of investment' and the necessity of the government to regulate society's propensity to consume partly through taxes, partly through fixing the rate of interest and partly through other means (Keynes, 1936, pp.377–9).

The model indicates the possibility of cost factors influencing prices. The concept of cost-push inflation was thus born, but it remains something that is denied by classical economists. If anything pushed up the money wage then the aggregate supply curve would shift upwards, prices would rise, the real money supply would fall and so interest rates would rise and output and employment would fall. This became an explanation of stagflation: the coexistence of stagnation and inflation, a phenomenon that was first observed in the early 1970s in many industrialized countries. In the Keynesian paradigm this phenomenon is attributed to the quadrupling of oil prices in the last quarter of 1973. This would shift the supply curve upward, increasing prices and reducing output and employment. See any standard textbook, such as Abel and Bernanke (1995, pp.332–6), Dornbusch and Fischer (1994, pp.230–35), Gordon (1993, pp.260–65) or Parkin and Bade (1986, pp.594–603) for a detailed treatment.

The importance of the money wage in determining costs has led to a different view of the economy held by certain Keynesian economists known as Post Keynesians who draw their inspiration from the work of Keynes, Joan Robinson (1903–83), G.L.S. Shackle (1903–92), Sidney Weintraub (1914–83) and Nicholas Kaldor (1908–86) amongst others. See Davidson (1994) and Snowdon *et al.* (1994) for summaries. Post Keynesian economists see the money wage as essentially an exogenous variable determined by trade union negotiation with employers. To classical economists it is 'just another price'. Increases in this money wage increase costs and hence prices and lead through the increase in demand for bank loans to an increase in the money supply. Money is thus endogenous in this view of the economy and is not the cause of inflation. Endogenous money arguments can be found in Kaldor (1985), Rousseas (1986) and Moore (1988).

We can add one more element to our Keynesian outline: the Phillips curve. This evolved out of an empirical relationship identified by A.W.H. Phillips in 1958 on the basis of British data over the period 1861–1957. The data showed an apparently stable inverse relationship between the rate of change of money wages and unemployment: when unemployment was high money wages had tended to fall and when unemployment was low money wages had tended to rise. A similar relationship between price inflation and unemployment had been spotted earlier by Irving Fisher. The relationship was popularized by Samuelson and Solow (1960) who extended it to the relationship between the inflation rate and the unemployment rate and compared the relationship for the USA and Britain. (Figure 3.17 shows a typical relationship.) They interpreted it as showing a 'menu of choice' between different levels of unemployment and the rate of inflation. If the government were to increase aggregate demand to reduce unemployment from, say, *A*, to point *B* then this would be at the cost of higher inflation. Although Samuelson and Solow did state that this relationship might not remain stable, they did present it as a trade-off between the two variables. Low inflation came at the cost of high unemployment and lower unemployment would cause higher inflation. The experience of the USA in the 1960s when unemployment fell steadily and inflation rates were successively higher provided strong support for the empirical validity of the Phillips curve and it continued for a while to be presented as a stable trade-off available for the government to exploit. The Phillips curve for the 1960s in America continues to be reproduced for examination because of the strong support it gave to the idea of a trade-off. See, for examples, Abel and Bernanke (1995, p.446), Dornbusch and Fisher (1994, p.217), Sachs and Larrain (1993, p.453), Parkin (1993, p.869) and Stiglitz (1993, p.977).

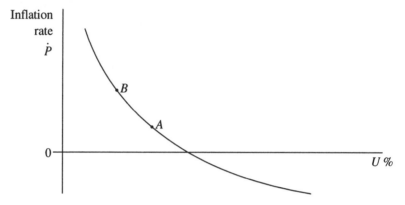

Figure 3.17 The Phillips curve

3.3   THE REVIVAL OF CLASSICAL ECONOMICS

We will now review the main development in anti-Keynesian economics based on the revival and modification of various aspects of the classical model, starting with the work of Nobel laureate Milton Friedman.

The Macroeconomics of Milton Friedman

Here we will review some important contributions of Milton Friedman that have been used to criticize the Keynesian income-expenditure/involuntary unemployment explanation of macroeconomic fluctuations and recessions: the permanent income hypothesis, the natural rate of unemployment, Friedman's aggregate supply curve: the fooling model, and the quantity theory and monetarism.

Permanent income hypothesis
The Keynesian consumption function with its hypothesized large marginal propensity to consume out of current income received strong empirical support when it was first tested. It is the basis for the belief in a large multiplier effect on income of changes in elements of autonomous expenditure. Subsequently certain pieces of evidence such as the finding that the average propensity to save had remained constant over a long period and the higher than expected average

propensity to consume in America after the Second World War led Friedman and others to propose alternative hypotheses (Friedman, 1957, pp.3–6). Friedman took his hypothesis from Irving Fisher. The basic idea is that household consumption in any period, such as a year, is not a function of the amount of income received during that year but depends on the household's wealth, which will be determined by its expected future earnings. Annual income, consumption and saving data are just convenient statistical presentations that should not lead us to believe that they are associated on an annual basis. If everyone was paid once a week on a Friday we would not expect a large amount of consumption to take place on that day but would expect consumption to be spread out over the week. Similarly a household's consumption in any year would depend on what it thinks its lifetime earnings would be. Friedman never clearly defined permanent income but we can think of it as the household's view of its expected long-term income. Friedman hypothesized that current consumption is a close proportional function of this permanent income. Permanent income is a non-observable theoretical concept that exists in the heads of the consumers but determines their behaviour. If permanent income changes then households will change their current consumption plans. This allows us to derive the hypothesis that changes in current income or other variables that change a household's view of its permanent income will change its current consumption. Those changes in income that do not change permanent income will not change current consumption. This leads to the conclusion that transitory or short-lived changes in current income, such as large bonuses, windfall gains or temporary tax cuts, would not change current consumption. Only changes in current income that change permanent income would affect current consumption. This implies that the marginal propensity to consume out of current income might be very small if those changes in current income were not thought to be permanent changes in future average income. Although it was not his main purpose, Friedman did draw the conclusion that this would imply a much smaller investment multiplier and hence a 'cyclically more stable system' than that implied by the Keynesian approach (ibid., pp.236–8).

Much of the empirical evidence offered by Friedman to support his theory relies on definitions of basic terms different from those relevant to the Keynesian theory and from those used in everyday language (ibid., p.28). In many studies he cites consumption is defined as the purchase of non-durable goods plus only the *services* (or depreciation) rendered by durable goods such as cars and furniture (ibid., pp.116, 132). So if a household enjoyed a surprise, temporary increase in current income Friedman's theory would treat this as transitory income and, as it would have little impact on permanent income, it would be 'saved'. He defined buying consumer durables as 'saving' – except for the current services rendered by them in the period under study. So the stockbroker in Singapore who in 1993 received a huge bonus and then bought five cars[6] would be considered by Friedman as saving nearly all this windfall gain, even though it was spent on goods, providing easy support for his theory. A Keynesian would define the purchase of goods, even durable goods, as consumption and would argue that consumption had risen even though the increase in income was transitory (Davidson, 1994, pp.43–4). This would support the Keynesian view that income increases do cause significant increases in current expenditures on consumption goods, thus giving rise to multiplier effects in the industries that produce such goods.

Despite disquiet with odd definitions and the limited empirical support for the theory, the idea of permanent income has become an important aspect of macroeconomic thinking. It has led economists to ask how current changes in variables change household wealth. If wealth is affected then we would expect consumption to change. We will show a later application of this idea below.

Natural rate of unemployment
In the classical model the labour market is always in equilibrium yet the recorded rate of labour unemployment varies. How can there be unemployment and why does it vary? Figure 3.18 illustrates Friedman's answer. *LF* represents the labour force, the number of people who wish to be economically active and work. N^s represents the supply of labour at any real wage; that is, the amount of work these people are prepared to do, given their preferences and the real wage that prevails. The gap between the two functions shows the extent to which people voluntarily choose not to work because they do not like the existing real wage. Equilibrium is given at point *A*, where the real wage is w^* and the amount of employment is N^*. Voluntary unemployment of the extent *AB* exists and the recorded rate of unemployment would be AB/LF_1. We can see that this is the same as in the classical model above, just allowing for the fact that when the labour market clears there will be some unemployment.

This theory has been taken by some to account for all of the changes in observed unemployment. The natural rate of unemployment is a non-observable concept but if we hypothesize that all unemployment is natural-rate unemployment then we predict that those things that will increase natural-rate unemployment will increase actual observable unemployment. Increases in unemployment would be due to a fall in N^*, *ceteris paribus*. Some factors causing this are a fall in the *MPN* of new workers entering the labour force: employment and the real wage will be lower and the gap *AB* will be bigger. Anything that shifted the supply curve of labour to the left would increase the natural rate of unemployment. Such influences might include an increase in the marginal tax rate on labour income or a change in workers' preferences for leisure rather than work. The decision to work rather than take leisure depends on the difference between income when not working and the real wage for working. Usually textbooks take the former to be zero, so the gain from working is the real wage.

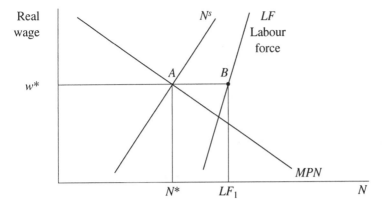

Figure 3.18 The natural rate of unemployment

However, in countries where there is an unemployment benefit (or insurance) system, the gain from taking a job is the difference between the real wage and the size of the unemployment benefit. If the unemployment benefit is large compared to the real wage then there will be little gain to be had from working. This would reduce the supply of labour at any real wage offered by the employer, increasing the gap *AB* and thus increasing the natural rate of unemployment. Hence increasing unemployment benefits and increasing tax rates on labour income have been identified as possible causes of the observed large increases in unemployment in European countries that have occurred since the mid-1970s. Another reason offered for high unemployment, and implied by the above model, is the lack of training and falling educational standards of new workers. Their *MPN* is low, so they are just not worth employing, contributing to a rise in the natural rate of unemployment.

We will offer some other reasons for changes in N^* later, but the point is that natural unemployment occurs when the labour market is in equilibrium. At this rate there is no tendency for the *real wage* to change. This theory accepts the flexibility of money wages to ensure that the equilibrium real wage can always be realized. Friedman (1968) added an ingenious twist to the classical theory to explain why employment and output might fluctuate. Friedman accepts the quantity theory of money (see below) but had spent much time gathering evidence that changes in the money supply do produce changes in real output within a short period of time (Friedman and Schwartz, 1963; Friedman, 1987). He also presented evidence to support his view that, contrary to the Keynesian income-expenditure theory, money was a better explanation of changes in income than real autonomous expenditures (Friedman and Meiselman, 1963). But how could changes in money produce changes in real income if the aggregate supply curve is vertical, as it is in the classical model? Friedman had to invent a theory that provided an upward-sloping aggregate supply curve (at least in the short run) that did not depend on what he would see as arbitrary ad hoc assumptions about rigid money wages and disequilibrium in the labour market. This he did in his 'fooling model' of labour supply.

Friedman's aggregate supply curve: the fooling model

Output fluctuates because N fluctuates. How could an increase in the money supply induce workers to do more work? An increase in the money supply would increase prices. How would this induce workers to do more work? The classical model would argue that it could not, as the money wage would always adjust to keep the real wage at the equilibrium rate. Consider the logic of Figure 3.19 and the problem it suggests for any theory wishing to show how employment could be pushed above N^*. Hypothetically adjust the price level so that it produces a real wage different from w^*. If the price level was too low, w would be too high and employment would be constrained to be on the demand curve for labour, and output would fall. If the price level were pushed upwards the real wage would fall and employment would fall, as we would be constrained by the low supply of labour.[7] In other words, we cannot get to the right of N^* by manipulating the real wage through changes in the price level. For employment to exceed N^* there must be two real wages: a high one, at X, to induce workers to supply more labour and a lower one, at Y, to induce employers to hire more workers. But how could there be two real wages? This is where Friedman's ingenious theory comes in. Of course, there would only be one actual real wage but there might be different *perceived* real wages for different people. The perceived real wage is another non-observable concept invented to explain observable behaviour. Friedman assumed it is the workers who would not realize what was happening to the real wage when the price level changed. Assume

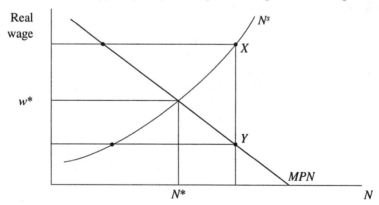

Figure 3.19 Disequilibrium in the labour market

that workers only slowly adjust their view of what the price level is. We can then assume that they think the price level is unchanged in the short run. If the price level really increases, employers will offer higher money wages to employ more workers who will think that the real wage has risen and will supply more labour. Employment and output will rise as a response to the increase in prices; the aggregate supply curve will be upward sloping.

Figure 3.20 shows this. At the price level of 1 and a money wage of $5, employment is N^*. There is a corresponding natural rate of unemployment which is not shown. If the price level doubles, the value of the MPN schedule shifts upwards to be twice as high as before. Workers still think the price level is 1. The money wage is pushed up to $7.5, so workers think the real wage has risen to $7.5; so they supply more labour and employment rises to N_1. Employers know that the real wage has, in fact, fallen to $3.75 and are happy to employ more workers. Workers have been fooled into supplying more work. If, in contrast, the price level had fallen to 0.5, employers would have hired fewer workers and the money wage would have fallen. With workers still thinking the price level is 1, they would take this to be a fall in the real wage and would supply less labour and output would go down. Hence output is a positive function of the price level and so fluctuations in the nominal money supply would cause changes in output, employment and the observed rate of unemployment. The labour market is always on both the demand and supply curves for labour, but there can only be long-run equilibrium when everyone's perceptions of the price level are correct. This approach stresses a new aspect of equilibrium: demand must equal supply *and* everyone's perceptions must be correct. This short-run equilibrium cannot last as workers will realize that the price level has, for example, doubled. In that case, the supply of labour will fall, the money wage will rise to $10 and we are back in the classical world where employment is

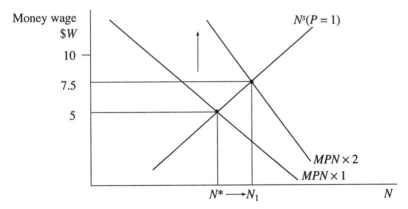

Figure 3.20 The fooling model

back at N^* and output is at Y^*. The increase in the money supply can only cause a short-run increase in output. In the long run money is neutral, as in the classical model.

This theory of the aggregate supply curve provided an explanation of short-run fluctuations in output caused by changes in the money supply that allowed the labour market to be in equilibrium in the sense that demand equalled supply but was based on misperceptions of the real wage. Unemployment would fall as prices and output rose. Some Keynesian economists have accepted this theory and some macroeconomics' textbooks even present it as a Keynesian theory (Froyen, 1993, pp.225–31), which it is not. It inspired Robert Lucas Jr., certainly no Keynesian, to use the idea of misperceptions to provide an alternative reason for an upward-sloping aggregate supply curve (see below).

The quantity theory and monetarism
Friedman argues that money is important in the sense that it is the primary explanation of short-run fluctuations in output employment and unemployment and is the ultimate determinant of a country's inflation rate: inflation is always and everywhere a monetary phenomenon. Differences in inflation rates across countries are primarily due to different rates of monetary growth. We can derive these propositions from the equation of exchange

$$MV \equiv PY$$

Take logarithms of both sides:

$$\log M + \log V = \log P + \log Y$$

Differentiate with respect to time

$$1/M \ (dM/dt) + 1/V(dV/dt) = 1/P(dP/dt) + 1/Y \ (dY/dt)$$

This means that in terms of growth rates

$$\dot{m} + \dot{v} \equiv \dot{p} + \dot{y}$$

where lower-case letters with a dot over them represent growth rates of the related variables, hence $\dot{p}$ is the rate of inflation. So far this is an identity, true by definition. For simplicity assume that V is constant, so that $\dot{v}$ is zero.[8] This gives us

$$\dot{m} = \dot{p} + \dot{y}$$

The rate of growth of the money supply, which by assumption is the same as the rate of growth of nominal income, equals the rate of inflation plus the rate of growth of real output. Rearranging gives us

$$\dot{p} = \dot{m} - \dot{y}$$

which now is a theory of inflation if we assume that the rate of growth of the money supply is exogenous to the model and that changes in $\dot{m}$ do not bring about equal changes in $\dot{y}$. The long-run growth rate of Y is given by supply-side factors and will not change when $\dot{m}$ changes, hence the only reason for changes in the inflation rate or differences across countries is the different rate of monetary growth. Take a country where output is growing at 3 per cent per annum; with a 10 per cent per annum rate of money growth, the rate of inflation would be 7 per cent per annum:

$$\dot{p} = \dot{m} - \dot{y}$$
$$7 = 10 - 3$$

If the rate of monetary growth were to increase to 20 per cent per annum then the inflation rate would increase to 17 per cent per annum. The monetarist policy implication is that to reduce the rate of inflation it is necessary to reduce the rate of growth of nominal money. Price stability can be secured by setting $\dot{m} = \dot{y}$ (or more strictly to the increase in the demand for real money, which would be $\dot{y} - \dot{v}$). Lucas (1987, p.106) has identified price stability obtained this way and real rates of interest of 3 per cent that go with it as one of the few true 'free lunches' discovered in 200 years of economic inquiry.

This is just another aspect of the neutrality of money: monetary changes do not change real variables. Such an increase in the rate of money growth would not change the real rate of interest (r). The nominal rate of interest would equal the real rate of interest plus the expected rate of inflation. If the current rate of inflation had prevailed for a time then the expected rate of inflation would equal the actual rate; hence nominal rate of interest $= r + \dot{p}$, or $r =$ nominal rate of interest $- \dot{p}$. This relationship was stressed by Irving Fisher and is sometimes called the Fisher equation.

If the real rate of interest is 3 per cent and the inflation rate is 7 per cent then the nominal interest rate will be 10 per cent. When the rate of money growth increased to 20 per cent in the analysis above the inflation rate increased to 17 per cent. In this case the nominal interest rate would rise to 20 per cent. The increase in the rate of growth of the nominal money supply by ten percentage points has increased the rate of inflation and the nominal interest rate by the same number of percentage points. One reason for differences between interest rates across countries is that nominal rates differ because of different inflation rates.

This theory is a long-run explanation of different inflation rates. We can combine it with the short-run fooling model and the natural rate of unemployment to derive Friedman's early prediction about the simple Phillips curve. Imagine the economy at the natural rate of unemployment U^* with employment at N^* and output at Y^*. Supply-side factors such as increasing labour productivity and labour supply mean that Y^* is growing at 3 per cent per annum. Assume that these effects keep the real wage constant. Assume that $\dot{m}$ is 3 per cent per annum, so inflation is zero; that is, prices are constant. The real wage is constant, so money wages are also constant. If the economy has been in this state for a while, people will have come to expect zero inflation. This is shown in Figure 3.21 where we have labelled the Phillips curve $\dot{p}^e = 0$, meaning expected inflation is zero and the economy is in a natural equilibrium at point A. Now the central bank increases the money growth rate to 5 per cent per annum. Aggregate spending now grows at 5 per cent. In the short run people think inflation is still zero. The increase in demand increases prices and fools workers into doing more work, employment rises and the rate of unemployment falls and the economy moves to a point like B. At point B, Y has risen above Y^* but will be growing at the trend rate of growth of Y of 3 per cent. However, at point B, people will eventually realize that inflation is 2 per cent. Money wages will start rising

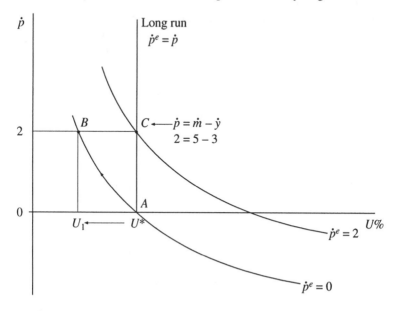

Figure 3.21 The expectations-augmented Phillips curve

by 2 per cent, so the real wage returns to its natural rate and employment falls back to N^* and so unemployment returns to U^*. However as $\dot{m}$ is still 5 per cent at point C, inflation is now permanently higher at 2 per cent ($\dot{p} = \dot{m} - \dot{y}$). People have adjusted to this, so we label the Phillips curve going through this point $\dot{p}^e$ = 2. Only at U^* are people's expectations of inflation correct and so U^* is the only possible long-run equilibrium. This result is the same as that of the static model of the natural rate above. Friedman thus argued that there was no long-run trade-off between inflation and unemployment: once inflationary expectations had adjusted people would not be fooled and the economy would return to U^*. An implication is that, if actual inflation is above expected inflation, unemployment will be below U^*. This is a testable implication if we are able to identify expected inflation. When actual and expected inflation rates are the same, we will be at U^*. The long-run Phillips curve is a vertical line at the natural rate U^*. This rate is compatible with any rate of inflation determined by $\dot{m}$, so that $\dot{p} = \dot{m} - \dot{y}$. If $\dot{m}$ remains constant then the inflation rate will remain constant.

The only way to try to keep the economy at a point like B, where $Y > Y^*$ and $U < U^*$, would be to keep on increasing the rate of monetary growth in an attempt to keep on fooling workers to supply more labour. This would produce an increasing rate of inflation. For this reason the natural rate of unemployment is sometimes also called the non-accelerating inflation rate of unemployment (NAIRU) although some economists see this more as an empirical concept that does not require belief in the natural rate theory with which it is sometimes identified. See Snowdon *et al.* (1994, pp.130, 323–4, 337) for different views. We will come across the NAIRU in Singapore in Chapter 8.

Lucas Supply Curve and Rational Expectations

The theories of Robert Lucas are similar to those of Milton Friedman, in that Lucas also created a theory of the upward-sloping supply curve of output based on people's mistakes or misconceptions, but he added a new twist to macroeconomics by reintroducing the concept of rational expectations. The supply curve implied by his analysis is now called the Lucas supply curve.

The argument is similar to that of Friedman but was derived from the problems faced by a single competitive producer in deciding whether to change output. Assume producers sell their output in competitive markets so price is a parameter. Simple microeconomics tells us that such firms will increase output when output price rises and reduce output when price falls. In microeconomics, where we do partial equilibrium analysis, a rise in price means a rise in relative price. Only a change in relative price should induce a change in output. At a time of general inflation it might be difficult, so the theory assumes, for a producer to tell if his relative price has really risen. Assume his output price rises by 5 per cent. Should he increase output? If this price increase is just the result of a general inflation of 5 per cent then there has been no increase in relative price, so he should not increase output. If he knew that all prices were rising 5 per cent then he would know there has been no increase in relative price, so he would not increase output. If actual price and expected (perceived) prices were the same there would be no tendency for output to increase. If, at the time of the 5 per cent increase in this producer's price, he thought that the inflation rate was zero then he would believe this *was* an increase in relative price and he would increase output. He might be mistaken, of course, as all prices *might* be rising 5 per cent, but this producer just did not know that. So if actual price exceeds expected price output will rise. Lucas believes in Friedman's idea of the natural rate, so output has a strong tendency to be at its natural rate when all expectations are correct. However output could be induced to increase if prices exceeded what people thought they were and would fall if prices were lower than perceived prices. The Lucas supply curve is summarized as:

$$Y = Y^* + b(P - P^e)$$

where P^e is expected price or what people think is happening to the general price level and b is just a coefficient showing how sensitive output is to this price difference. Sometimes the second term in the equation is described as the 'price surprise' that induces people to change output. If people think their output price is just rising at the same rate as all prices this term will be zero and output will be at Y^*. If prices are rising but people believe, correctly or perhaps not, that their price is rising faster than general prices, they will increase output. Hence misperceptions of what each individual producer's relative price level is can induce changes in output around the natural level Y^*. These changes in prices would of course be the result of changes in the money supply and so this theory explains why changes in the money supply could cause changes in output: it is all based on people confusing the change in the general price level caused by any change in the money supply with an increase in their relative prices.

Lucas added an important idea to this theory. If people knew what was happening to the money supply then, if they understood how the economy worked, they would know what the rate of change in the general price level would be and thus would never be fooled into changing output through a misunderstood change in relative price. It was reasonable to assume that people would try to predict what was happening to the general price level so they would not confuse general price increases for relative price increases. The term 'rational expectations' is the assumption that people do try to predict or forecast important variables on the basis of what they think the correct model determining the variable is. This view of behaviour was thought to be an improvement on the assumption associated with the Friedman fooling model that people adapted their view of the price level slowly on the basis of recent changes in the price level itself.

The assumption of rational expectations was thought to be a great improvement on this inadequate assumption, as it now assumed that people make predictions for important variables and their predictions are those of the relevant model. The idea of rational expectations had been introduced into macroeconomics in 1932 by Jan Tinbergen (Keuzenkamp, 1991), subsequently one of the two first recipients of the Nobel prize in Economic Sciences. Lucas and others, however, drew the theory from the microeconomic work of John Muth, published in 1961, and he is usually mistakenly credited with creating the idea.

We can see its relevance through a simple example. Assume people understand the government's policy concerning the rate of money growth. They will then predict what the rate of inflation would be, say 3 per cent. If they heard that the government was to increase the rate of growth of the money supply by five percentage points then, assuming they believe in the long-run neutrality of money, as Friedman and Lucas do, they would predict that the inflation rate would be 8 per cent. So when prices started to rise they would not be fooled into believing that their relative price was rising. Output would not be pushed above Y^* when people knew what the real monetary growth rate was. The term 'anticipated' is used to describe that part of the money supply growth that is known to people. Hence 'anticipated' monetary growth will not push Y away from Y^* as people will just predict how this will affect inflation and will not be subject to a price surprise. Assume now, however, that the government has announced that it will increase the money growth rate by five percentage points but actually increases it at a much faster rate. Then people will believe that anticipated money growth is going to produce 8 per cent inflation. Because of the actually higher money growth rate, prices will start rising at a faster rate than this and so people will be fooled into increasing output. 'Unanticipated', or unknown, growth in the money supply could lead to an increase in output. A new proposition was derived from this view. It argued that only unanticipated policies would have an effect on real output. This meant that, if people understood how the government carried out stabilization policies, they would be able to take into account the effects of these policies now and they would have no influence on output. This came to be known as the 'policy ineffectiveness proposition' and was used as a criticism of Keynesian stabilization policies.

For historical studies aimed at analysing this new theory, this provided a testable implication if it was possible to decompose past actual monetary growth into that part it was reasonable to assume people could have anticipated and into that part they could not have anticipated. The unanticipated part was then used in regressions to see whether it 'explained' actual subsequent output growth. Early studies, by Robert Barro in particular, seemed to support the view, whereas later studies tended not to do so. At first the new theory was enthusiastically adopted by those who liked its elegance and precision and many expository books used the phrase 'rational expectations revolution' to describe the impact of the new theory, but soon people were beginning to question its plausibility. It argues that recessions, including large depressions such as the great depression, were caused by people mistaking what was happening to relative prices. On the other hand, it based the policy ineffectiveness proposition on the view that people would monitor monetary and other policies and take their predicted effects into account now. This seemed just too implausible to many older economists, although most of the younger embraced the idea. As it was first incorporated into a classical model it suffers from all the implausibility of that model. It can only explain unemployment as voluntary, or as a result of people's mistakes. There is no room for the Keynesian concept of involuntary unemployment, a concept still upheld as useful by Keynesian economists. The idea of rational expectations can be incorporated into non-classical models, of course, but it is usually associated with the market-clearing classical model.

There have been a few applications of the rational expectations idea, one to consumption behaviour, as we have seen. Friedman's permanent income hypothesis argued that current consumption was a stable function of permanent income. Permanent income would be what people expected their future average income to be, based on a prediction of their future income using relevant information. All relevant systematic influences on a person's future income would be incorporated into that prediction. Hence the only reason for changes in permanent income and therefore in consumption would be pieces of random news. This would mean that consumption behaviour would be very stable, with the best predictor of future consumption being present consumption, and consumption would not be a close function of a current variable such as income. Consumption does tend to be the stablest item of expenditure in the economy, something true for Singapore, as we saw in Chapter 2. However statistical studies have shown that consumption is a closer function of current income than this theory would show. As one of the developers of the theory, Robert Hall, says: 'One problem is that consumption is a bit too responsive to temporary changes in income, although clearly not as responsive as in the simple Keynesian consumption theory' (Hall and Taylor, 1993, p.291).

The Keynesian, Friedman and Lucas theories share the common feature that they argue that changes in demand (money supply) could produce changes in output, something that could not happen in the classical model. Friedman and Lucas share the view that these output changes are based on people's mistakes and cannot be permanent changes as, once expectations have adapted, or if policy is anticipated, the economy will return to its natural rate, or never deviate from it. In their view the economy is much more stable than is implied by the Keynesian model and there is no need for government stabilization policies. Another school of macroeconomics developed from incorporating other aspects of Lucas's work into the logic of the classical model. We briefly review its features in the next section.

Real business cycle theory

In the classical model demand cannot change output: the aggregate supply curve is vertical. The only possible explanation of cyclical movements in output is that the level of Y^* itself changes in a cyclical matter. There are no deviations of Y from Y^*. We have seen that factors changing Y^* are changes in productivity which shift the *MPN* schedule or changes in labour supply. A school of economists have taken up the challenge of explaining why output fluctuates solely as a result of these supply-side factors. They deny that any demand-side changes, including changes in the money supply, could affect output. These models are known as real business cycle models.

One aspect stresses shifts in *MPN* and these are referred to as technology shocks. The logic of these models is often presented using a Robinson Crusoe economy as the model (Plosser, 1989). They are abstract to the point of utter simplicity. They tend not to incorporate real-world phenomena such as markets or money but to generalize from the behaviour of a representative agent. As Plosser (ibid., p.56) puts it: 'Imagine Crusoe observes a temporarily high value of productivity.' We have to imagine that the microclimate near his island changes and brings more fish. The model then just traces out mathematically his optimal response over time in terms of work, consumption and saving (which here is investment by definition). The dynamic responses to such a shock last for many periods. Obviously a beneficial shock that increases *MPN* would increase work and output. A negative shock would reduce work and output. Robinson Crusoe's responses are the best for him, so they are optimal. This is obvious and trivial. As Plosser puts it: 'Any attempt by a social planner to force Crusoe to choose any allocation other than the ones indicated, such as working more than he currently chooses, or saving more than he currently chooses, are likely to be welfare reducing' (ibid., p.56). Again any unemployment we observe in the real world has to be assumed to be voluntary if this theory is to help us. Attempts to apply such a view of the world to the real economy have not been very convincing for most economists who have not been infected by the 'real' bug nor have a vested interest in maintaining this line of research. As Tobin puts it commenting on such an approach to macroeconomics: 'That's really the enemy at the other extreme of macroeconomics' (quoted from Snowdon *et al.*, 1994, p.132). The 'other extreme' is 'New Keynesianism' See later.

Many economists just cannot find evidence of technological shocks that can explain the recent recessions, such as those of the early 1980s and 1990s, in a number of industrial economies, let alone the great depression. Real business cycle economists look for anything that could be a shock to productivity: a natural disaster, large changes in oil prices, a new source of important raw materials, a change in government regulations, and so on. Keynesian economists had already incorporated supply-side shocks such as those caused by the OPEC oil price increases. Such incorporation into a Keynesian model explains why there can be a recession with increasing inflation, something that the demand-driven Keynesian model could not explain very well. Most critics charge that real business cycle economists have not provided enough evidence that it is supply shocks that cause most cycles. Mankiw (1989, p.85) argues that the 'existence of large fluctuations in the available technology is a crucial but unjustified assumption of real business cycle theory'.

There are some aspects of real business cycle theory that do not rely on supply-side shocks to technology to justify their view that actual cycles are not caused by demand fluctuations but are the result of people's optimal responses to changing circumstances, some of which may be caused by demand-side changes. These theories look for reasons for shifts in labour supply to explain the cycle. We will mention the most prominent here.

One ingenious argument, derived from Lucas's early work, is the idea of intertemporal substitution of labour for leisure. It is argued that the supply of labour is a positive function of the real interest rate (Barro, 1990, pp.66–7). If there was an increase in government spending or in the government deficit that pushed up interest rates this would induce workers to do more work now and output would go up at the same time as government spending and the interest rate. This combination of events is found in the real world and is implied by the simple demand-driven Keynesian model, but the supporters of the classical view such as Barro (ibid., pp.289–91) would argue that their explanation is superior as it is based on a sound theory of individual maximizing behaviour.

Why would workers do more work when interest rates rise? Think of a self-employed insurance salesman who can decide his own working hours. He decides the optimal number of hours to work this year and next year. When is the best time to work a lot? Say he expects to earn $100 an hour either this year or next year. The benefit of working an extra hour this year and taking an extra hour of leisure next year is this year's wage times $(1+r)$. If the rate of interest is 5 per cent, an extra hour's work this year can give him $105 worth of extra consumption next year. The cost of taking an hour of leisure next year is the $100 he will not earn, but this is a future value. In present value terms it is $95.2 (100/(1.05). On the basis of these benefits and costs and his preferences, he will choose how many hours to work and not to work in each year. Assume that, as he is deciding, he hears that the rate of interest has risen to 10 per cent. Now the benefit from working an extra hour this year has risen to $110. The cost of an extra hour's leisure next year has gone down, to $91 (100/1.1). As the benefit to working more this year has risen and the cost of future leisure has gone down this person will decide to do more work this year and less next year. He substitutes work for leisure this year and leisure for work next year. Hence the amount of work done this year is a positive function of the interest rate. During booms, when people work longer hours than usual, interest rates are high and in recession, when many people are not working at all, interest rates tend to be low. This is indirect support for the view. Again, however, many people cannot accept that large business cycle fluctuations are due to people voluntarily changing their optimum work–leisure combinations as interest rates change. Most mainstream macroeconomists take the view that there is not enough direct evidence that this effect really occurs on a large scale and has enough empirical support (Hall and Taylor, 1993, p.461).

There is another argument invoked to explain fluctuations in labour supply and how these might be associated with demand-side policies. Imagine the government increases its expenditure and runs a larger budget deficit. In the simple classical model interest rates rise, the composition of output changes but there is no increase in output. The government is taking more of output, so there is less for the private sector; so private sector wealth falls. If the government finances its expenditure by increasing taxes then it is more easy to see that private sector wealth will fall. It is argued in real business cycle theories that, despite the fact that the result cannot be derived from a simple Robinson Crusoe model because of the opposite results of wealth and substitution effects (Barro, 1990, pp.43–4), a reduction in wealth increases labour supply as a fall in wealth means people can afford less leisure. Abel and Bernanke (1995, pp.362–5) present this negative wealth effect on work as an argument of the new classical model. Labour supply thus increases, so output rises as a consequence of the increased budget deficit or increased government expenditure or an increase in taxes!

These aspects of the new classical or real business cycle model provide reasons for changes in output that are not the result of Keynesian multipliers, although they would be observed to happen at the same time as changes in government expenditures or investment. Real business cycle theory originally ignored money or assumed that in the real world it is endogenous, that is being determined by what is happening in the model and just changing in response to the demand for money during the business cycle. Hence money cannot cause anything.

Implications of real business cycle theory are that prices would be counter-cyclical. As output rises, *if the money supply is constant*, prices must fall in the classical model, and vice versa. Most economists believe that, with the exception of obvious supply shocks, prices are procyclical, rising in booms, for example. Some real business cycle economists have gone back over the evidence and now argue that everyone has been wrong, confusing inflation and price levels, and that, in fact, prices are countercyclical: 'The price level in the post-war period for the main countries is actually counter-cyclical, whereas most people tend to view it as pro-cyclical and then to try to explain this. In some of these cases there has been a basic misunderstanding of the facts' (Robert Barro, quoted from Snowdon *et al.*, 1994, p.274). Real business cycle theorists claim that their models are consistent with the fact that over the business cycle wages are procyclical, whereas the implication of the Keynesian, Friedman and Lucas theories is that they would be countercyclical ('real wage movements pose problems for any business cycle theory I know about' – Robert Lucas Jr., quoted from Snowdon *et al.*, 1994, p.224).

Most older economists cannot accept the New Classical view that unemployment is voluntary and that the business cycle is just the result of people deciding the best intertemporal supply of effort. Plausibility has never been a strong feature of mathematical models, but simple evidence is enough to refute many elegant theories. As Tobin (1992, p.398) puts it: 'We do not need fancy econometrics to mobilize evidence against the "real business cycle" view that observed fluctuations in output and employment are movements in price-cleared equilibrium.' He then lists six facts that clearly contradict the real business cycle view. The most obvious are that much unemployment results from people being fired, not voluntarily leaving jobs and unable to find new ones (Abel and Bernanke, 1995, pp.367–9; Gordon, 1993, p.204) and that the ratio of vacancies to unemployment varies over the cycle such that when unemployment is high there are fewer job vacancies. This is incompatible with the view that unemployment is voluntary. Again the classical view is that monetary changes should not affect output, but Tobin accepts as 'overwhelming' the evidence that money does affect real variables. He writes that 'the list could go on' and concludes by asking: 'Why do so many talented economic theorists believe and teach elegant fantasies so obviously refutable by plainly evident facts?' (Tobin, 1992, p.399). The prose is simpler than that of Keynes but the incomprehension and amazement is just the same as that expressed by Keynes 60 years ago.

One last New Classical view that has been influential is the so-called 'Ricardian equivalence' hypothesis or sometimes the 'Barro–Ricardo equivalence theorem', a view revived by Robert Barro (1974) from an idea of David Ricardo, who did not think the idea was relevant to actual behaviour. This is the view that private sector saving behaviour is a function of government saving. It is easy to understand this in the context of the permanent income view of consumption behaviour, although Barro did not present the theory this way. Think now in terms of our simple classical model of the interest rate and assume the government reduces taxes. Its deficit rises, so it has to sell bonds. On the assumption above the interest rate would rise but, argues Barro, people will see their taxes falling now but will think to themselves that taxes will have to rise in the future so that the government can pay off the debt it is now issuing. They see their future tax burden rising and so will save any tax cut so they have the money available in the future to pay the increased taxes. This means that their consumption will be relatively stable over time and total saving does not change; private saving offsets the government dissaving. In our model above this means that the supply of loanable funds schedule (the saving schedule) shifts to the right by an amount equal to the increase in the budget deficit and so interest rates do not rise. Evidence on this proposition is mixed: while some countries seem to show such behaviour, many others do not. One reason for doubting its relevance is the American experience in the 1980s, when there were tax cuts and a rising government budget deficit. People should have saved the tax cut but, in fact, the personal saving ratio in America during this period fell considerably (Dornbusch and Fischer, 1994, p.318). This evidence is enough for some writers such as Gordon (1993, p.400) and Dornbusch and Fischer (1994, p.320) to reject the relevance of the hypothesis. One response is to argue that the saving data are misleading. The idea of forward-looking behaviour in which people try to anticipate government actions has, however, become entrenched in macroeconomics as a result of this idea and that of rational expectations.

The Singapore view is that 'there is little evidence of this ["Ricardian equivalence" hypothesis] phenomenon in Singapore ... Private individuals do not seek to lower their saving rates in response to increases in government saving' (*Monetary Authority of Singapore Annual Report 1993/1994*, p.48).

3.4   NEW KEYNESIAN ECONOMICS

We conclude with a broad review of this so-called school of economists, although there are differences among them and their similarities to Keynes are slight: 'If I had a copyright on who could use the term "Keynesian" I wouldn't allow them to use it' (James Tobin, quoted from Snowdon *et al.*, 1994, p.132). They see themselves as theorists trying to provide a firm microeconomic foundation for the existence of sticky prices and wages to justify the Keynesian argument that changes in demand will be translated into changes in output. This could explain recessions in the economy and, as there would be costs to the economy in terms of lost output and high unemployment, there remains a role for the government to carry out macroeconomic stabilization policy. This New Keynesian conclusion separates them from the New Classic school of Lucas and others but puts them in a very similar position to that of Friedman, as G.N. Mankiw agrees when he argues that monetary changes are the main determinant of demand change, that money is neutral in the long run and the economy does have a tendency to return to the natural rate of output when there is a demand change that pushes it away from this point. These economists are willing to use rational expectations arguments but not necessarily concerning the same variables as in the New Classical approach. Furthermore they often use monopolistic competition, or imperfect competition, models of the firm, unlike the standard classical assumption of perfect competition taken by most textbook expositions. Dornbusch and Fischer (1994) and Gordon (1993) drop the assumption of competition. Some use the representative agent model of generalizing from the behaviour of one 'agent' and this must be take as a major shortcoming of some New Keynesian models. Gordon (1990) provides a survey, as does Snowdon *et al.* (1994, chap. 7) and a good textbook by such economists (Abel and Bernanke, 1995) provides the arguments in more detail.

One influential argument ('the "rage of the 80s"': Gordon, 1990, p.1157) explaining unemployment is the efficiency wage hypothesis. This is the idea that workers' productivity is a positive function of the wage they are paid, an argument that can be found in the writing of Adam Smith. In its modern form it generates the proposition that, as firms will set the wage to maximize the amount of effort they get from each dollar of wages, this 'efficiency wage' will not necessary lead to the labour market being in equilibrium and there could be unemployment. There is no mechanism for the wage rate to fall as this would increase the cost per unit of effort for employers, and unemployment could persist. See Abel and Bernanke (1995, pp.398–404) and Gordon (1993, pp.225–8) for textbook treatments. Another argument relates to 'menu costs', the costs of changing prices. If these costs exceed the expected gains in profit when demand conditions change, firms may keep prices unchanged.

The result of these various disconnected theories is that New Keynesian economists are prepared to summarize their view of the economy in terms of our simple aggregate demand and supply model by drawing the aggregate supply curve as a perfectly horizontal line – taking us right back to the over-simplified 45-degree diagram explanations of Keynes of the 1950s or the *IS/LM* curve model. The main difference is that New Keynesians would argue that the aggregate supply curve cannot be permanently fixed at any given price level. Assume there is a fall in demand. Output falls along the horizontal aggregate supply curve in the short run and unemployment rises. After a while prices fall because of the fall in demand and the economy tends to move back to the natural rate of output (Abel and Bernanke, 1995, pp.413–20; Gordon, 1993 pp.228–32). The short-run response is the same as in the simple Keynesian model but the long-run outcome is that of the classical model. The main difference is, of course, that New Keynesians see a role for government stabilization policy through either monetary or fiscal policy.

3.5   CONCLUSIONS

Modern macroeconomics is represented by a number of schools whose approaches are very different. Even the usefulness of basic ides is questioned. A classical economist would ask how it is possible for people to be unemployed against their will. If an accountant cannot get a job as an accountant he can work as a teacher or a taxi driver. Jobs are always there. People are rational; the outcome of this rationality must be optimal. It can be proved to be so for Robinson Crusoe, so it must be for everyone. A Keynesian will reject representative agent models and retain the idea of involuntary unemployment and associate the extent of employment with the extent of aggregate demand. Keynesians just cannot understand why some other economists believe the labour market is always in equilibrium and adjustments to changes in demand happen quickly enough to ensure that output is always at its natural level. Monetarists stress that inflation is a monetary phenomenon; Keynesians still identify cost-push factors. An interesting illustration of this was provided when Milton Friedman was asked in late 1994 whether he thought inflation would increase in the American economy. He replied that he did not expect there to be any increase in inflation during the following two years because there was then no rapid increase in the money supply. When asked the same question, John Kenneth Galbraith, who is identified with the Post Keynesian approach, agreed that there would be no increase in inflation, but his reason was based on the fact that there was 'substantial slack in the labour market', which made the resurgence of trade union power unlikely (Bloomberg Business News report in the *Business Times*, 16 December 1994). These are very different ways of looking at the causes of inflation.

Policy makers still think in terms of Keynesian models in which demand matters and unemployment is involuntary. As Krugman (1994, chap. 8) puts it: 'In the long run Keynes is still alive' and he chronicles the re-establishment of Keynesian ways of thinking. In terms of thinking about the economy it is clear that many economists prefer to teach the *IS/LM* curve model, even to their graduate students in America. Despite its limitations as demand-side theory only, it is the 'tool of first resort' for James Tobin and 'I don't think there is a better model for getting the intuition of the short-run adjustment of the economy right' is the view of Stanley Fischer (quoted from Snowdon *et al.*, 1994, pp.129, 35). We will thus use this model in the next chapter to analyse the nature of an open economy.

SUGGESTIONS FOR FURTHER READING

Most of the above arguments will be covered in any good macroeconomics textbook. In particular we recommend Abel and Bernanke (1995), Dornbusch and Fischer (1994) or Gordon (1993) as those using mainly American evidence and Parkin and Bade (1986) as one that uses British evidence. Barro (1990) is the leading New Classical textbook.

We recommend most highly Snowdon *et al.* (1994) for a review of different schools in macroeconomics, their differences and the views of their main developers.

NOTES

1. When the real wage rises the price of leisure (not working) rises. The substitution effect says that people will consume less leisure (because it is more expensive) and thus do more work. However, when the real wage rises, real income will rise even if people do the same amount of work. If leisure is a normal good people will want more leisure: that is, to do less work. We

assume that the substitution effect dominates so that people do more work as the real wage rises.

2.   In a letter to William Beveridge, dated 28 July 1936, in *The Collected Writings of John Maynard Keynes*, Vol. XIV, Part II, p.57. We can devise many other multipliers based on different assumptions. We could make taxes a function of income, in which case there would be another leakage at the margin, making leakages greater and the multiplier smaller. The multiplier is always the reciprocal of the proportion of an increase in income that is not spent in the domestic economy $(1 - c)$. If, for example, the addition of taxes linked to income reduced the proportion of any increase in income spent in the domestic economy to 0.4, c, the multiplier would be 1.67, not 2.5 as in the text. If we added the possibility of leakages for imports then the multiplier would be even smaller. This we do in the next chapter. If we make investment a positive function of the level of spending and this was correlated with the level of income the multiplier would be larger because, as income rose, investment would rise, thus producing extra multiplier effects. Some models do incorporate this effect.

3.   We can formalize these results in the following way. Substitute the expression for the *LM* curve into that for the *IS* curve and solve for *Y*. This would give us

$$Y = [a + \bar{I} + \bar{G} - c\bar{T} + (i/m_2)(M/P - m)]/[(1 - c) + i(m_1/m_2)]$$

This shows that *Y* is a positive function of all the autonomous expenditures and an inverse function of lump-sum taxes, a positive function of the nominal and real money supply. *Y* would fall if *m*, the autonomous demand for money, rose. The impact of these changes on *Y* is determined by the *IS/LM* multiplier. For example, an increase in *G* would increase *Y* by the change in *G* multiplied by

$$1/[(1 - c) + i(m_1/m_2)]$$

This is clearly smaller than the simple Keynesian multiplier, $1/(1 - c)$, because of the addition of the second term. This term represents how much r rises as *Y* rises (the slope of the *LM* curve, m_1/m_2) and by how much this would crowd out *I* through the i term. The larger this term the smaller the full multiplier will be. The multiplier will be small if i is large (investment is a sensitive inverse function of r) or if m_1/m_2 is large, which will occur, *ceteris paribus*, if m_2 is small, there is low responsiveness of money demand to r and hence a steep *LM* curve.

The multiplier for a change in the nominal money supply is

$$(i/m_2)/[(1 - c) + i(m_1/m_2)]$$

4.   What Keynes (1936, p.129) actually wrote was:

> If the Treasury were to fill old bottles with bank-notes, bury them at suitable depths in disused coal mines which are then filled up to the surface with town rubbish, and leave it to private enterprise on well-tried principles of *laissez-faire* to dig the notes up again (the right to do so being obtained, of course, by tendering for leases of the note-bearing territory), there need be no more unemployment, and, with the help of the repercussions, the real income of the community, and its capital wealth also, would probably become a good deal greater than it actually is. It would, indeed, be more sensible to build houses and the like; but if there are political and practical difficulties in the way of this, the above would be better than nothing.

It is clear that Keynes saw this policy as an alternative to public works policies of housebuilding, not just as a means of increasing the money supply. His policy would mean that the successful businessmen would go out and buy diggers and tractors, hire miners, security guards, accountants and so on, using bank loans if necessary, which would be easy to get as this is an investment project with a guaranteed known return. This would increase real investment and, through the multiplier, which Keynes refers to as 'repercussions', would shift the *IS* curve and increase output. When the money is recovered then the money supply will increase, thus reinforcing the multiplier effects of the first increase in investment expenditures. The increase in the money supply is the secondary, not primary, consequence of the policy. Hiding the money just creates an investment opportunity that is bound to be profitable. In a recession these opportunities are scarce.

5. It is interesting to note that, during the recession of the early 1990s, public works projects were a policy reaction of governments in the USA, Japan and the European Union.

6. This is a true event. We have forgotten which five cars he bought. Perhaps this is an example of the 'rampant consumerism' that the Singapore government was railing against in 1994 and 1995 and trying to limit, by restricting advertisements for credit cards and introducing limits on the amounts banks could lend to personal borrowers.

7. This is an example of disequilibrium in a market when we would always observe the amount traded to be the minimum of either the demand or supply at that disequilibrium price. This is called the min. condition or the 'short-side rule'.

8. This is a typical economist's assumption. We know it is not true, but we can keep this fact in the back of our head and allow for large changes in it in any discussion. For example, if V is rising, $\dot{v}$ is positive and nominal income (MV) will be rising faster than at the rate $\dot{m}$, so inflation will be higher than otherwise.

4.   Macroeconomics for an open economy

An open economy is one in which international trade is a significant part of economy activity and one which is open to flows of capital either into or out of it. Singapore is clearly such an economy. As we have seen, the total of trade far exceeds GDP and net exports have become a significant component of aggregate demand. There are no restrictions on the flow of money across borders through the foreign exchange market. We need a framework to help us understand how these trade and capital flows affect the nature of the relationships between the main macroeconomic variables discussed in the previous chapter and how this changes the nature and effectiveness of various government polices.

We first discuss the nature and determination of a country's exchange rate and how it influences trade flows. We show how trade and capital flows are summarized in a balance of payments account and how different policies towards the exchange rate lead to different outcomes for a country's balance of payments. We then present a simple aggregate demand model that incorporates the effects of changes in exchange rates and capital flows on demand and the way a government's policies are constrained by the type of exchange rate system it adopts.

4.1   EXCHANGE RATES

An exchange rate is just the price of one currency in terms of another. We will refer to Singapore as the domestic economy with its domestic currency and the rest of the world as the rest of the world. We can look at this price from the point of view of the domestic country or from that of the rest of the world or a particular foreign country. On 9 March 1995, for example, the price of one American dollar was S$1.409. This means that Americans, or anyone else using American dollars to buy Singapore dollars, had to pay US$0.710 for each Singapore dollar; 0.710 is the reciprocal of 1.409.

We can disuss the exchange rate in terms either of how much domestic currency you have to pay for a unit of foreign currency (the price of foreign exchange) or of how much you get in terms of foreign currencies for each unit of domestic currency (the price of the domestic currency for foreigners or the value of the domestic currency measured in foreign currencies). We need to keep both concepts in mind.

Economists simplify drastically the factors determining the exchange rates and use simple demand and supply analysis because an exchange rate is just a price. We will think in terms of the demand for and supply of Singapore dollars in our analysis below, so we must use an exchange rate concept that is the price of Singapore dollars. The demand for Singapore dollars arises from the demand from the rest of the world for Singapore exports (including services such as shipping, insurance and tourism) and for assets in Singapore. These assets could be financial assets (shares in a company listed on the stock exchange, or a bank account denominated in Singapore dollars) or real capital, such as a new factory built by a foreign company, or a house. We accept that this demand for Singapore dollars will be an inverse function of the price of Singapore dollars measured in US dollars, for example. Such a demand curve is shown in Figure 4.1. The horizontal axis is the quantity of Singapore dollars, so the vertical axis must be the price of Singapore dollars. At an exchange rate of US$0.70, Singapore goods and services would be more expensive than at a rate of US$0.50, so we believe the demand for Singapore dollars would be lower, as people would not be as prepared to buy Singapore goods and services, since those from Hong Kong or Malaysia, for example, would be cheaper. The supply of Singapore dollars is a positive function of the price of Singapore dollars. At a price of US$0.70, Singaporeans can buy more foreign goods for each Singapore dollar than at a price of US$0.50 for each Singapore dollar, so we assume they will buy more goods from the USA or go there more often for their holidays.

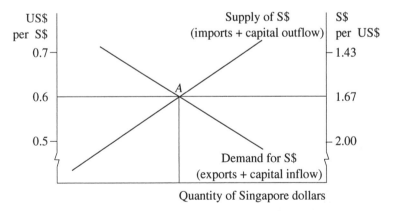

Figure 4.1   Equilibrium in the foreign exchange market

The foreign exchange market is in equilibrium at point *A* where the demand and supply for Singapore dollars are equated. At this equilibrium a Singapore dollar is worth US$0.60 and so an American dollar costs S$1.67. We can see why the price of the Singapore dollar might rise. Such an increase is called an appreciation of the currency, as it becomes worth more in terms of foreign currencies. Anything that increases the demand for Singapore dollars or reduces the supply will cause its price to rise. Anything that reduces the demand for Singapore dollars or increases their supply would reduce its price. Such a fall in price is called a depreciation, as the currency is now worth less in terms of foreign currencies.

Figure 4.2 shows just one possible reason for an appreciation of the Singapore dollar: the demand for Singapore dollars has risen with respect to the supply and its price rises to US$0.65, meaning that an American dollar now costs S$1.54. A lower price of American dollars in terms of Singapore dollars shows that the Singapore dollar has appreciated. Of course, as a certain currency is appreciating against one currency it could be depreciating against another.

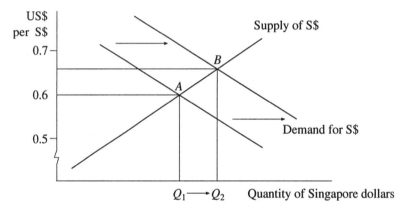

Figure 4.2   The effect of an increase in demand for the currency

These demand curves are non-observable but give us clues as to why a currency might appreciate. We will show some other consequences of such changes that confirm that it is relative shifts in demand and supply that are responsible for changes in exchange rates. There are many factors lying behind the demand and supply curves, of course. We give one simple illustration here. In October 1993 Singapore Telecom sold shares to the public including a tranche reserved for foreigners. We would expect the demand for Singapore dollars to rise before this date as the capital inflow would rise. Over the period July 1993 to October 1993 the Singapore dollar appreciated by 3.1 per cent against the American dollar (from S$1.6211 to S$1.5716) and 2.6 per cent against the pound sterling. So, at a time when we might expect to see an increase in demand for Singapore dollars, the Singapore dollar did appreciate, just as the simple model predicts. This is an example of a very short-term change in the value of the currency. Later in this book we will have to examine factors that determine long-run changes, such as the facts that the Singapore dollar has appreciated from S$2.52 to the American dollar in January 1974 to S$1.465 in December 1994 and from S$5.59 to the pound sterling to S$2.283, and depreciated from S$0.890 to the Deutschmark to S$0.932.

Other factors lying behind shifts in the demand and supply for a currency might be the following. An increase in domestic prices at a more rapid rate than in the rest of the world would lead to a fall in the demand for a country's exports and a switch to imports rather than domestic goods, thus reducing the demand for and increasing the supply of its currency and thus leading to its depreciation. If a country were to liberalize its financial sector, allowing more shares on its stock exchange to be owned and traded by foreigners, for example, this could increase the demand for a country's currency, tending to make it appreciate. This phenomenon is occurring in Asia as countries such as China and India open up to the world and in Malaysia, Thailand and the Philippines also. These countries are among the so-called 'emerging (stock) markets' and are attracting the attention of foreign investors (both in financial assets and in real capital projects) and are receiving large inflows of capital. Such large flows could result in either appreciating currencies or domestic money supply growth, or a mixture of both,[1] for reasons we will explain shortly. An increase in domestic interest rates or policies that make investment more profitable, such as tax reductions or concessions, might increase inflow of capital, thus increasing the demand for a country's currency.

The model above assumed that the exchange rate is determined solely by the activities of the private sector. The exchange rate is a market-determined rate in that there has been no government intervention. The market has been left to find its own equilibrium. This is called a 'clean float'. Let us look at what this would imply for the balance of payments account.

A balance of payments account is just a summary of all international transactions, denominated in domestic currency, organized in terms of credit and debit items. Credit items are those that give rise to the demand for domestic currency and debit items are those that give rise to a supply of domestic currency. Consider Figure 4.3, where the foreign exchange market is in equilibrium. Let us assume that this summarizes all international transactions. The principal flows omitted here are unrequited transfers of money.[2] The demand and supply of domestic currency by the private sector are equilibrated at 100. The demand for domestic currency consists of exports (55) plus the capital inflow (45). The supply of Singapore dollars consists of imports (40) and capital outflow (60). The balance of payments accounts categorize debits and credits as either current account items (essentially trade in goods and services) or capital account items (capital flows). In these circumstances the balance of payments would look like this:

Current account		Balance
Credit: exports	55	
Debit: imports	40	
		+ 15
Capital account		
Credit: capital inflow	45	
Debit: capital outflow	60	
		−15
Overall balance		0

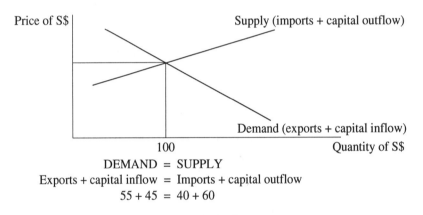

DEMAND = SUPPLY
Exports + capital inflow = Imports + capital outflow
55 + 45 = 40 + 60

Figure 4.3   Balance of payments equilibrium and the foreign exchange market

Here the current account is in surplus and the capital account is in deficit by the same amount. It can be seen quite clearly that this must be so. Total credits equals total debits. We have just rearranged the items according to whether they are current or capital items. The surplus (deficit) of one account must be exactly offset by an equal deficit (surplus) in the other account. An interesting question concerns which account determines which. The answer is that they are mutually determined. It is often said that because a country has a deficit on its current account through importing more than it exports (as in the USA, for example) it must have a credit on its capital account (capital inflows exceed outflows, so it is borrowing from abroad) implying that the former determines the latter. We could equally say that, as the country has a capital account surplus (people find it a good country to buy assets in) it must have a current account deficit (it can import more than it exports).

4.2   EXCHANGE RATES AND TRADE

Changes in a country's exchange rate affect exports and imports through the possible change in their prices, either in foreign or in domestic prices. If a country's currency depreciates this means that its exports could be sold at lower foreign prices but still produce the same price in domestic currency for the exporter. Assume that a Singapore good costs S$10 to make and deliver to the customer in America. If the exchange rate is SS1.50 to the American dollar then this good could sell for US$6.67 and provide the Singaporean exporter with S$10 (6.67 times 1.50). If the Singapore dollar depreciates to S$1.60 to the American dollar this good will now provide S$10.70. In fact the exporter could reduce his American dollar price to, say, US$ 6.50 and obtain S$10.40 for the good. This price cut would allow him to outcompete American competitors and those from other countries that competed with him in foreign markets. It would lead to an increase in real exports. Conversely this depreciation would make foreign goods more expensive in Singapore. Originally an American compact disc might sell for S$22.5 when the exchange rate was S$1.50. When the exchange rate changes to S$1.60, this good may rise in price to S$24, thus reducing the demand for it.

An appreciation of a country's currency would make its exports more expensive and its imports cheaper. Think of a Singapore good selling for US$10 in America. At an exchange rate of S$1.60, the exporter obtains S$16 to cover his Singapore dollar costs, including his profits. If the Singapore dollar appreciated to $1.50 to the US dollar he would only get S$15 and his profit margins would be reduced if he could not reduce his costs. If he could not cut his costs by increasing productivity or cutting wages he would be tempted to try to sell his good in the domestic market or to increase its US dollar price. This would tend to reduce exports. An imported good selling for S$20 at an exchange rate of S$1.60 could fall in price to S$18.75 when the Singapore dollar appreciated, thus encouraging a larger volume of imports.

So the basic assumption of the models we will develop below is that an appreciation of a currency will tend to reduce a country's exports and increase its imports. A depreciation of the currency would tend to increase its exports and decrease its imports, thus increasing net exports. These conclusions are based on the assumption that price is the main determinant of export or import sales and there have not been offsetting cost changes that nullify the change in prices.

4.3 THE GOVERNMENT AND THE FOREIGN EXCHANGE MARKET

In the simple model of the foreign exchange market above the exchange rate was determined solely by private sector transactors. Such activity might lead to large fluctuations in the exchange rate, affecting the volume of imports and exports. For this reason some governments try to control the exchange rate. One extreme form of control would be to set a fixed price for its currency and to intervene in the foreign exchange market to keep the price at or near this level. This is just a price support scheme. The private sector demands and supplies would be shifting around, sometimes creating excess demand, when the currency would tend to appreciate, or excess supply, when the currency would tend to depreciate. The government's central bank or monetary authority could smooth out any such fluctuations by selling or buying domestic currency according to the state of disequilibrium at the desired exchange rate.

Consider Figure 4.4. Assume the government wanted to keep the exchange rate at US$0.55 on a particular day when the private sector demanders and suppliers would produce excess demand at this rate and an equilibrium rate of US$0.60. To prevent the currency from appreciating the monetary authority would have to sell its own currency to the extent of *AB*, supplementing the deficient private sector supply and meeting the excess demand at point *B*. In return for the domestic currency that it sells, the monetary authority would receive American dollars from private sector sellers and thus be able to accumulate foreign currency reserves as long as this situation prevailed.

If, however, the monetary authority wanted the currency to be worth more, say US$0.70, it would face a situation on that day of excess supply of domestic

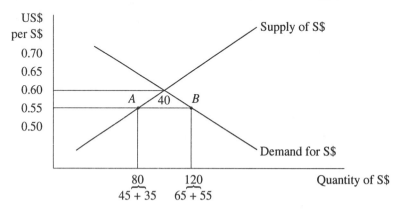

Figure 4.4   Government intervention in the foreign exchange market

currency at this rate and it would have to intervene by buying its own currency using US dollars to prevent the price from falling. It could do this if it had a stockpile of US dollars.

Let us look at the nature of this country's balance of payments when the monetary authority intervenes to affect the exchange rate. We will take the first example where the monetary authority is selling its own currency and the volume traded is a point *B* in Figure 4.4. The total volume traded is 120 with the private sector supplying 80 (imports 45 plus capital outflow of 35) and the total private sector demand is 120 (exports 65, capital inflow 55). The country's balance of payments accounts would look like this:

		Balance
Current account		
Credit: exports	65	
Debit: imports	45	
		+ 20
Capital account		
Credit: capital inflow	55	
Debit: capital outflow	35	
		+ 20
Overall balance		+ 40
Official transactions		− 40
Balance		0

There is a current account surplus of 20 and a capital account surplus also of 20. The overall balance is in surplus to the extent of 40. This is possible because the monetary authority is selling its domestic currency to the extent of 40, so we could say that the balance is zero; a balance always balances but the private sector's transactions do not balance when there is intervention. The monetary authority's intervention is represented by its official transactions. Here it is negative as it is a supply of domestic currency and thus represents the extent of the accumulation of foreign currency. So the accumulation of foreign currencies is represented by a negative figure for official transactions in the balance of payments accounts. Perhaps the reader would like to work out what the balance of payments accounts might look like if the monetary authority was buying its own currency to maintain a high price for it.

Intervention in the foreign exchange market has important implications for a country's money supply process. If the monetary authority finds that at the exchange rate it would like to see prevail there is continuous excess demand then it must sell domestic currency. This would make the domestic money supply increase alongside an increase in the country's foreign exchange reserves. If the country were in a situation where, at the desired exchange rate, there was excess supply of its currency then it would have to buy its own currency thus reducing its own domestic currency supply. If a country tries to fix its exchange rate it loses control over its domestic money supply unless it takes measures to offset these effects arising in the foreign exchange market. For example, in some countries, when the monetary authority intervenes to prevent its currency from appreciating it is selling domestic currency. This will tend to increase the domestic money supply. At the same time the authority could sell government bonds to the private sector, thus 'mopping up' this increase in the money supply and offsetting the expansionary effect on the money supply. This action is called 'sterilization'. The extent to which it is possible and happens varies from country to country. For countries subject to perfect capital mobility and fixed exchange rates sterilization is not feasible (Rivera-Batiz and Rivera-Batiz, 1985, pp.236–7).

The nature of Singapore's money supply process and the role of foreign exchange transactions will be discussed in Chapter 5.

4.4   AGGREGATE DEMAND IN THE OPEN ECONOMY

We now return to our *IS/LM* curve model and incorporate the effects of trade flows and the implications for equilibrium of different polices towards the exchange rate. We start with an *IS* curve relevant to an open economy.

We assume exports are a function of the level of foreign demand which depends on foreign income levels and the exchange rate. So at any exchange rate, *exr*, exports, $\overline{EX}$ are exogenous. Imports consist of an autonomous element, $\overline{IM}$, and an induced part that is a function of domestic demand which is a function of domestic income. The higher is domestic income, the greater the extent of imports, through the marginal propensity to import, *j*. Total imports depend on the exchange rate also. We can represent this by writing the functions as

Exports $\overline{EX}(exr)$
Imports $\overline{IM}(exr) + j\,(Y)$

Aggregate demand is

$$Y = C + \bar{I} + \bar{G} + X - M$$

We use the model of the previous chapter and so when we substitute for the terms we get

$$Y = a + c(Y - \bar{T}) + \bar{I} - i(r) + \bar{G} + \overline{EX}(exr) - \overline{IM}(exr) - j(Y)$$

If we solve for Y we get

$$Y = \frac{a - c\overline{T} + \overline{I} + \overline{G} + \overline{EX}(exr) - \overline{IM}(exr)}{(1-c)+j} - \frac{i(r)}{(1-c)+j}$$

This is an *IS* curve relevant to an open economy. We can see that the multiplier, meaning the horizontal shift of the *IS* curve here, is smaller than that of the previous chapter. There c was 0.6 and so the multiplier was 2.5 (1/0.4). Here, with a marginal propensity to import of 0.2, for example, the multiplier is 1.67 (1/0.6).

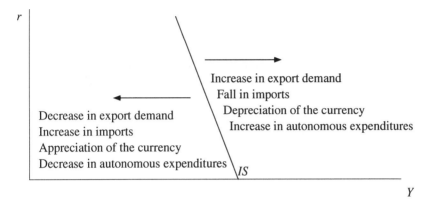

Figure 4.5   The open-economy IS *curve*

It is smaller because we have another leakage when domestic incomes rise. This makes the proportion of any increase in income spent in the domestic economy smaller and so the multiplier is smaller. Figure 4.5 shows this *IS* curve. It will shift for a number of reasons:

1. An increase in exports, or an decrease in autonomous imports will shift it to the right, thus increasing aggregate demand. A decrease in exports or an increase in autonomous imports will shift it to the left.
2. A depreciation of the currency, through its tendency to increase exports and reduce imports, will shift it to the right. An appreciation of the currency, through its tendency to reduce exports and increase imports, will shift it to the left.
3. An increase in the elements of autonomous expenditures such as a, $\overline{I}$ or $\overline{G}$ or a reduction in $\overline{T}$ will shift it to the right. A decrease in these expenditures or an increase in $\overline{T}$ will shift it to the left.

Now we can combine this *IS* curve with other elements of the model. We assume that this is an open economy with no restrictions on capital flows. We also assume that its financial markets are very liquid and well regulated so that its financial assets are perfect substitutes for those that can be held in any other country.[3] This means that, if there is no expectation of an appreciation or depreciation of the country's currency, its rate of interest must equal that in the rest of the world, r_w.

We will first show how this open economy adjusts to disequilibrating changes under a fixed exchange rate regime and then the situation when exchange rates are allowed to float.

4.5   THE FIXED EXCHANGE RATE REGIME

Figure 4.6 shows our open economy in equilibrium at point A, where domestic demand conditions and the money supply generate a level of income of Y_1 and an interest rate equal to that in the rest of the world. We assume that the supply of output is perfectly elastic at the pre-existing price level. Assume also that there is an increase in government expenditure or a reduction in taxes, or anything that increases exogenous expenditures and thus shifts the *IS* curve to the right. The level of income increases, as do domestic interest rates at point B. Financial assets in this country become very attractive to foreigners who now buy this country's currency in order to obtain these assets. There would be a tendency for the currency to appreciate but with a fixed exchange rate regime the monetary authority must intervene and buy this excess demand for its currency. This makes the domestic money supply increase, shifting the *LM* curve to the right, reducing the domestic rate of interest to equal the world level. Equilibrium is restored at point C with a higher level of income and money supply.

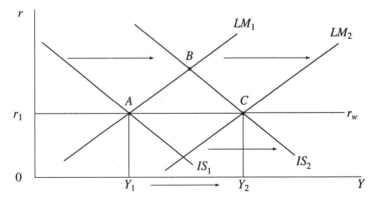

Figure 4.6   The effect of an increase in government expenditure with a fixed exchange rate

The money supply has become endogenous, automatically increasing as a result of the increase in domestic interest rates and monetary authority intervention. In this case there would be a full fiscal policy multiplier effect on Y of the increase in $\bar{G}$ or $\bar{I}$.

Now imagine something that would shift the *IS* curve to the left, such as a fall in export demand or a fall in investment. The domestic rate of interest falls below the world rate, people prefer to hold assets in other countries and so sell this currency, which tends to make it depreciate. Under the fixed exchange rate regime the monetary authority has to intervene by buying the increased sales of domestic currency. The domestic money supply falls and the *LM* curve shifts to the left, restoring the domestic rate of interest to that in the rest of the world. There has been a full negative multiplier effect on Y. All the necessary equilibrating adjustments happen through endogenous changes in the money supply and are represented by shifts in the *LM* curve as the domestic money supply changes. The shifts in real expenditures that move the *IS* curve have had large effects on output.

Now consider what would happen if the monetary authority tried to expand demand by increasing the money supply. This is shown in Figure 4.7. The *LM* curve shifts to the right, pushing down the domestic rate of interest below the world rate. There is a tendency for people to sell this currency and so the monetary authority has to intervene by buying it. The domestic money supply falls and the *LM* curve returns to its original position, so there has been no effect on output. Monetary policy has had no effect on domestic demand or output. The government cannot set the money supply at any amount other than that required to make the domestic interest rate equal to the world rate. In this regime of a fixed exchange rate shifts in the *IS* curve are the reason for changes

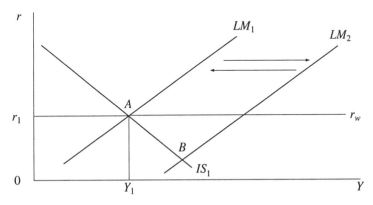

Figure 4.7 The effect of an increase in the money supply with a fixed exchange rate

in output; money has no role. From 1945 to 1971, most advanced industrial countries operated a fixed exchange rate regime under the Bretton Woods system whereby governments were obliged to intervene to keep their exchange rates from fluctuating outside a pre-agreed band which could only be changed by formal devaluation or revaluation.[4] It was in the 1950s and 1960s that most Keynesian macroeconomic textbooks were being written and it is no surprise that they stressed the importance of fiscal multipliers in determining demand as they knew that the money supply would be endogenous under the fixed exchange rate system.

Now consider Figure 4.8, where we analyse what would happen if people came to believe that the domestic currency would appreciate against foreign currencies. Say that initially $r = r_w$ at 5 per cent per annum and people now think this currency will appreciate by 3 per cent over the next year. The domestic interest rate could now fall to 2 per cent as now people holding this currency would receive a 2 per cent rate of interest plus the 3 per cent currency appreciation, equalling the opportunity cost represented by r_w. How would the domestic rate of interest be pushed down to 2 per cent? In the fixed exchange rate regime the answer is easy to see. On coming to believe that this currency will appreciate, people start to buy the currency, tending to make it appreciate. The monetary authority intervenes, selling domestic currency, so the *LM* curve shifts to the right, increasing *Y* and pushing the rate of interest down to 2 per cent. The expectation of currency appreciation is another explanation, along with low inflation rates which make nominal interest rates low, for the existence of low interest rates in some countries.

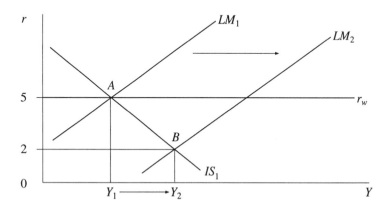

Figure 4.8 The effect of expected currency appreciation with a fixed exchange rate

4.6   THE FLEXIBLE EXCHANGE RATE REGIME

For simplicity we assume there is a completely clean float and a flexible exchange rate. We will analyse the same changes as under the fixed exchange rate regime.

In Figure 4.9, we show what would happen if there were an increase in government spending, G. The IS curve shifts to the right, pushing up the domestic rate of interest to point B. At this high rate of interest people want to buy financial assets there, so they buy this country's currency. The currency does appreciate. This appreciation reduces exports and increases imports. These effects reduce aggregate demand and the IS curve shifts to the left, reducing output and reducing the domestic rate of interest back to the original unchanged world rate. Equilibrium has been restored through an appreciation of the currency and a fall in net exports (NX). The fiscal expansion has no effect on output at all. We are back in the classical world. Here an additional flexible price, the exchange rate, has prevented any change in real expenditure from increasing output. We have seen that Y remains constant but the government is buying more, so we must identify who is buying less. Clearly in this model net exports have been reduced through the appreciation of the currency, so the composition of the unchanged output changes with the government buying more and the rest of the world less.

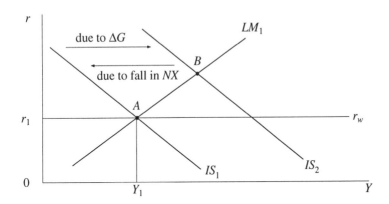

Figure 4.9   The effect of an increase in government expenditure with a
flexible exchange rate

With flexible exchange rates, shifts in the IS curve cannot change output because they bring about equilibrating changes in the value of the currency that offset the initial effect of the IS curve shift. A rightward shift in IS pushes up domestic interest rates, which makes the currency appreciate, thus reducing net exports and shifting the *IS* curve back to the left. A leftward shift in the *IS* curve reduces the rate of interest, leading to a currency depreciation that will stimulate net exports, shifting the *IS* curve back to the right. So, for example, a fall in investment would lead to a fall in domestic interest rates, a depreciation of the currency and thus an increase in net exports which would offset the initial decline in investment. With flexible exchange rates the economy is very stable in the sense that changes in factors that shift the *IS* curve cannot change output.

We can analyse the effects of changes in the money supply under flexible exchange rates. Assume there is an increase in the money supply, as shown in Figure 4.10. The *LM* curve shifts to the right and the domestic rate of interest falls below the world rate. The currency depreciates, which increases exports and reduces imports. The *IS* curve therefore shifts to the right, producing equilibrium at point *C*, where the interest rate has returned to the world level. An

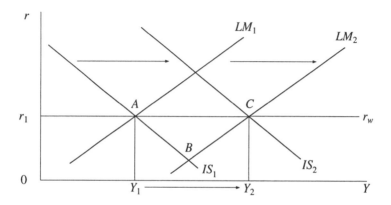

Figure 4.10 The effect of an increase in the money supply with a flexible exchange rate

expansionary monetary policy has had a large impact on output as it has caused a depreciation of the currency, which induces a rise in net exports, further increasing demand. Conversely a reduction in the money supply would shift the *LM* curve to the left, increasing the domestic rate of interest and causing the currency to appreciate. This would reduce exports and increase imports, thus shifting the *IS* curve to the left and reducing output. Again monetary policy has had a strong effect on output. In the flexible exchange rate system it is the *IS* curve that does all the required equilibrating adjustment through the effect of changes in the exchange rate on net exports.

We can analyse the effects of an expected appreciation of the domestic currency. The domestic interest rate must fall to 2 per cent, as shown in Figure 4.11. Initially the original domestic interest rate with an expectation of currency appreciation attracts a capital inflow, which leads the currency to appreciate. This reduces net exports, shifting the *IS* curve to the left, reducing the rate of interest to 2 per cent and restoring equilibrium. This could cause a recession in the economy.

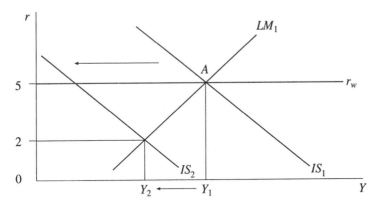

Figure 4.11 The effect of expected currency appreciation with a
*   flexible exchange rate*

We have analysed these effects in strictly *ceteris paribus* terms, changing one variable and assuming there was no policy response. In the last case, for example, we assumed that as the exchange rate appreciated and the economy slipped into recession the government did nothing. This is unlikely and it is clear that an expansionary monetary policy could offset the contractionary effects of the currency appreciation. We have also assumed that exchange rates are either fixed or perfectly flexible. In fact, they are often a mixture of both. In the short run the monetary authority or central bank often intervenes to prevent large fluctuations in the exchange rate, but will allow the market to determine the long-run trend in the rate. This is usually called a 'managed float'. The relevance of this possibility and its consequences for Singapore will be illustrated in the next chapter.

4.7   PURCHASING POWER PARITY CONDITIONS

We have also assumed that the price level is fixed, as in the simple *IS/LM* curve model. There is another possible adjustment mechanism when prices can change. We will briefly review the mechanism here using very simple numerical examples that reveal some very important ideas. Assume all goods are tradeable and there are no transport costs. The world price level is US$1. Return to the fixed exchange rate mechanism. The exchange rate is $1 for US$1. That means our goods would be able to sell for US$1 on world markets as they would have to under our assumption that all goods are tradeable. The 'law of one price' prevails: when we measure the prices of goods in a common currency they must be the same. Now there is a worldwide inflation except in the domestic country and the world price level doubles to US$2. At the fixed exchange rate our goods are very cheap. One US dollar only buys half a good in the rest of the world but still buys one good in our economy because the exchange rate is fixed. There would be a large increase in the demand for our exports and hence an increase in the demand for our currency. With a fixed exchange rate the monetary authority must intervene by buying the foreign currency, which makes our money supply increase. As long as our prices remain at $1 there is sustained excess demand for our currency and a continuous increase in our money supply. In the long run our price level must rise to $2 as then, at the original unchanged exchange rate of one to one, our goods now cost US$2. The law of one price has been upheld by a doubling of our price level. In other words, in a fixed exchange rate system, inflation in the rest of the world can be imported into the domestic economy. Another implication is that countries in a fixed exchange rate system cannot have different rates of inflation and, by implication, must have similar monetary growth rates. Again there cannot be an independent monetary policy.

Now consider what would happen in the case of a flexible exchange rate system when there is a doubling of the world price level. Our goods are attractive so the demand for our currency rises. The currency appreciates and will keep on doing so until $1 equals US$2, that is until it has doubled in value. The law of one price is upheld by the appreciation of our currency and all goods now sell for US$2. The implication is that the currencies of high inflation countries will tend to depreciate (the rest of the world here) and those of low inflation countries will appreciate (the domestic economy). These very simple numerical examples omit other factors that could influence exchange rates, such as interest rate changes, but do give us some empirical implications to look at:

1. Countries with fixed exchange rates should have similar inflation rates. If they differ significantly the high inflation country will have balance of payments deficits and can only maintain the exchange rate if it has large reserves or if it introduces controls on currency flows. Otherwise it will probably have to devalue.
2. Currencies of high inflation countries will depreciate against those of low inflation countries.

We now have to distinguish between two concepts of the exchange rate: the nominal rate and the real rate. The nominal rate is the simple exchange rate concept we have been using above, but it can be calculated as a weighted average against a number (a 'basket' is the term used) of foreign currencies. The real exchange rate is the nominal exchange rate adjusted for differences in prices in different countries and this shows the relative price levels when they are measured in one common currency. If purchasing power parity were always observed then the real exchange rate would never change; either the exchange rate (under the floating system) or the price level (under the fixed or managed system) would adjust to ensure that relative prices stayed the same. How these exchange rates have changed in Singapore and how this has affected the economy will be discussed in Chapter 6.

The implications of purchasing power parity for changes in exchange rates under the flexible system or for the consequences of inflation rate differentials are taken seriously by many classical economists as strong long-run forces. For many, the purchasing power parity proposition is a proposition as important as the neutrality of money, and both are held as axioms by classical economists. There is, however, much evidence that for long periods exchange rates do differ markedly from their purchasing power values; that is, the real exchange rate does change. See Rivera-Batiz and Rivera-Batiz (1985 pp.475–86) for a review and Krugman (1994, pp.216–19) who argues that the fact that the real exchange rate tends to move with the nominal rate in many cases is one of the best pieces of evidence for a Keynesian way of looking at the economy, as it shows that prices do not adjust in the way the classical model assumes.

SUGGESTIONS FOR FURTHER READING

Any good macroeconomics textbook recommended in the previous chapter; and Sachs and Larrain (1993) or Bird (1987).

NOTES

1. Different countries are responding in different ways. In 1994 China started blaming large capital inflows for its rapid monetary growth and high inflation rate. In Malaysia and the Philippines the governments have implemented administrative measures to make their assets less attractive to foreigners. The Manila stock exchange index was one of the fastest growing in 1993. In 1994 its currency continued to appreciate significantly against the American dollar.
2. If Mrs Tan in Bedok sent her son who is studying in London $500 a month, this would be a transfer and a debit item. If Dr Tay, who is an engineer working in America, sent his parents in Tampines US$1000 a month this also would be a transfer but a credit item.
3. There are models that allow for situations in which there is less than perfect capital mobility or where financial assets in different countries are not perfect substitutes. In that case we must have a balance of payments equilibrium condition that shows us what the domestic interest rate must be at every level of domestic output so that the balance of payments is in equilibrium. In these circumstances the equilibrium condition, called a *BP* curve, is an upward-sloping line when plotted in the *IS/LM* curve diagrams. For this approach, see a good macroeconomic textbook such as Gordon (1993, pp.134–5) or Luckett *et al.* (1994, pp.135–44). It is felt that

an upward-sloping *BP* curve is relevant for a large open economy and the horizontal one for a small open economy, although many American textbooks do their analysis solely in terms of the perfect capital mobility assumptions. See Gordon (1993, pp.129–33), Sachs and Larrain (1993, pp.394–425) and Dornbusch and Fischer (1994, pp.167–84). Luckett *et al.* (1994, p.147) conclude that 'Singapore's *BP* curve is relatively flat.' We have confined ourselves to the analysis of perfect capital mobility.

4. Although most countries switched to floating exchange rates after 1973, several European countries who are members of the now Economic Union, under the leadership of Germany, readopted a fixed system called the Exchange Rate Mechanism. The UK had problems maintaining the value of sterling within its agreed band and left the system in September 1992 after trying to support the pound through large-scale intervention.

5. Money in the economy

In this chapter we examine the nature of Singapore's monetary system, its monetary data and the development of the main monetary aggregates, the nature of monetary policy in Singapore and some other related topics.

5.1 SINGAPORE'S MONEY

Although Singapore became independent from the Federation of Malaysia on 9 August 1965, it did not have its own currency until 12 June 1967 when the Board of Commissioners of Currency, Singapore (BCCS) was established. Since 1938 Singapore used Straits dollar notes, as did Sarawak and North Borneo. During the Japanese occupation Japanese government notes (never coins) replaced Straits dollars at par. Although issued at par they depreciated to 110 to one by 1945 (Drake, 1981, p.12). After the war Singapore, now a British Crown Colony and no longer part of the Straits Settlements, was part of a monetary arrangement with the Federation of Malaya, the colonies of Sarawak, North Borneo and Brunei and had its currency issued by the Board of Commissioners of Currency, Malaya and British Borneo. After Singapore became independent in August 1965 it waited two years before issuing its own currency. The new Singapore currency replaced the old notes that circulated in Malaysia and Brunei and they were gradually withdrawn from circulation and ceased to be legal tender in Singapore on 16 January 1969 (Soh, 1990, pp.18–20). After this date, Singapore, Malaysia and Brunei maintained free interchangeability of their currencies until 1973, when all Singapore's monetary arrangements with Malaysia were suspended. Brunei and Singapore have continued this inter-changeability until today, meaning that Singapore notes can be used in Brunei and vice versa and they are exchangeable at par and circulate as 'customary tender' in both countries (Chan and Ngiam, 1992a, p.21). The way the monetary authorities run the system requires repatriation of each country's notes on a regular basis and the resulting data show that it is overwhelmingly Brunei notes that are repatriated rather than Singapore notes. The currency of Brunei is the *Ringgit* (the same name as Malaysia's currency unit) but is usually referred to as a 'dollar' and represented by the standard $ sign. In 1993, $526.6 million of Brunei notes (2.8 per cent more than in 1992) were repatriated from Singapore compared to only S$14.3 million from Brunei (30 per cent less than in 1992) (*Annual Report and Accounts of the Board of Commissioners of Currency* 1993, p.13).

A legacy of Singapore's membership of the British Empire, along with the other British colonies of the region, is that it was part of a Currency Board system.[1] This was true for Singapore for the period 1899–1942 (Japanese invasion in 1942) and then from 1946 to 1973 (floating of the Singapore dollar in June 1973). After the floating of sterling, in June 1972, Singapore switched to the US dollar as the reserve currency until June 1973. Many books about Singapore still imply that it operates a Currency Board system today, a view perhaps fostered by the fact that currency issue is the responsibility of the Board of Commissioners of Currency, Singapore, not a central bank, and that Singapore's international reserves are very large. We should examine this view.

Currency Boards were a common feature of the monetary systems of British colonies (as we have seen above, a Currency Board operated in the Straits Settlements and Malaya), as well as of a few Italian colonies and in other places for short periods during emergencies, such as in North Russia from 1918 to 1920. They were generally abandoned when the colonies became independent or after the floating of most major currencies in 1972. The idea of a Currency Board system has come back into fashion recently as the system is admired by those who distrust the central banking system and so have recommended its readoption to cure the inflationary problems of Latin American countries, as well as to establish new currencies in the newly independent countries of the former Soviet Union (Hanke *et al.*, 1993).[2]

Let us briefly review the nature of a Currency Board system and show why it does not exist in Singapore today. A Currency Board is just an organization, either governmental or private (and licensed by the government) that issues its own currency and coins in exchange for another currency, known as the reserve currency, at a fixed and unchangeable rate. There could be more than one Currency Board in any country, thus providing competing currencies. The reserve currency could be a commodity such as gold, but payments are usually made in notes of the reserve currency. Anyone presenting the reserve currency to the Board could obtain local currency in order to conduct business and pay taxes in the country and would be assured that the Currency Board would redeem its notes in terms of the reserve currency at the fixed exchange rate. When Singapore was part of a Currency Board system the reserve currency was the pound sterling until June 1972 and the American dollar after that. The result of the system is that the value of the currency is fixed in terms of the reserve currency and the free market exchange rate could not diverge from this rate. In a Currency Board system the rate decided by the Currency Board determines the market rate, not the other way around. Its value against other currencies changes as the value of the reserve currency changes. Currency Boards do not have the power to increase the note issue unless there is a demand for the currency from people who sell it units of the reserve currency. Nor can they be forced to lend to the government to cover any part of its deficit. This is why they are advocated by those who think central banks are not independent of their governments and will collude in monetary financing of any budget deficit the governments choose to run. Nor can they act as lender of last resort to the banking system. The Currency Board uses its holdings of the reserve currency to buy low-risk, liquid securities, mostly denominated in the reserve currency. Of course, a successful Currency Board would not have to redeem much of its note issue. The Currency Board thus earns income from the interest on these reserves. The currency is always fully backed by these foreign reserves. The currency thus issued provides the cash reserves for the banking system. If the country has a commercial, fractional reserve banking system, which is almost always the case, and is true of Singapore, then the money supply (that is, currency plus bank deposits) will greatly exceed the amount of currency in existence, so the total money supply of a country cannot be fully backed by foreign reserves.

Singapore's official foreign reserves exceed the value of its note issue. In 1993, for example, reserves equalled S$77.9 billion and total currency in existence was S$9.675 billion; the amount in active circulation was S$8.94 billion. This relationship between total official foreign reserves and currency is often quoted in this context (Lee, 1985, p.39), for example, but a more relevant figure would be the currency fund of the BCCS. At the end of 1993, when gross currency was S$9.675 billion, the external assets of this fund stood at S$10.262 billion, representing a backing of 106.1 per cent (*Annual Report and Accounts of the Board of Commissioners of Currency 1993*, p.5). This fact, together with its history of being part of a Currency Board system, results in statements that imply that this is still so. For example, citing the Monetary Authority of Singapore's *The Financial Structure of Singapore*, Luckett *et al.* (1994, p.123) write: 'Technically the BCCS is obliged to redeem Singapore currency against US dollars on demand, or issue currency on demand on [*sic*] exchange for US dollars or other convertible currency, or gold.'

These writers then discuss the pros and cons of a Currency Board system, which suggests that they think it is relevant to modern Singapore. Whatever is technically true of Singapore is one thing; what is the practice is a different issue altogether. Since March 1982 when the Currency Act was amended the BCCS no longer announces official conversion rates for the Singapore dollar into foreign currencies (Soh, 1990, p.32). This was just recognition of reality as the Singapore dollar had been floating since June 1973. The position now is that 'the rates of exchange used by BCCS for its transactions have been based on current rates in the foreign exchange market' (*The Financial Structure of Singapore*, p.14). In other words, the rate used by the Currency Board is taken from the market rate, not the other way around, as would be the case under a true Currency Board system.

We take the view that for a currency to be considered a Currency Board currency we should be able to obtain answers to three simple questions: what is the reserve currency; at what rate can the local currency be converted into that currency; and who is allowed to obtain the reserve currency from the issuer of local currency (Peebles, 1994)? In contrast to the situation in Singapore, the answers to these questions in Hong Kong are very straightforward: US dollars; HK$7.80 per US dollar; the three note-issuing banks.[3] Hong Kong reverted to a Currency Board system in October 1983 during the panic selling of Hong Kong dollars during Sino-British talks on Hong Kong's future (Peebles, 1988, pp.147–9). We know of no one who can provide similar straightforward answers to our three simple questions in Singapore, let alone be willing to convert Singapore dollars into another currency at a pre-announced rate. The Currency Board legacy and recent monetary policies do mean that international reserves exceed the note issue. It is probably for this reason that people believe that, if it had to, the Singapore government could eventually redeem all the note issue in terms of foreign currencies. On a day-to-day basis it does not and there is no fixed value of the Singapore dollar against any reserve currency. Singapore does not have a Currency Board system. In fact, the only currency which can be obtained for Singapore dollars at a known and unchangeable rate is the Brunei *Ringgit*. Singapore has a Currency Board but it does not have a Currency Board system. The Singapore dollar has appreciated steadily against nearly every other currency, a fact we return to in Chapter 6. Some people may prefer this situation to having it linked to one currency but there are often complaints from the business sector about the 'strength' of the Singapore dollar. How the economy has adapted to this situation will be discussed in Chapter 6.

5.2   SINGAPORE'S MONETARY DATA

The main monetary series available in Singapore are defined as follows:

- Currency: we have used the series 'currency in active circulation'. This is the total amount of Singapore currency in existence minus the amount that is held by the commercial banks (as vault money, presumably) and other financial institutions and the amount that consists of commemorative, numismatic and bullion coins. Active currency averages about 92 per cent of total currency in existence in any year.
- M1: This is active currency plus demand deposits held by the private sector.
- M2: This is M1 plus quasi-money which consists of fixed savings and other deposits at banks plus negotiable certificates of deposits denominated in Singapore dollars and issued by Singapore banks.
- M3: This is M2 plus net deposits with non-bank financial institutions such as POSBank and finance companies.

These categorizations are not ideal for statistical purposes – they never could be – so some studies are likely to rearrange the data to create other series. At least one Singapore economist has recommended taking a part (he thinks at least one-half) of POSBank deposits and classifying them as transactions deposits and adding them to the existing M1 series to obtain a series more suitable for statistical analysis (Lee, 1990, pp.244–5).

Table 5.1 shows the development of these series in order to provide insight on their relative importance as part of Singapore's money supply and Table 5.2 shows their annual average growth rates.

Table 5.1   Monetary series, selected years (million dollars, end of year)

	Currency	M1	M2	M3
1962	390.9	783.6	1 349.8	n.a.
1965	472.6	890.5	1 657.3	n.a.
1970	681.9	1 574.3	3 782.6	4 044.7
1971	806.0	1 759.9	4 204.6	4 574.7
1972	1 004.8	2 384.8	5 281.7	5 744.5
1973	1 144.4	2 632.7	6 103.2	6 723.4
1974	1 306.4	2 858.8	6 924.8	7 696.7
1975	1 637.7	3 472.2	8 164.2	9 114.2
1976	1 946.8	4 000.0	9 202.5	10 751.6
1977	2 242.6	4 412.1	9 806.3	11 912.1
1978	2 582.8	4 925.9	10 862.3	13 683.1
1979	2 941.2	5 706.1	12 899.5	16 473.1
1980	3 137.0	6 134.6	16 065.0	20 531.4
1981	3 381.8	7 242.1	19 671.1	24 991.5
1982	3 996.0	8 156.8	22 804.0	29 676.1
1983	4 335.3	8 607.7	25 525.7	33 742.9
1984	4 619.2	8 866.3	27 120.8	36 053.0
1985	4 739.0	8 785.0	28 147.7	37 028.5
1986	5 033.4	9 821.3	30 954.9	40 184.8
1987	5 439.8	11 030.5	37 089.2	47 147.9
1988	5 996.7	11 957.7	42 087.6	52 823.5
1989	6 609.9	13 744.6	51 545.5	64 007.8
1990	7 108.5	15 260.9	61 845.1	75 792.4
1991	7 497.1	16 430.0	69 542.3	84 199.7
1992	8 279.2	18 515.6	75 728.5	91 082.1
1993	8 942.1	22 882.2	82 130.3	100 969.4

Sources: *Economic and Social Statistics Singapore 1960–1982; Yearbook of Statistics Singapore*, 1979/80, 1991 and 1993; Lee (1990, p.134).

The series M1 is the monetary concept most likely to be correlated with expenditures and the volume of transactions in the economy as it consists of the principal means of payments: currency and bank deposits. M2 includes fixed and savings deposits at banks that cannot be immediately used for transactions purposes. M3 is a broader measure. For purposes of economic analysis in which we relate monetary series to economic activity, M1 and M2 are the most useful variables to use. These series are highly correlated so either series would give the same picture of the annual developments in monetary aggregates. One monetary study of Singapore reached the conclusion that for purposes of analysis 'the choice between the three measures [is] of little consequence' (Simkin, 1984, p.11) and concentrated on M1. We will do this later. Another study argued that more attention should be paid to M1 in Singapore on the basis of its relatively more stable velocity and its sensitivity to business conditions (Lee, 1990, p.195).

Table 5.2   Annual average monetary growth rates (per cent per annum)

	1965–93	1965–73	1973–93	1965–80	1980–93
Currency	12.2	12.5	10.1	15.7	8.0
M1	12.1	15.1	10.4	14.9	9.4
M2	14.9	18.0	14.1	16.0	13.3

Source: Calculated from the data in the sources for Table 5.1.

Figure 5.1 shows the annual growth rates of M1 and M2 and we can see that they tend to move together. The only series to show an absolute fall in annual terms is M1, which fell in 1967 and 1985. We can see a slowdown in the rate of growth of both series in the early 1980s until their lowest growth rates were achieved in 1985. After this year of recession monetary growth rates increased.

If we compare monetary growth over different periods as in Table 5.2 we can see faster growth for M2 for all periods and a slowdown in monetary growth after 1980 for all series. This is especially noticeable for currency, which grew much more slowly after 1980.

Let us look at the composition of Singapore's money supply and relate it in a general way to the level of economic activity. In 1965 currency in circulation made up 53 per cent of M1 and was equal to 16 per cent of that year's GDP. By 1993 currency made up only 39 per cent of M1 and equalled only 10 per cent of that year's GDP. We can thus see a decline in currency holding in terms both of its proportion of the money supply and of its relationship to total annual incomes. This decline in the relative importance of currency has not been smooth and in the late 1970s the ratio of currency to M1, which had averaged 43 per cent in the period 1967–73, rose to 52 per cent in 1978. This change was identified by Drake (1981, p.20) who called it a 'remarkable change in the composition of the money

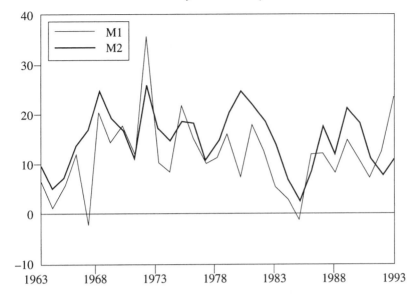

Figure 5.1 Monetary growth rates, 1963–93 (per cent per annum)

stock'. He advanced a few guesses as to its cause, ranging from a possible increase in smuggling or underground cash-using economic activity, to the increase in tourism, a possible increase in gambling and the growth of small cash-using businesses relative to large. He indicates that this change may also be due to an increase in the demand for Singapore currency from people in neighbouring countries (ibid., pp.20–21). The interesting thing is that this ratio remained at around 50 per cent until 1989, then declined, with the biggest decline being from the 45 per cent ratio of 1992 to 39 per cent in 1993. We could speculate that this is due to the increased availability of automatic teller machines and the increased use of non-cash means of payment such as cash cards and stored value cards for use on trains and buses, as well as credit cards. During the late 1980s and into the 1990s interest rates on deposits were falling, so high interest rates cannot be invoked to explain this fall in the currency component of money supply.

Despite this fall in the currency component of the money supply, the ratio of currency to GDP in Singapore is not less than that in developed countries, which shows that Singapore has a long way to go before it becomes anything approaching a 'cashless society', if that were possible or even desirable. In the USA in 1993, currency, a lot of which is circulating outside America, was only 5 per cent of that year's GDP and in the UK and Australia the ratios were 3 and 4 per cent, respectively, showing that they use much less cash in their transactions than Singapore (ratios calculated from *International Financial Statistics*, April 1994).

An easy way to see these monetary developments is to look at the monetary velocities with respect to annual GDP. These are shown in Figures 5.2 and 5.3. The velocity of currency is obviously the highest as it is the smallest component of the money supply. After 1980 it shows a general upward trend, indicating a fall in the amount of currency relative to GDP. This pattern is found in most developed economies as the use of cash declines in favour of cheques and, in Singapore, in favour of cashless transfers at point of sale. Velocity of M1 shows similar fluctuations but no clear trend after 1980. The trend in velocity of both M2 and M3 is clearly downwards, indicating more rapid growth in these monetary aggregates than in GDP. This is most apparent for M3. Again this is a common feature of monetary development as the broader measures include stores of value and wealth as well as the means of transactions and, as incomes and wealth rise, people hold relatively more financial assets, such as fixed savings deposits and deposits in non-bank financial institutions. Bordo and Jonung (1987, pp.101–34) show that this is the pattern for most 'industrial-market (rich) countries'. This trend of falling velocity for such series as M2 or M3, which means an increasing ratio of these series to GDP, has been clearly observed in all the ASEAN countries with the exception of the Philippines and by the mid-1980s Singapore and Malaysia had ratios of M3 to GDP of 104 and 106 per cent, respectively (Schulze, 1986, p.61). This trend has continued with the more rapid growth of M3 than of M2 and M1 in Singapore.

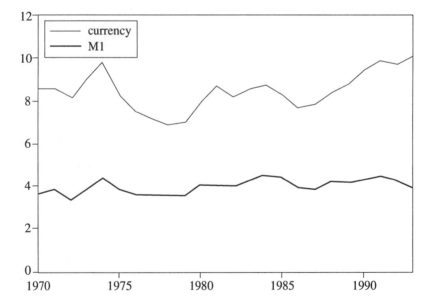

Figure 5.2 Velocity of currency and M1, 1970–93

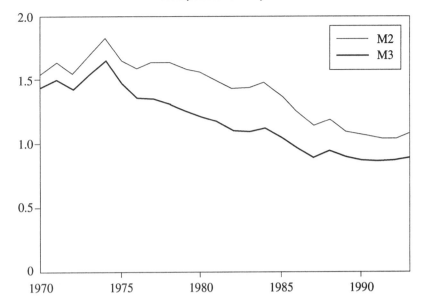

Figure 5.3 Velocity of M2 and M3, 1970–93

For easy reference and help in putting the size of Singapore's money supply in context, the velocities of the four monetary series with respect to annual GDP and the ratio of these series to GDP in 1993 were:

VCurrency	9.95	Currency/GDP	10.0%
VM1	3.89	M1/GDP	25.7%
VM2	1.08	M2/GDP	92.3%
VM3	0.88	M3/GDP	113.4%

Lee (1990, p.192) plots velocity for three series but his data ignore the usual convention and are on a quarterly basis, making his numbers one-quarter of the size of the numbers here. To put these figures in context, let us invoke a comparison with Singapore's model, Switzerland. There, in 1993, the velocity of currency was 13.4, showing that there is much less currency there, and the velocity of M2 was 0.82, meaning that M2 was 122 per cent of GDP (calculated from *International Financial Statistics*, July 1994, pp.518–20).

5.3   SOURCES OF MONETARY GROWTH

In any modern society where the bulk of the money supply consists of bank deposits there are three main reasons for the money supply to change: new bank lending to the private sector, new bank lending to the public sector and changes in foreign assets of the banking system. This latter item mainly refers to the accumulation of or reduction in the foreign reserves of the monetary authorities through their intervention in the foreign exchange market, but also includes the activities of banks. Singapore's statisticians have always provided such a categorization for changes in M1 and it is summarized for recent years in Table 5.3. The period includes the recession of 1985–6.

The arithmetic and the logic of the table is that the annual change in M1 equals the net lending by the banking system to the private sector (column 2) plus that to the public sector (column 3), plus the change in foreign assets of the monetary authorities (which here are the MAS and the BCCS) and the banks plus unidentified 'others' (columns 4,5,6). The item 'others' is very large for some years and prevents an accurate account of what was happening.

Table 5.3   Changes in money supply, selected years (change during the year, million dollars)

	M1	Private sector	Public sector	Net foreign assets of banking system		Others
				Monetary authorities	Banks	
1983	450.9	3 085.7	–4 461.9	3 793.9	–2 826.0	859.2
1984	258.6	1 690.1	–4 199.2	2 889.3	–1 600.2	1 478.6
1985	–81.3	–919.2	–3 083.1	2 088.8	1 017.9	814.3
1986	1 036.3	–3 074.3	1 640.9	691.9	3 788.5	–2 010.7
1987	1 209.2	–2 716.9	849.4	945.1	1 810.2	321.4
1988	927.2	24.0	–4 651.1	1 628.8	1 995.3	1 930.2
1989	1 786.9	296.3	–6 159.4	2 981.9	2 618.6	2 049.5
1990	1 516.3	–1 742.7	–2 504.9	7 799.1	–3 045.3	1 010.1
1991	1 169.1	400.1	–1 191.8	5 062.3	1 670.8	–4 772.3
1992	2 085.6	2 023.7	–3 554.2	7 514.2	1 172.7	–5 070.8
1993	4 366.6	8 397.1	–4 473.0	9 773.7	–4 391.4	–4 939.8

Source: *Yearbook of Statistics Singapore*, 1993, Table 12.3.

We can see, for example, that in 1985 M1 fell by 81 million dollars; M2 increased by 1.0 billion dollars, however. This change in M1 is explained by negative net lending to the private sector (an excess of their deposits over new loans) and a negative net lending figure for the public sector. Offsetting this was the accumulation of foreign reserves by both the monetary authorities and the banks and a positive figure for 'others'. The net effect was a fall in M1 in which the largest negative figures were lending to the public and private sectors, respectively. As the economy started to recover in 1986 the figure for loans to the private sector remained negative but the figures for loans to the public sector and the monetary authorities' accumulation of foreign reserves contributed to large monetary growth.

The year 1993 shows some interesting features. It shows the largest annual increase in M1 ever, dominated by large net lending to the private sector (offset by negative lending to the public sector) plus very large accumulation of foreign assets by the monetary authorities. Inspection of the monthly data gives us a good idea of what was happening in this year and returns us to our case study of the effect of the sale of Singapore Telecom shares in October 1993. Table 5.4 shows what was happening to the money supply around this period. We can see that in the single month of October M1 increased by S$5.52 billion, with lending to the private and public sectors as well as the monetary author-ities' accumulation of foreign assets all playing a role. The 'other' item is very large and negative for this month. The largest single factor was loans to the private sector. An examination of the loans of the banking system show that in October bank loans totalled S$4.66 billion, with S$2.20 billion going to pro-fessional and private individuals and S$1.05 billion to financial institutions. In October CPF withdrawals for the purpose 'others' totalled S$4.14 billion, compared with an average over the previous three months of S$130 million (*Monthly Digest of Statistics*, August 1994, Tables 14.10 and 14.17). This shows that both bank loans and CPF assets were being used to bid for Telecom shares and possibly to buy into the booming stock market. In November M1 fell by S$3.44 billion. We can see how this share offer affected the money supply process and the exchange rate: people borrowed from the banking system as foreigners were buying the Singapore dollar. The dollar was allowed to appreciate but the monetary authorities intervened and sold Singapore dollars. As the monetary authorities were buying foreign currencies both currency in circula-tion and the banks' reserves with the monetary authorities rose. In fact, in October 1993, banks' reserves with the MAS rose by S$1.27 billion, compared with an average monthly rise over the previous three months of only S$127 million (*Monthly Digest of Statistics*, August 1994, Table 14.7). This represents MAS intervention in the foreign exchange market. Both private and public actors con-tributed to the large short-run increase in M1. In that month the inter-bank lending rate fell to 0.19 per cent, compared to 2.54 and 2.31 per cent in the previous two months. The pattern we see is of an appreciating currency, growing reserves and money supply and falling interest rates. Does this pattern hold up for longer periods?

Table 5.4 Changes in the money supply, 1993, selected months (change during the month, million dollars)

	M1	Private sector	Public sector	Net foreign assets of banking system		Others
				Monetary authorities	Banks	
July	54.1	116.6	−1 661.0	683.8	43.3	871.4
Aug.	290.6	287.0	43.9	1 104.0	−457.1	−687.6
Sept.	414.3	1 230.3	−577.4	782.7	−971.4	−49.9
Oct.	5 521.0	6 935.3	3 095.2	1 502.2	−75.1	−5 936.6
Nov.	−3 442.3	−6 392.0	−3 296.9	529.7	1 034.2	4 682.7
Dec.	825.2	1 971.5	639.1	1 477.7	−1 864.8	−1 398.3

Source: Monthly Digest of Statistics, August 1994, Table 14.3.

Figure 5.4 shows relevant monthly developments from mid-1991 to mid-1994. The exchange rate is the Singapore dollar price of the US dollar and the interest rate is the inter-bank overnight rate, one that is very sensitive to short-term change in liquidity. We can see clearly the combination of growing M1, falling interest rates until the end of 1993, when M1 growth stopped, and yet an appreciating currency from S$1.78 in June 1991 to S$1.53 in June 1994. We can see the jump in M1 in October 1993, the plunge in the interest rate in October and the appreciation of the currency from about July until October 1993, which was reversed for a few months then continued in the first half of 1994.

The Singapore dollar continued to appreciate against the American dollar throughout 1994, as the latter was very weak. So it is possible for a currency to appreciate even though domestic interest rates are falling. The appreciation together with government announcements that its policy would be to let the currency appreciate would allow domestic interest rates to be lower and people would still be willing to hold the currency in anticipation of further appreciation. The relationship is: balance of payments surplus, meaning there is excess demand for the Singapore dollar, and MAS intervention that moderates its appreciation but increases domestic money supply, which in turn pushes down domestic interest rates. Other interest rates such as the prime lending rate fell over this period from 7.71 per cent in June 1991 to 5.73 per cent in June 1994.

There is another way of analysing reasons for monetary growth and that is by using an identity called the money multiplier. This approach recognizes that money consists mainly of bank deposits that have to be backed by reserves, of either currency or reserves held with the monetary authorities, which in total

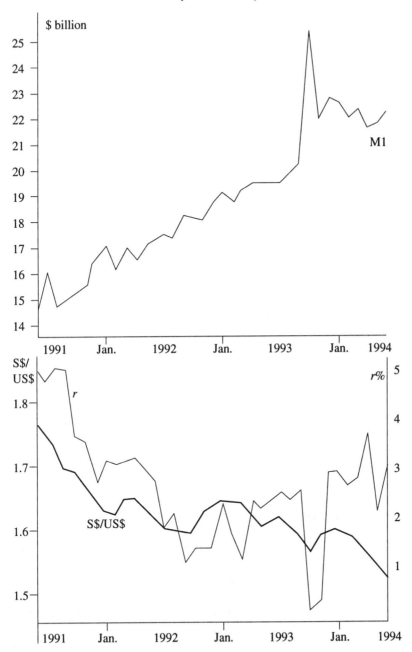

Figure 5.4 M1, interest rate and the exchange rate, 1991–4

are called high-powered money, or the monetary base, in this type of analysis. The money multiplier attempts to link monetary growth to the growth in the monetary base, given the required reserve ratios of high-powered money to deposits and the behaviour of the private sector in determining how much money it wishes to hold as either currency or deposits.

We need some definitions. Let high-powered money H equal currency, $CURR$, plus banks' reserves with the monetary authorities, BR:

$$H = CURR + BR$$

Let total bank deposits be BD and define the following ratios which notation we take from Lee (1990, p.181) which might be familiar to many readers from there and from Friedman and Schwartz (1963, p.794):

$p = BD/CURR$, which is called the public's cash ratio and is determined by what proportions of their money holdings they wish to hold in these forms; $b = BD/BR$, which is the bank's reserve ratio, being based on the extent to which banks have to or choose to hold reserves to back the deposits of the public. M is $CURR$ plus BD.

Given these definitions, it can be shown (Friedman and Schwartz, 1963, pp.788–94) that:

$$M = H\,[b(1+p)/(b+p)] \text{ or } M = H(mm),$$

meaning that the money supply is a multiple of the total amount of high-powered money. The multiple is called the money multiplier (mm) and is not to be confused with the national income determination multiplier of Chapters 3 and 4. This identity makes sense if the ratios b and p are relatively stable or predictable, in which case changes in H will bring about predictable changes in M. The identity can be used to identify historical reasons for any change in M, whether due mainly to changes in H or to changes in the behavioural ratios p and b. It also gives insights into the tools of monetary policy. If mm were stable, power over H would enable the monetary authorities to control the money supply. Changes in p or b would change the money multiplier and thus the extent of M for any given amount of H. For example, if the money authorities increased the reserves banks had to hold against their deposits (this would be represented by a fall in b in this model) then the money multiplier would be lower and hence M would fall for a given H. If people held less currency compared to bank deposits over time, and this might be induced by the monetary authority's changing interest rates (here p would increase), this would increase the money multiplier and allow M to grow more rapidly than H.

This approach is best applied to the determination of M2 and this is done in Table 5.5 for illustration. M2 consists of all bank deposits such as demand, fixed and saving, as well as certificates of deposit. We have chosen two years for illustration. Lee (1985; 1990) covers the period 1968 to 1982. We can see that the money multiplier has increased over the period under question (Lee, 1985, p.59 put it at 4.03 at the end of 1982) mostly owing to the fall in the ratio of currency held by the public to bank deposits (increase in p). Over this period about 75 per cent of the change in M2 was due to the change in high-powered money or the monetary base. Lee (1985, p.42; 1990, p.183) showed that 105 per cent of the increase in M2 over the period 1968–82 was caused by the increase in H. These results, based as they are on just two end-point observations, show that change in the monetary base is the main determinant of the change in the money supply in Singapore. This monetary base comes into existence mainly by intervention in the foreign exchange market by the MAS.

Table 5.5   The money multiplier, selected years

	1983	1993
M2	25 526	82 130
BD	21 190	73 188
CURR	4 335	8 942
BR	1 558	5 199
H(CURR + BR)	5 893	14 141
p (BD/CURR)	4.889	8.185
b (BD/BR)	13.601	14.078
Money multiplier (*mm*)	4.33	5.81

Source: Calculated from data in *Yearbook of Statistics Singapore 1993*, Tables 12.2 and 12.6.

5.4   SEASONALITY IN CURRENCY

Figure 5.4 also shows that there is a jump in M1 towards the end of each year. This raises the question of seasonality in the money supply. The use of money for transactions will obviously be high when there are a lot of transactions. In many economies it is clear that the use of currency increases during holiday periods, when retail sales are high. This is mostly during the build-up to Christmas. In Singapore retailers do mark Christmas as a holiday season and we might expect retail sales to be high during December. In addition to Christmas, the Chinese Lunar New Year, which falls in either late January or early February, is widely celebrated, although often these days outside Singapore. During this period debts are traditionally supposed to be settled and young unmarried people receive cash gifts in small red packets (*hong bao*). All these factors might lead us to expect an increase in currency in circulation in December and January of each year.

Table 5.6 shows the monthly percentage increases in currency in circulation and retail sales in the relevant period for those recent years for which monthly data are available. Generally there is an increase in currency in circulation and retail sales in December and January, then a fall in both in February. On average, M1 in December and January is about 7 to 8 per cent higher than its average over the previous two months: people intended to make more transactions so they ensured they had sufficient means of payment to do so. As the use of automatic deductions from one's bank account through the NETS system develops this phenomenon is less likely to be apparent. Furthermore credit card transactions are more common these days and on average credit card billings during December–January are 30 per cent higher than in other months, indicating that all means of transacting are more frequently used during this holiday period. Such seasonal factors are found in other Chinese societies. In Hong Kong, for example, there is a marked increase in the demand for currency during the New Year holiday period, but this is fully anticipated by the banks and they are always able to meet large cash withdrawals (Peebles, 1988, pp.150–51).[4]

Table 5.6   Currency in circulation and retail sales, monthly increases (per cent)

	1991–92		1992–93		1993–94	
	Currency	Retail sales	Currency	Retail sales	Currency	Retail sales
October	0.3	18.1	1.9	–5.9	0.6	0.3
November	1.7	–0.7	0.4	1.2	0.9	4.3
December	4.6	2.8	4.5	16.3	4.9	21.0
January	8.0	17.6	4.2	18.1	0.8	4.5
February	–4.8	–29.0	–3.9	–28.4	0.5	–22.4
March	–1.4	–12.7	0.1	16.2	–0.6	33.2

Sources: *Monthly Digest of Statistics*, various issues.

This seasonal variation in the amount of transactions money (currency or M1) that is regularly observed in many countries around Christmas time is taken as evidence of the endogeneity of money, or of 'reverse causation' (Abel and Bernanke, 1995, p.371). Quite clearly there is no exogenous increase in money supply that makes people go out and spend more at Christmas time; it was the anticipation of the festival that made them obtain currency and then spend it. This is just an example of people converting one form of money, bank deposits, for example, into another more useful form, currency, the means of transaction. There is no implication that at Christmas time a broader measure of money, such as M3, would increase because people intended to spend more money in the shops. In fact, in recent years in Singapore, the average amount of M3 in December and the following January only exceeds the average amount of the previous two months by 0.4 per cent. In Singapore, however, the entire money supply is most likely to be endogenous, responding to change within the economy because of the nature of this economy. We have seen the theoretical reasons for this in Chapter 4, where an open economy with a fixed or managed exchange rate will see its money supply respond endogenously to capital flows and the balance of payments.

Let us summarize the nature of this monetary system and the implications it has for monetary policy.

5.5   MONEY AND MONETARY POLICY

Let us first establish the nature of the relationships between monetary aggregates as implied by Chapter 4 and the evidence above. We would expect to see a close relationship between the accumulation of official foreign reserves and the balance of payments position. We would expect to see the increase in foreign reserves to be connected with changes in banks' reserves with the monetary authorities and the change in currency. Changes in banks' reserves with the monetary authorities and the increase in currency, which increases the monetary base, would allow banks to create credit, so we would expect to see the broader money supply connected to changes in reserves and ultimately the balance of payments position.

Table 5.7 summarizes the data for recent years. The first column, BOP, shows the overall balance of payments position as presented in the balance of payments accounts. This figure includes a 'balancing item' so that it corresponds to the identified amounts of accumulation of foreign exchange assets. Because of this it is a statistical artifact that is almost identical to the amount of accumulation of official foreign exchange assets. The 'balancing item' is large for certain years. The variable BOPA is the overall balance of payments after this 'balancing item' has been deducted. It is thus the figure one gets from the underlying data of the identified current and capital account items. It is closely correlated with BOP ($r = 0.98$). The implications of this difference will be discussed in Chapter 6. The other columns show the annual increases in official foreign reserves, the annual change in the banks' reserves with the MAS, and the annual increases in currency and M1, respectively. We can see that, as the

BOP figures increased over time, the rate at which foreign reserves increased also increased, as did the size of the annual increases in bank reserves and money growth. We can formalize these relationships using simple regressions. We concentrate on the period since 1980 because, as will be explained in the next chapter, this is a period when the MAS was managing the exchange rate. Furthermore all exchange controls were abolished in June 1978. This means that Singapore was more similar to our simple open economy model of Chapter 4 after about 1980. All variables in Table 5.8 are in current million dollars and the period is 1980–93, giving 14 observations.

Table 5.7   Balance of payments and money growth in recent years (million dollars)

	BOP	BOPA	Official foreign reserves	Bank reserves with MAS	Currency	M1
				annual change		
1983	2 237.7	3 914.7	1 837.4	140.1	339.3	450.9
1984	3 250.6	2 549.0	3 012.7	184.7	283.9	258.6
1985	2 941.7	1 529.1	4 302.9	87.8	119.8	−81.3
1986	1 208.6	−274.0	1 086.6	77.8	294.4	1 036.3
1987	2 328.5	657.8	2 284.2	245.3	406.4	1 209.2
1988	3 343.6	3 776.6	2 834.9	217.7	556.9	927.2
1989	5 334.2	6 320.6	5 330.6	943.2	613.2	1 786.9
1990	9 892.5	12 239.3	9 914.1	172.2	498.6	1 516.3
1991	7 262.8	8 509.8	7 281.5	741.1	388.6	1 169.1
1992	9 959.0	15 162.1	9 985.6	537.1	782.1	2 085.6
1993	12 153.7	18 566.3	12 078.4	434.4	662.9	4 366.6

Source: *Yearbook of Statistics Singapore 1993*, Tables 4.9, 12.2, 12.3, 12.4, 12.6.

The first regression is virtually an identity because of the way the BOP data have been computed. That is why the slope coefficient is unity. The second shows that there is a relationship between the accumulation of foreign reserves and the underlying balance of payments position as identified by BOPA. Similarly the annual increases in the three measures of the money supply are significantly related to the BOP, with the size of the slope coefficients getting larger the broader the measure of the money supply. The relatively weak relationship between changes in currency and the BOP has been identified and noted before by Lee (1985, p.39; 1990, pp.178–9). For example, 62 per cent of the variation in M1 is explained by the BOP and a one billion dollar increase in the BOP would be associated with a 224 million dollar increase in M1. Similarly M2 would rise by 529 million dollars, and 45 per cent of its variation is explained by BOP. For similar regressions for the period before 1982, see Lee (1985, p.39; 1990, p.178).

Table 5.8   Regression results

Foreign	=	−75.08	+	1.008BOP	$R^2 = 0.99$	DW = 2.2
reserves	=	(−0.37)		(29.31)*		
Foreign	=	1351.3	+	0.600$BOPA$	$R^2 = 0.93$	DW = 1.8
reserves		(3.70)		(12.90)*		
Currency	=	259.0	+	0.036BOP	$R^2 = 0.44$	DW = 1.8
		(3.80)		(3.09)*		
M1	=	128.8	+	0.224BOP	$R^2 = 0.62$	DW = 1.5
		(0.41)		(4.40)*		
M2	=	2463.0	+	0.529BOP	$R^2 = 0.45$	DW = 0.8
		(2.50)		(3.13)*		
Banks'	=	162.9	+	0.033BOP	$R^2 = 0.22$	DW = 2.8
reserves		(1.54)		(1.84)**		
Banks'	=	209.0	+	0.020$BOPA$	$R^2 = 0.21$	DW = 2.8
reserves		(2.37)		(1.79)**		

Note: Figures in brackets are *t*-ratios; * indicates significance at the 1 per cent level, ** at the 10 per cent level.

As we saw above, a possible reason for monetary growth in some countries is central bank lending to the government to cover part of its deficit, that is monetizing the deficit. We have also seen that in Singapore the government does not run a budget deficit, so this is not a candidate for explaining monetary growth. The possibility that the government's fiscal position influences monetary growth in six South-East Asian countries has been examined by Thanisorn (1993). He uses atheoretical regressions on quarterly data aimed at explaining monetary growth and the fiscal position and then examines causality between these two variables. The main conclusion relating to Singapore is that 'One can say with confidence at the 5-percent level of significance that the fiscal deficit (surplus) does influence the money supply growth in Singapore during the period 1974:2 to 1989:4' (Thanisorn, 1993, p.20). However this statistical connection is qualified later and a possible reason for the result is offered: 'In the case of Singapore, the increase in budget deficit may influence the foreign capital inflows which in turn raise the money growth' (ibid., pp.21–2). So, again, we see a case where the statistical evidence should not be taken to mean direct causation, here running from the government's budget position to money supply growth. Even here, the extent of the capital inflow has been identified as an important reason for money growth in Singapore.

Another aspect of money in Singapore that has attracted some research is the nature of the demand for money functions. Daquila and Phua (1993) summarize earlier results and seek to extend the analysis by econometrically estimating what they term Keynesian and Monetarist models of money demand. In the Keynesian version they expect the demand for real money to be a positive function of current real income and an inverse function of the rate of interest and the expected rate of inflation. In the monetarist model they expect money demand to be more closely dependent on permanent income and wealth than on current income. They also expect money demand to be a positive function of the expected rate of inflation on the basis of the argument that, if 'prices of goods are expected to increase, people will demand more money now and buy those goods' (ibid., 1993, p.184). Anyway, that is what they believe. We hope you do not believe it.

They state that they used 'Forty-eight (48) quarterly observations' over the period 1977 to 1988 (p.185). However the original source of their estimates is Phua (1989) who presented estimates for 1979 to 1988 (which gives only 40 observations) and the regression results of Daquila and Phua (1993, pp.186–90) and stability tests are identical (to the fourth decimal place) for all estimates to those of Phua (1989, pp.48–60). The stability tests reported in Daquila and Phua use data from 1979–88; there is no mention of 1977 data here. So it seems the study must be for 1979 to 1988, using 40 observations. All terms are in natural logarithms, so they can easily identify elasticities of the determinants of money demand. They use the three-month time deposit rate and deflate the nominal money series by the consumer price index.

Some of their results are interesting and merit comment. In the Keynesian model they claim interest elasticities of demand for real money of 0.945 for M1, 0.805 for M2 and 0.802 for M3. They comment that these are high income elasticities (Daquila and Phua, 1993, pp.186, 192). This cannot be accepted and the results are very surprising. Their approach closely follows that of Lee (1990 p.170) who had estimated these three elasticities over the period 1968–82 as 0.962 (M1), 0.950 (M2) and 1.084 (M3). Lee (1984, pp.155–7) also presents the same and other results which show that the income elasticity of M3 is greater than that of M1. Koh (1988) who had used quarterly data over the period 1978–87 – almost the same as Daquila and Phua's period – also econometrically estimated income elasticities using the same equations. His estimates were 0.717 (M1), 1.398 (M2) and 1.463 (M3). Daquila and Phua (1993) are aware of all these results and cite them. The pattern in previous studies is that the income elasticity of M3 exceeds that of M1 and that those of M2 and M3 exceed unity.[5] The estimates of Daquila and Phua (1993) for all series are less than unity and that for M3 is less than M1! What their estimates imply is that as real GDP increased, the amount of M1 grew more rapidly than M3. We have seen above that this is just not the case: M1 grew less rapidly than GDP (its velocity therefore rose) but the broad measure M3 grew more rapidly than M1 and GDP so we would expect this income elasticity to be more than unity. Checking the original source from which their results were derived (Phua, 1989, pp.64–6) we can easily establish this from their own data. At the end of their period real GDP was 2.05 times its initial value, whereas real M1, M2 and M3 were 1.76, 2.87 and 2.77 times their initial values, showing that real M1 grew at a slower rate than real GDP, whereas real M2 and M3 grew more rapidly than both GDP and M1, and M2 grew slightly more rapidly than M3. We would expect to see this reflected in higher income elasticities for M2 and M3 than for M1 and of M2 than M3, but their results suggest the opposite. Something is wrong with their analysis.

Perhaps a problem is the way Daquila and Phua identified expected inflation. They take it to be the same as the current rate of inflation, but this is defined in a very strange way. They define inflation as the successive differences in the CPI (Daquila and Phua, 1993, pp.182–3; Phua, 1989, p.36). As they want to run their regressions in logarithmic form they then take the natural logarithm of this number and their equations clearly show that the variable is $\ln \Delta$ CPI (Daquila and Phua, 1993, pp.186–8; Phua, 1989, p.51). Now during this period prices fell in 1985 and 1986, so some of the differences in the CPI would be negative, but you cannot have a logarithm of a negative number. Perhaps their notation is incorrect and what they mean is they used the successive difference in the logs of the CPI, which is the usual practice, as this number is approximately equal to the percentage change in the series. Lee (1984; 1990) quite clearly uses this way of modelling the inflation rates and it is $\Delta \ln$ CPI in all his work, as it is in Koh (1988). To investigate this we ran the same regression using the data of Phua (1989), deflating the nominal money series by the CPI and then putting them into the same units (million dollars) as the nominal money series. Daquila and Phua (1993) seem just to divide by the CPI and it is not clear what units they are in. This would influence the estimate of the intercept term but not the various slopes. We define expected inflation as the difference in the log of the CPI as in Lee (1984; 1990). Using simple ordinary least squares estimates in order to make a preliminary description of the relationship, we obtained income elasticities for the three money series of 0.60(M1), 1.34(M2) and 1.33(M3).[6] These are more in line with what we know happened to the quantities of money in the economy and their velocities: M1 grew less rapidly than real GDP but M2 and M3 grew more rapidly than GDP and M2 slightly more rapidly than M3.

We reproduce the equation for M3 here with *t*-ratios without the sign in brackets:

$$\ln M3 = -1.60 + 1.33\ln GDP - 0.092\ln r - 2.055 \,\Delta\ln CPI$$
$$(2.50) \ (19.91) \qquad (3.89) \qquad (2.75)$$
$$R^2 = 0.98 \ DW = 1.21 \ n = 39$$

Money demand is significantly inversely related to the interest rate (r) and the rate of inflation as they expected but our estimate of income elasticity is much higher than theirs and is consistent with what we would expect knowing the history of the Singapore economy. The interest elasticity for M3 is low and our re-estimates imply that M3 is a less sensitive function of the rate of interest than M1 (see note 5). This is consistent with all other previous estimates such as those in Lee (1990, p.170) and Koh (1988, p.187), both of which Daquila and Phua know and cite. However Daquila and Phua present results showing M3 to be a more sensitive function of the interest rate than M1. We would expect M1 to be more sensitive to interest rates than M3. M1 mainly includes the means of transactions, some of which (such as cash) bear no interest. When interest rates rise people try to economize on holdings of these forms of money and hold broader measures that bear interest. Hence an increase in the rate of interest would lead to a fall in M1 but M3 would not change. For further review of these and other aspects of the results of Daquila and Phua (1993) and evidence to support the generalizations made here, see Peebles (1995).

Daquila and Phua (1993) also estimate a monetarist model (Phua, 1989, pp.53–8). They conclude that all their estimates are good and support both the Keynesian and Monetarist approaches and that the demand functions have been stable (Daquila and Phua, 1993, pp.192–3). There is no attempt to discriminate between the models or to derive any implications for the working of the economy. They mention that their results imply a low interest elasticity of demand for money in Singapore, a result that is consistent with that of Lee (1984; 1990).[7] Before we conclude anything about the implications of this for the slope of the *LM* curve and the working of the economy, we must remember the special nature of the monetary system of the economy: money is not exogenous and the money supply, and hence the *LM* curve, does the adapting to keep the economy in equilibrium, with Singapore interest rates similar to those elsewhere in the world.

In light of the evidence about the nature of the relationship between money and other macroeconomic aggregates, and given its experience with running the monetary system, the official view of the MAS as to the nature of monetary policy in Singapore has been made clear and repeated a number of times. In the mid-1980s it was expressed this way by the then Chairman of the MAS, Dr Goh Keng Swee:

> In Singapore, which of the monetary aggregates does the MAS watch, M1, M2 or M3? The answer is none ... So the MAS is probably the only central bank that does

not have to watch the Ms. What does it watch? It watches the foreign-exchange rate. (Quoted from Lee (Tsao), 1987a, p.132)

Similarly, he also said:

Monetary policy as it is understood in modern industrial countries – that is, control of the money supply – has no place in Singapore. Nobody in the Monetary Authority bothers if M1, M2 or M3 is going up or down. (Quoted from Simkin, 1984, pp.10–11)

Any attempt at independent control over the money supply would affect domestic interest rates. In the light of our simple model of a very open economy in Chapter 4, we know that this cannot occur.

An attempt by the MAS to raise or lower domestic interest rates on any sustained basis, with foreign rates unchanged, would be thwarted by a shift of funds into or out of Singapore. Put another way, high capital mobility implies that the MAS can seek to influence either the exchange rate or domestic variables like interest rates, but not both. The choice of the exchange rate as the focus of monetary policy must imply a loss of control over domestic interest rates. (Teh and Shanmugaratnam, 1992, p.292)[8]

Figure 5.5 shows the evidence behind such a statement, in which we can see how the Singapore interest rate (here the six-month Singapore Interbank Offer

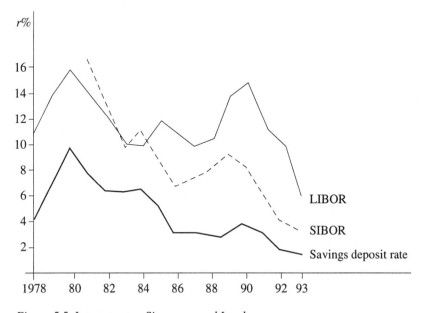

Figure 5.5 Interest rates, Singapore and London

Rate (SIBOR) moves with the six-month London Inter-bank Offer Rate (LIBOR).
We can see that since the mid-1980s the Singapore interest rate has been below
the foreign rate, possibly reflecting the expected appreciation of the Singapore
dollar. The graph shows how the saving deposit rate moves with these other
rates and has fallen considerably recently.

In these circumstances the government has chosen a policy of managing the
exchange rate. It is under no international obligation to do this but has chosen
to give up an independent monetary policy in order to manage the exchange
rate so as to control the extent of imported inflation. As the current chairman
of the MAS, Dr Richard Hu Hsu Tau, has put it:

> We have only one monetary policy, which is the exchange rate. Because we have
> completely open financial markets without foreign-exchange controls or capital
> controls, we don't even control interest rates. Our only control is managing the
> exchange rate and that is basically to prevent the Singapore dollar from rising too
> fast. (*Euromoney*, February 1995, p.85)

The effect of this exchange rate policy on the economy will be examined in the
next chapter.

The most commonly heard phrases describing monetary and exchange rate
policies are the need to restore liquidity to the system, or to plough back and
recycle the cash withdrawn from the system by the CPF scheme and public sector
surpluses which are held with the MAS. These sums withdrawn are seen as a
serious loss of liquidity in the monetary system which would push up interest
rates and lead to excessive appreciation of the currency (Teh and Shanmugaratnam, 1992, p.293). The liquidity is reintroduced into the system by
intervention in the foreign exchange market when the currency starts to appreciate
too quickly.

As a consequence of the nature of Singapore's monetary system, a question
for Singapore students is based on the proposition that, as Singapore cannot have
an independent monetary policy, there is no need for the MAS to exist. The
students are expected to explain the first proposition and, we surmise, to argue
that there is still a need for the MAS as it has taken upon itself all the regulatory
and prudential functions relating to the monetary, banking, financial, stock trading
and insurance sectors that in many other countries are the responsibility of many
different regulatory agencies. The MAS likes to remind people that, as Singapore
is such a small place, it can easily pick up rumours of what is happening and
can act quickly to prevent any abuses of its regulations.[9]

The concept of monetary policy discussed above is the control of the monetary
aggregates. There are other aspects of monetary policy, of course. An important
one in the early days of Singapore's development was ensuring that credit went
to those sectors that the government wished to see develop. At first this was

done by the Economic Development Board and this body continues to lend to small enterprises today. This function shifted to the Development Bank of Singapore (DBS). As function changed so did leadership, as the first Chairman of the EDB, Hon Sui Sen, became president of the newly created DBS and then later the Minister of Finance.

Another tool of monetary policy is moral suasion, that seemingly vague term that is usually the last in the textbook list of tools of monetary policy. It is last as it is not usually very common or effective in a large country such as the USA or UK. In Singapore, however, this moral suasion can be applied strongly and banks usually know it is in their interest to follow the new directives. If they do not they will be told off publicly and held up as a bad example and ultimately there is the threat of losing their operating licence (Luckett *et al.*,1994, p.163).

An interesting example of moral suasion was seen in mid-1994 when the MAS seemed to be alarmed by the perceived threat of excessive consumer spending, although at this time retailers were complaining of poor business and many large retail groups were reporting large losses. The MAS imposed restrictions on credit card advertising and let it be widely known that it did not approve of the way credit cards were being advertised as a means of buying things and that advertisers should only stress 'the convenience of having a credit card, rather than the spending aspect' (*Business Times*, 2 December, 1994, p.1). Credit card advertisements disappeared from the print and broadcasting media very quickly and applications for new cards were said to have fallen in the following two months (*Business Times*, 2 December 1994, p.1).[10] This policy was reinforced in February 1995 by the MAS putting limits on the extent of unsecured personal loans. These were referred to as 'stringent guidelines' (*Business Times*, 4–5 February 1995, p.1). Banks and finance companies were told they should limit such loans to those earning more than S$30 000 a year and the loans should not exceed two months' salary. The main purpose was to 'rein in excessive credit-based consumption and not to check inflation' in the words of the Minister of Finance, who believed that there was 'no worry at all' about inflation in Singapore at that time (*Business Times*, 10 February 1995, p.3). The main purpose was thought to be to reduce borrowing for the purpose of buying cars and thereby to moderate the rise in COE prices. Loans for car buying were not to exceed 70 per cent of the price of the car with its COE and had to be repaid within seven years. We can see such policies as aimed at restricting one type of spending using quantitative limits on certain types of lending rather than through using a more broadly based restrictive policy using higher interest rates for example. The government seems set to reduce what it considers to be an excessive rate of consumption, especially if it is financed by borrowing, but this is in a country where the ratio of personal consumption to GDP is almost certainly the lowest in the world, as we saw in Chapter 1.[11]

In a review of the standard tools of monetary policy listed in any textbook, Luckett *et al.* (1994, pp.158–64) conclude that such tools as changing the banks' reserve requirements, open market operations and changing the discount rate have not been actively used in Singapore. This is also the conclusion of Lee (1990, p.136) who argues that Singapore cannot effectively use open market operations and a discount rate policy because money and capital markets have not been fully developed. In a review of the use of open market operations in South-East Asian countries, Tumnong (1991, pp.92–3) concluded:

> In Singapore, its relatively undeveloped securities market severely limited the scope of open market operations. Accordingly, the conduct of monetary policy in Singapore hinges on the management of the exchange rate as an instrument of domestic price control, complemented with domestic money market operations to ensure an appropriate level of liquidity in the banking system.

In fact, discussion of monetary policy tools in books about Singapore is often very short and lacking in actual cases, and hardly any examples of such tools as 'persuasion and directives' (Lee, 1990, p.137) or 'moral suasion' are actually given although this is identified as 'a powerful tool' (Luckett *et al.*, 1994, p.163). We have given some recent examples above.

In these circumstances it is difficult to analyse money in Singapore using statistical approaches that have been applied to other economies. This is an important conclusion of Lee and Li (1983), whose results are summarized in Lee (1990, pp.196–204). These authors use causality tests to establish the relationship between money and other macroeconomic variables such as prices and output. Their results present a mixed picture, but one feature stands out, and that is one-way 'causality' from the nominal and real money series to nominal GDP. The authors warn that this should not be taken to mean that money 'causes' output or prices. In reality, money and output are both mainly determined by exogenous factors outside the economy. An increase in export demand, for example, would lead to an increased payments surplus, an increase in the money supply and an increase in bank credit. The increase in exports would lead to an increase in economic activity. Statistical studies would seem to suggest that money 'caused' output to rise but, in fact, both events are the consequence of events outside the economy (Lee, 1990, p.204).

5.6   CENTRAL BANK INDEPENDENCE, INFLATION AND GROWTH

As many countries experienced high inflation rates in the 1970s and early 1980s, interest arose in the relationship between the degree of central bank independence and the rate of inflation in different countries. It was pointed out that the German central bank was one of the most independent in the world and that Germany had one of the lowest inflation rates. In contrast, in countries where the central bank was not really free from government control or manipulation through which government budget deficits were financed from central bank loans, inflation rates were high. In some countries political pressures arose which tried to enact constitutional reform to make the central bank more independent and obliged to maintain low inflation rates. Canada and New Zealand were two countries where such changes were implemented and in New Zealand the governor of the central bank is now required by law to conduct monetary policy in an open manner and is personally accountable for the effects of monetary policy (Cukierman, 1992, p.263). The new law came into effect in 1989 just before parts of the world economy slipped into recession, creating a low inflationary environment. New Zealand had previously been a high inflation country with a central bank that was regarded as one of the world's least independent.

Establishing the quantitative relationship between central bank independence and inflation, which would be the economist's way of analysing the above proposition, is not easy as it is difficult to quantify the extent of independence, although there are a number of proposals for measuring this in a single index. One influential study that analyses this issue for 16 industrialized countries shows a clear inverse relationship between the degree of central bank independence and inflation. It shows New Zealand as being the least independent, with the second highest rate of inflation (for the period 1955–88) and Switzerland and Germany as the most independent and having the lowest inflation rates (Alesina and Summers, 1993, p.155). The authors' scatter diagram has been reproduced in such works as Abel and Bernanke (1995, p.565) and Snowdon, *et al.* (1994, p.213), which indicates the impact it has had. Alesina and Summers also show that the variability of inflation is also negatively correlated with the degree of central bank independence, but there is no evidence that real interest rates or growth performance are related to the degree of central bank independence. They take this to be 'a fragment of evidence in support of theories emphasizing the neutrality of money' (Alesina and Summers, 1993, pp.156–9).

Singapore does not feature in their work, but it is included in another attempt at analysing the degree of central bank independence. Cukierman (1992, pp.378–82) constructs an indicator of independence based on various legal criteria, with unity representing maximum independence. Singapore's index is 0.27, the same as that of Sweden, Finland and New Zealand. The study is based on the experience of the 1980s. Switzerland and West Germany are ranked as having the most independent central banks (index of 0.68 and 0.66, respectively) and there were 45 countries whose central banks were more independent than Singapore's according to this indicator. A first glance at the legal position of the MAS, which we must take as being Singapore's central bank, would indicate that it might not be very independent from the government. After all, its chairman is also the minister of finance, as well as the chairman of the board of the BCCS. If Singapore's ranking is the same as that of New Zealand, which had an average inflation rate of 12 per cent per annum during the 1980s, why has Singapore's inflation rate been much below what one would expect from this situation? The answer is, we hope, clear from our discussion above. Singapore does not have a government budget deficit and monetary growth is largely out of the control of the MAS. There is no prospect of nationwide trade union demands for higher wages. Excess demand for the currency allows the Singapore dollar to appreciate, offsetting any increase in foreign prices. The MAS is committed to achieving low inflation. In fact, its mission statement, as printed in its *Annual Report*, is as follows: 'The MAS seeks to promote sustained and non-inflationary growth of the economy as well as to foster a sound and progressive financial-services sector' (*Monetary Authority of Singapore: Annual Report 1993/94*).

In the following chapter we examine the exchange rate policy of the MAS. When discussing his interviews with bankers and foreign exchange traders in Singapore, Darren McDermott referred to the head of foreign exchange at a German bank and wrote that: 'Like nearly everyone contacted for this article, he asked for anonymity; traders believe the MAS won't brook any commentary on its actions' (*Asian Wall Street Journal*, 14 December 1995, p.24). We think this is an exaggeration and hope it does not apply to humble academics who have no immediate financial interest in what happens on these markets.

SUGGESTIONS FOR FURTHER READING

Tan Chwee Huat (1992) is a good review of financial institutions in Singapore and Lee (1990) is an examination of the workings of the monetary systems of both Singapore and Malaysia and their history and connections. Luckett *et al.* (1994) covers related material in a very concise manner.

Drake (1981) covers the early history of Singapore's money and, for historical interest, the papers in the MAS *Papers on Monetary Economics* of 1981 are recommended.

The MAS *Annual Reports* are highly recommended, as are *The Financial Structure of Singapore*, published by the MAS and the *Annual Report and Accounts of the Board of Commissioners of Currency*, Singapore.

NOTES

1. Despite Singapore's close connection with the pound sterling, Singapore journalists and economic commentators use their own non-standard forms such as 'the sterling pound', 'the sterling' or even 'the UK sterling'.

2. Hanke has been active in advocating a currency board for Mexico, for example, following its financial crisis in early 1995.

3. 'Unlike Hong Kong, Singapore does not maintain a fixed exchange rate peg' (Teh and Shanmugaratnam, 1992, p.292).

4. In Mainland China, however, under the planning system the pattern was somewhat different, even through to the late 1980s. In the early part of the year people bought goods from state shops for the New Year holiday and seeds and fertilizers for the spring planting and this made the quantity of cash in circulation go down, not up. Towards the end of the year the government bought the crops and this made the amount of currency in circulation go up (Peebles, 1991, pp. 209–10).

5. A later study by Tseng and Corker (1991, p.18) estimated the long-run income elasticity of M1 as 0.86 and that of M2 as 1.37 for 1975 to 1989, using 60 quarterly observations. This confirms the pattern.

6. The results for the 39 observations over the period 1979:II to 1988:IV using Phua's data are as follows, with t-ratios without their sign in brackets. Money series are in million constant price dollars and real GDP is in million dollars in constant 1985 market prices. Phua (1989) gives his sources as the *Yearbook of Statistics Singapore*, although this source does not contain monthly or quarterly data. See Peebles (1995) for a review of the possible data sources.

	intercept	$\ln$GDP	$\ln r$	$\Delta\ln$CPI	R^2	DW
$\ln$M1	3.797	+ 0.600	– 0.147	– 0.083	0.95	1.14
	(6.31)	(9.54)	(6.57)	(0.117)		
$\ln$M2	– 1.903	+ 1.336	– 0.112	– 0.974	0.98	0.98
	(2.66)	(17.92)	(4.22)	(1.16)		
$\ln$M3	– 1.600	+ 1.329	– 0.092	– 2.055	0.98	1.21
	(2.50)	(19.91)	(3.89)	(2.75)		

The income elasticty for M1 seems rather low, but that is the figure we got. We cannot reproduce the results of Daquila and Phua (1993) or anything like them using their data, which we had to get from Phua (1989) as Daquila and Phua (1993) did not publish any original data.

7. Caution is advised when reading Lee's interpretation of his results. He obtained an interest elasticity for M1 of –0.127, for example, and states that this 'implies that a 1.3 per cent increase in interest rate would lead to a 10 per cent decrease in real money balance' (Lee, 1990, p.172). This means that a 10 per cent increase in the rate of interest would lead to a 1.3 per cent fall in the amount of real money people wished to hold.

8. The second author is Director of the Economics Department of the MAS.

9. Singapore's financial district is called by some people 'the golden shoe' after its supposed resemblance to the shape of a shoe. One event that is singled out to show the success of the MAS's regulatory role is the fact that it did not grant a banking licence to the Bank of Credit and Commerce International (BCCI) in the 1980s. This bank later collapsed as the result of some fraudulent business. Singapore's financial sector and its regulators were put on the global map in late February 1995 when it was discovered that at Baring Securities (Singapore), a part of Barings Bank, the oldest and most profitable British merchant bank, one trader had positions in futures on the Japanese stock index that would result in a loss of at least 600 million pounds sterling, over one billion Singapore dollars, and more than the whole capital of Barings bank. Eventually total losses were put at at least 916 million pounds. The trader disappeared and was arrested in Germany a week or so later. These losses bankrupted Barings Plc which was put under administration in the UK and quickly sold to the Dutch insurance and banking group ING. The main question asked was how a single trader could put his company in such a position without Barings knowing. Another question raised by, amongst others, the *Asian Wall Street Journal* (editorial, 2 March 1995) was why the MAS did not act earlier, as it was said that there had been rumours of Barings' exposure for some time before the actual disappearance and 'débâcle'. It appears that there had been a warning of the dangerous position of the Singapore office and SIMEX had warned Barings' London directors of the

situation in February. The official position is that the débâcle was due to the lack of control within the Barings group (*Business Times*, 6 March 1995, p.1).

10.   This approach to control is found outside the financial sector. In 1994 the Prime Minister used part of his nationally broadcast National Day address to point out how deeply offended he was by an advertisement that put American forms of speech into the mouth of an Asian child who, he thought, was being cheeky to his father in saying that, if the father could play golf so many times a week, he should be able to have some of the nutritional supplement that was the point of the advertisement. This advertisement, made in Asia by Asians, was immediately withdrawn. Dozens of crass advertisements, some produced by the government, continue to be aired.

11.   The policy was defended in a few speeches by BG (NS) Lee Hsien Loong, Deputy Prime Minister, when he defended the very short notice at which the policies were announced (although the government did make clarification over the confusion it caused, and later allowed bridging loans for house purchase to be exempt) and warned of the dangers of excessive conspicuous consumption in Singapore which 'will lead to unhappiness and resentment'. BG Lee advised Singaporeans that Singapore was different from Hong Kong, where 'it is socially acceptable to display one's wealth, in fine clothes, fine dining, Rolls-Royce' (*The Straits Times*, 14 February 1995, p.28).

6. Trade and exchange rates

This chapter focuses on the macroeconomic issues which arise from Singapore's participation in international trade, including those associated with the balance of payments and the foreign exchange market. However, since it is difficult to discuss these issues without understanding the rather special features of Singapore's trade structure and trade policy, we begin by identifying the key characteristics of Singapore's trading structure, especially its high degree of openness to international trade and factor flows, its exceptionally high import content of exports, and the transformation of the economy since the mid-1960s through a process of rapid industrialization and export-led growth. This is followed by a brief survey of the key principles which have guided Singapore's trade policy and the perceived difficulties which have arisen in recent years. The scene is then set for a discussion of the balance of payments and the foreign exchange market, including the problems faced by policy makers since 1980 as they attempted simultaneously to achieve domestic and external economic goals. We also address two of the more controversial issues in Singapore's macroeconomic trade policy, namely the pursuit of high and growing international foreign exchange reserves, and the decision to curb the process of making the Singapore dollar an international currency.

6.1 THE CHARACTERISTICS OF SINGAPORE'S TRADE

The total volume of Singapore trade is very large compared to its annual production, making it one of the most open economies in the world. Table 6.1 emphasizes this openness compared to other countries in the region. Both merchandise imports and exports exceed GDP resulting in a trade to GDP ratio of 2.94 in 1992, one of the highest in the world. In 1988 Singapore had the highest level of import penetration in East Asia, reflecting both its extreme openness and its very low level of protection.[1] The high import ratio is partly a consequence of resource deficiency: Singapore has a negligible agricultural base (this was so even in 1960) and is heavily reliant on the international market for raw materials and foodstuffs, including water from Malaysia and Indonesia. A second, well-known, reason for Singapore's heavy import dependence is its very high import content of exports, especially petroleum-related products (mainly fuel for ships and aircraft), since all petroleum is imported. The average total weighted import requirements per unit of domestic exports (excluding re-exports) for 1988, computed from the 1988 input–output table, is 0.692 (Tan, 1995, Table 2.2).

Table 6.1   Dependence on trade and international comparisons

	(1) Trade to GDP ratio 1992	(2) IP ratio 1988	(3) Intra-industry trade: % of trade with		
			USA	EC	Japan
			1990		
Singapore	2.94	121.2	47.5	41.4	21.7
Hong Kong	1.97	79.6	29.7	37.9	12.4
South Korea	—	23.0	33.1	27.9	38.1
Taiwan	—	27.2	30.1	30.1	37.2
Indonesia	0.48	18.4			
Malaysia	1.37	55.7			
Thailand	0.66	26.1			
Philippines	0.48	58.8			
Japan	0.16	—			
China	0.35	13.7			

Note: The trade to GDP ratio is for merchandise trade measured in nominal US\$; IP measures import penetration ratios (3-year moving averages) $\equiv M/(P + M - X)$, where P refers to production and M and X are imports and exports; the intra-industry trade indices are for manufactured goods and are measured according to the Grubel and Lloyd 1975 formula.

Sources: Calculated from the *World Development Report* (1994, Table 3 and Table 13); Hill and Phillips (1993, Table 4); and Chow *et al.* (1994, Table 1).

A third, and more subtle, reason for Singapore's high level of import penetration arises from the rapid growth of intra-industry trade in the last two decades. This is two-way trade in similar goods, rather than in different goods, and is especially prominent in highly differentiated consumer goods.[2] Anyone who lives in or visits Singapore cannot fail to notice the increasing propensity of Singaporeans to consume branded goods from the rest of the world, especially fashion goods and electronic and computer products, while simultaneously exporting similar (but differentiated) goods to cater for foreign tastes. As Table 6.1 shows, this phenomenon has not been confined to Singapore, but by 1990 almost half of Singapore's trade with the USA and EC in manufactured goods consisted of intra-industry trade, and a fifth of the trade with Japan. In 1966 these figures were about 10 per cent and less than 1 per cent, respectively. According to Chow *et al.* (1994), this transformation is best explained in Singapore's case by increasing specialization in differentiated goods, the broadening of the economic base and level of technological sophistication, and the process of vertical integration by multinational corporations as components are shipped into Singapore for assembly and exported back to industrial countries.

Another facet of Singapore's high level of openness stems from the crucial role played by foreigners and foreign resources in the Singapore economy. The main features of this have already been described in Chapter 1, including the relationship between national income aggregates such as GDP, GNP and IGNP, and savings and investment flows; the importance of foreign workers; and the high degree of foreign ownership of Singapore's production and cumulative equity capital stock. Especially important in the trade context are the heavy net inflows of capital, labour and technology into Singapore. Foreign investment commitments in manufacturing averaged S$2.93 billion between 1988 and 1993 (Table 6.2), representing 83 per cent of total foreign and domestic commitments, up from 77 per cent in the 1980s. Most investment came from the USA and Japan and found its way into electronics and chemicals, both of which have significantly increased their share of the total at the expense of petroleum and machinery. The net inflow of long-term capital is also overwhelmingly foreign direct investment (FDI) rather than portfolio, with Singapore recording the highest ratio of the countries listed.

A less obvious indicator of Singapore's exposure to the global economy relates to the tourism sector. Singapore cannot claim to be a natural tourist destination like Hawaii or Cyprus, nor does it have a strong cultural appeal to tourists in the same way as Bali or East Malaysia, and it lacks the abundant beach resorts of nearby Malaysia and Thailand. Yet tourism is a major industry in Singapore and in relative terms is one of the largest in the Asia Pacific region. According to the World Tourism Organization (1988), Singapore ranked second out of 11 Asia Pacific countries in 1986 in terms of tourism receipts and was exceeded by only Malaysia and China in terms of visitor arrivals in that year. By 1993 over 6 million visitors were coming to Singapore (compared to its resident population of 2.9 million), increasingly from fast-growing Asian countries, generating travel receipts of approximately S$9 billion and contributing about 11 per cent to GDP (Wilson, 1994a, Table 1). Despite a slowdown in the mid-1980s (and in 1991), growth rates for both visitor arrivals and travel receipts have returned to respectable levels since 1988. Moreover travel receipts underestimate the contribution of tourism since they only measure the direct foreign exchange effects and ignore the strong multiplier linkages which the tourism sector has with the rest of the economy. According to Khan *et al.* (1989), regardless of a significant leakage of tourism spending through imports, Singapore's strong input–output linkages and high value-added tourist activities (including shopping) explain the significant contribution made by tourism to national output, income and employment.

Table 6.2   Foreign investment flows into Singapore

| | 1983–89 | 1988–93 |
	Period average	
Foreign commitments in manufacturing		
S$ billions:	1.29	2.93
Share of total (%)	77.02	83.01
Share by country (%)		
USA	43.26	41.69
Japan	25.61	30.93
Share by industry (%)		
Electronics	22.88	37.90
Chemicals	7.49	17.39
Transport/equipment	6.13	5.41
Petroleum	13.01	7.80
Machinery	38.60	11.61

Share of FDI in cumulative total long-term capital inflows		
	1975–84	1985–92
	Period average (%)	
Singapore	97.7	133.1
Indonesia	11.3	23.1
Malaysia	44.7	115.7
Philippines	7.4	26.8
Thailand	14.4	47.7
Korea	2.0	0.0

Notes: The share of foreign commitments by country is of total foreign commitments; the share by industry is of total foreign and local commitments.

Source: Investment commitments are calculated from the *Yearbook of Statistics*, various issues; the FDI ratio for 1975–84 is from Lim and associates (1988, Table 9.4), the ratio for 1985–92 is calculated from the IMF *Balance of Payments Statistics Yearbook 1993*.

Because much of Singapore's trade historically has taken the form of 'entrepot' trade, the published trade statistics distinguish between 'total exports' and 'domestic exports', with re-exports or 'pure entrepot exports' as the difference between the two series. It is also current convention to further distinguish between domestic oil exports, which are oil imports refined in Singapore, and non-oil domestic exports. To measure the value-added contribution of exports to GDP, however, even this distinction is probably too narrow because re-exports are officially defined as goods which are exported from Singapore in the same form as they have been imported, subject only to repacking, splitting into lots, sorting or grading. To take the high import content of exports into account, some economists have calculated an alternative series for domestic exports by using the input–output tables to net out imported intermediate inputs.[3] The authors refer to this series as 'net domestic exports' or 'made in Singapore', but, to avoid confusion with the standard concept of net exports used in this book, we will refer to this measure of exports as 'value-added domestic exports'.

What this value-added series shows is that, although the ratio of officially measured domestic exports to total exports has risen from 32.8 to 64.2 per cent between 1964 and 1992, reflecting the decline of traditional entrepot exports and the diversification of the production structure towards manufactured goods, Singapore is still very much a re-export economy in the broad sense since value-added merchandise exports constituted only 20.5 per cent of total exports in 1992. The remaining 79.5 per cent is accounted for by traditional entrepot exports and imported intermediate goods, including oil, processed into exports (Tan, 1995, Table 2.14).[4] It is because of this that Lloyd and Sandilands (1986) described Singapore as a 'very open re-export economy' or VORE. For most countries the import content of exports is relatively small, but for Singapore almost all the output of goods and services by the private sector and almost all intermediate capital inputs are tradeable goods. Water is imported from Malaysia for treating and some is re-exported; even land is traded in so far as earth is imported from Malaysia and Indonesia and placed offshore for land reclamation. The result is a very high share of international trade in commodities in both domestic production and consumption.

One of the most striking characteristics of Singapore's economic history since the mid-1960s has been the rapid transformation from an entrepot trading economy to an industrialized economy producing labour-intensive goods and subsequently capital and skill-intensive goods and sophisticated business and financial services. These changes in the structure of production, output and employment have already been highlighted in Tables 1.1 and 1.2. Table 6.3 shows the parallel changes in the structure of merchandise exports between 1964 and 1992 using both domestic exports and the value-added export data referred to in the previous paragraph.[5] Notice the shift over time from entrepot trade to manufactures of machinery and transport equipment. This is associated with industrialization, initially based upon low-skill-intensive exports of textiles and garments and simple electrical goods in the 1960s, to capital-intensive petrol refining in the 1970s, and to more sophisticated electronic goods in the 1970s and 1980s. Although petroleum refining and bunkering for ships and aircraft increased in importance in the 1970s, in value-added terms their contribution was less significant, falling to 7.6 per cent by 1992.

Table 6.3   The structure of Singapore's exports: 1964 to 1992

| | Domestic exports | | | Value-added exports | | |
| | Percentage of total | | | | | |
	1964	1975	1992	1964	1975	1992
Entrepot	43.3	4.7	0.7	16.8	3.8	1.0
Petroleum	22.3	52.0	20.7	22.0	20.0	7.6
Manufactures	21.9	38.7	75.3	41.6	69.5	87.2
Of which machinery & transport equipment	2.7	21.4	57.8	4.6	36.0	61.4
Other	12.5	4.6	3.3	19.6	6.7	4.2
Total	100	100	100	100	100	100

Note: Entrepot trade corresponds to SITC 2; petroleum to 3,9; manufactures to 5–8; machinery and transport equipment to 7; domestic exports are gross merchandise exports minus re-exports; value-added exports are domestic exports net of import content.

Sources: Tan (1995, Tables 2.3 and 2.4).

This structural transformation has been matched by changes in the geographical structure of Singapore's trade with the outside world. Table 1.4 records the key changes in the destination of Singapore's merchandise exports and the major sources of imports between 1960 and 1993. OECD countries now account for the highest proportion of total exports (43.7 per cent), especially the USA and Japan. This rises to 53.9 per cent if domestic exports are used, with the US share rising to 25.5 per cent. The decline in ASEAN's share since 1960 is contrasted with the rise in that of the Asian NICs, although ASEAN remains the most important market for traditional entrepot exports (30.6 per cent) compared to the OECD (23.2 per cent). Malaysia alone accounts for 20.3 per cent of entrepot exports.

As far as imports are concerned, again OECD dominates (52.2 per cent), especially Japan (21.9 per cent), with ASEAN second in importance (23.9 per cent) but declining since 1960 compared to OECD and the Asian NICs. Notice that Japan is much more important as a supplier of imports, particularly transport and machinery equipment, than as an export market. Singapore is not alone in experiencing difficulties when trying to 'penetrate' the Japanese domestic market.[6]

One way to capture these shifts in trade patterns is to calculate trade intensity indices which measure bilateral or regional trade flows relative to the country or region's share of world trade and indicate whether trade growth is primarily the result of scale expansion or more intense commercial ties. Table 6.4 shows some indices computed by Hill and Phillips (1993). East Asian developing countries, it seems, trade more intensively among themselves in 1988 than they do with the industrial economies, or than the latter do among themselves. The relatively low indices for ASEAN4 exports to and from other ASEAN4 countries compared to trade between ASEAN4 and Developing East Asia emphasize the relatively low value of intra-ASEAN trade as well as the key role of Singapore as an entrepot importer and exporter as far as the ASEAN4 are concerned. This does not, however, preclude important trade and income interdependencies between Singapore and other ASEAN countries. These will be measured in Chapter 8 in the context of regional macroeconometric models.

Table 6.4   Trade intensity indices by region, 1988

From/to	ASEAN4	Developing East Asia	Industrial economies
ASEAN4	1.5	2.4	0.9
Developing East Asia	2.2	2.3	0.9
Industrial economies	0.3	0.3	1.0

Note: ASEAN4 comprises Indonesia, Malaysia, Thailand and the Philippines; developing East Asia includes ASEAN4 plus China, Hong Kong, Singapore, Korea and Taiwan; the indices are based on 3-year averages of merchandise export flows.

Source: Hill and Phillips (1993, Table 8).

So far we have looked at the characteristics of structural change for Singapore in a static or comparative static fashion, but some economists, using a growth accounting methodology derived from Chenery *et al.* (1986), have argued that Singapore represents a classic case of successful export-led growth. Table 6.5 identifies the sources of manufacturing growth and overall GDP growth decomposed into export expansion, expansion of domestic demand and import substitution, taking averages over a number of time periods since 1964. Again all data are in value-added terms to take into account Singapore's high import content of exports. The key observation from this table is the overwhelming contribution of manufacturing export growth to manufacturing growth, and growth in exports of goods and services to overall GDP growth, especially from the 1970s on.[7] Note that service exports refer to total services, and not just services associated with commodity trade, and account for about half of the contribution to growth in GDP of goods and services together. In other words, Singapore's growth is both commodity-led and service-led. Domestic demand, on the other hand, was most important in the 1960s through infrastructure and housing expenditure. Import substitution is negative except for a small contribution to overall GDP growth between 1980 and 1992 as the result of a slowdown in export growth during this period. Negative import substitution is the counterpart to the import penetration discussed earlier.

Table 6.5   Sources of economic growth for Singapore, 1964–92

	Contribution from expansion in:		
To	Exports	Domestic demand	Import substitution
Manufacturing GDP: (%)			
1964–70	24	121	–46
1970–80	76	44	–20
1980–92	98	15	–12
1964–92	89	42	–31
Overall GDP: (%)			
1964–70	35	99	–35
1970–80	76	50	–26
1980–92	58	29	12
1964–92	62	63	–26

Note: Manufacturing GDP is value-added of the manufacturing sector at factor cost; GDP is overall GDP at factor cost; for manufacturing GDP the contribution of export expansion is based upon value-added commodity exports; for overall GDP exports include value-added service exports from both commodity and non-commodity trade.

Source: Tan (1995, Tables 3.4 and 3.8).

6.2   TRADE POLICY

Since the mid-1960s Singapore's trade regime can best be described as that of an outward-oriented, very open re-export economy pursuing selective export promotion. According to the World Bank's *World Development Report 1987* classification, Singapore would fall into the category of strongly outward-oriented (as opposed to moderately outward-oriented, moderately inward-oriented or strongly inward-oriented) in so far as there is no discrimination between production for the domestic market and for export, or active pursuit of import substitution.

Although there have been changes in trade policy since 1960,[8] including a brief period of import substitution in the early 1960s, five fundamental principles have guided trade policy in Singapore. Firstly, there has been a commitment to free trade in the fundamental sense of a low level of protection and continual exposure of consumers and producers to international price signals. Secondly, the trade authorities have pursued an active export promotion strategy, primarily through improvements in infrastructure and selective fiscal incentives. Thirdly, in sharp contrast to most developing countries, an 'open arms' policy towards multinational corporations (MNCs) was extended at a very early stage in the industrialization process. Fourthly, an integral part of trade policy in Singapore has been the liberalization of trade through economic integration, primarily through ASEAN. Finally, macroeconomic policy, including the foreign exchange regime, has been directed towards maintaining external competitiveness and the flow of foreign investment into Singapore, principally by maintaining low inflation and domestic price stability. Although the exchange rate has been fixed or later 'managed', rather than free-floating since 1960, the fixed or 'target' rate has never been allowed to depart substantially from a market-determined value or to be distorted by unnecessary controls on foreign exchange movements. We will illustrate each of these principles in turn. Exchange rate policy is discussed in Section 6.4 below.

With independence from the British in 1959, the ruling People's Action Party intensified the process of industrialization to diversify away from the narrow entrepot base which was seen as being constraining in terms of potential income and employment growth, and subject to high earnings instability. Between 1960 and 1965 trade strategy was geared towards import substitution based upon expected economic integration with the large Malaysian market nearby. This was accelerated when Singapore joined the Federation of Malaysia in 1963. Fiscal concessions were given to 'pioneer' industries, together with subsidies on factory sites, and quotas were imposed on selected import-competing industries. When Singapore left the Federation of Malaysia in 1965 and became a republic, it entered a transitional phase in its economic history as trade policy switched from inward to outward orientation. With no guarantee of free access to the Malaysian market, and lacking a large pool of indigenous industrial entrepreneurs compared to Hong Kong (from mainland China), import substitution was unsustainable in an economy with a small domestic market and a dearth of natural resources.

The focus switched towards the promotion of labour-intensive exports, the attraction of foreign investment and the gradual lowering of protection. Initially quotas were reduced (72 by 1967) but replaced by tariffs (398 by 1967), but even during the period of peak protection between 1965 and 1967, most ad valorem tariff rates were below 25 per cent and average nominal (3 per cent) and effective (6 per cent) tariff rates were low by international standards (Tan and Ow, 1982). By 1973 the number of tariffs had fallen to 197 and quotas had been reduced to just three. Tariffs continued to fall in the 1970s, accelerated by the ASEAN Preferential Tariff Arrangement in 1978. At the present time (1994) most tariffs are below 5 per cent and are levied on selected items such as cars. Non-tariff barriers are negligible.

As far as trade promotion is concerned, in 1968 the Economic Development Board was reorganized and legislation was introduced in 1967 and 1968 to provide tax incentives to encourage export promotion and foreign participation. Emphasis was placed on government-provided infrastructure. In 1968 Jurong Town Corporation was established to develop and manage industrial estates, offering prepared industrial land sites, ready-built factories, and port and cargo-handling facilities nearby.

By the early 1970s export-oriented labour-intensive industrialization was well on track, with virtually full employment. Although multinationals located in Singapore had already begun to raise capital intensity, the domestic labour market became increasingly tight and the threat of competition from lower-wage, competing countries, together with the possibility of increased protectionism by developed countries, led to a shift in emphasis in trade policy towards the promotion of technology and skill-intensive exports of goods and services with higher value-added. A restructuring programme, together with a 'high wage' policy, was introduced in 1979, having been delayed by the 1973 oil shock and ensuing recession. Tax incentives were also introduced to increase research and development.

In 1981 the National Productivity Board was established to increase labour productivity, and in 1983 the Singapore Trade and Development Board was set up as a trade promotion agency to provide trade information, offer financial assistance to help companies globalize and more recently to introduce computers to speed up customs procedures and trade documentation. Since 1986 policy has continued the stress on higher value-added skill and technology-intensive exports such as microelectronics, biotechnology, and financial and business services. The goal now became to broaden the manufacturing and service base into a 'total business centre' providing conference facilities and industrial estates as self-contained business centres. Singapore firms have been encouraged (with their families) to venture abroad and MNCs have been enticed to use Singapore as their regional headquarters.

This positive attitude towards MNCs has been an important feature of Singapore's trade policy. There was never any post-colonial ideological resistance to the attraction of foreign capital to Singapore and the PAP realized early on the potential ready-made package of scarce resources which MNCs can bring with them. This package includes technology, capital inputs, established brands and marketing outlets, managerial skills and an in-built capacity to respond to changes in comparative advantage. MNCs, in their turn, were attracted by Singapore's strategic location, political and social stability, tax incentives (pioneer status, accelerated depreciation allowances), infrastructure and relatively cheap but educated labour force (Chia, 1985; 1986b; 1993).

Overall Singapore represents a model of successful outward-oriented export-led growth. Outward orientation and export promotion have allowed it to overcome the limitations imposed by a small domestic market, earning foreign exchange to purchase intermediate goods imports and an increasing quantity and variety of consumer goods from the international market at the lowest prices. The transformation to an NIC has taken place along the lines of shifting comparative advantage[9] taking full advantage of the complementary resources provided by MNCs, especially in manufacturing and financial and business services. None of the negative features associated with the presence of foreign multinationals appear to be important in Singapore (Chia, 1985). Reducing 'dependence' on MNCs is seen rather as a positive step to increase the supply of indigenous industrial entrepreneurs and MNCs.

As far as economic integration is concerned, Singapore has consistently pursued trade liberalization through multilateral institutions such as GATT (the General Agreement on Tariffs and Trade) and APEC (Asia-Pacific Economic Cooperation Forum), and has been a beneficiary from liberalization in other countries, including the Generalized System of Preferences (Lim and associates, 1988, chap. 10). In addition, it has been an active participant in attempts to foster regional integration in South East Asia through ASEAN, the ASEAN free trade area (AFTA) and the Indonesian–Malaysian–Singapore growth triangle.[10]

Since its inception in 1967, the Association of South-East Asian Nations (ASEAN) has achieved very little in terms of tangible economic gains for its members,[11] apart from containing intra-ASEAN conflict and providing some common policies on food, energy and tourism (Wong, 1988). Intra-ASEAN trade still constitutes less than 20 per cent of total ASEAN trade. Attempts to lower tariff rates through the Preferential Trading Arrangements since 1978 have been disappointing and schemes to promote industrial cooperation have failed to produce the desired effects. This contrasts sharply with the success of the Indonesian–Malaysian–Singapore growth triangle since 1989. The idea is to pool economic resources in a complementary fashion to stimulate growth in Johor, just across the causeway from Singapore in Malaysia, and in the Indonesian Riau islands south of Singapore. Progress has been slow in Johor, but impressive on the Indonesian island of Batam, where an industrial park has been established to produce labour-intensive manufactured goods. In contrast to Johor, where Singapore and Malaysian interests tend to be more competitive than complementary, development on Batam has benefited from the combination of Indonesian land and labour and the provision of infrastructure and financial services by Singapore.

Beginning in 1991, ASEAN members made a concerted effort to speed up the process of tariff reduction by committing themselves to an ASEAN free trade area (AFTA), through a Common Effective Preferential Tariff Structure (CEPT). Although the full implementation of the scheme has been delayed, the goal is to reduce tariff rates on manufactured goods, including capital goods and processed agricultural products, to between zero and 5 per cent within ten years. Some product categories are 'fast tracked' to reduce the implementation time. The political commitment to AFTA has been surprisingly strong and there is some optimism that this will be translated into effective action and some gains in terms of increased intra-ASEAN trade and attraction of FDI to the region. The proviso, however, is that negotiations over the tariff 'exclusion list' are successful, and that resistance to the removal of protection in less competitive countries, such as Indonesia and the Philippines, does not further delay implementation. Singapore probably has the most to gain, given her very low level of tariff protection and efficient manufacturing sector.

There are two aspects of Singapore's trading position which have raised concern in recent years, and which impinge directly upon macroeconomic trade policy: the 'sandwich' problem and the perceived vulnerability of the Singapore economy to external shocks. The first problem stems from the fear that Singapore is steadily losing a comparative advantage in low-skill labour-intensive goods and some capital-intensive goods to other NICs and emerging NICs, but has not yet reached the stage at which it can compete with advanced industrial countries in technology and skill-intensive goods (Sandilands and Tan, 1986). On the other hand, if Singapore gives up its manufacturing base in favour of specialization on services, this may make the economy more susceptible to external shocks. These problems may be more apparent than real in view of Singapore's remarkable adaptability and resilience in the face of a changing world environment. To some observers (Lee (Tsao) Yuan 1994) there is no reason why Singapore cannot continue to compete effectively in high value-added manufactured goods and services (such as conferencing) by keeping the design, marketing and distribution functions in Singapore, while at the same time reducing costs by shifting more labour-intensive production offshore to Johor (Malaysia) and Batam (Indonesia). Increased service orientation also need not be incompatible with an expansion of the manufacturing sector as long as high-quality manufactured goods require highly specialized service inputs and customization.

The second problem arises from Singapore's vulnerability to a fall in external demand. There is some evidence that changes in exports or import prices have proportionately stronger multiplier repercussions on the domestic economy than domestic changes in monetary or fiscal policy (see Chapter 8), but the conventional export instability debate (Wilson, 1994c) is not especially applicable to Singapore in view of its strong automatic stabilizers through imports and savings, and strong balance of payments position. Although the 1985 recession is often cited as an example of Singapore's vulnerability to external shocks, that recession, in fact, required rather a special combination of unfavourable circumstances. Of the three occasions between 1964 and 1992 in which value-added commodity exports experienced negative growth, in two cases (1975 and 1982) value-added service exports cushioned the impact on GDP growth to give positive growth in exports as a whole, and the growth in domestic demand was also positive. Only in 1985 did both categories of exports exhibit negative growth, generating a negative value for external demand as a whole, and at the same time domestic demand growth was also negative (Tan, 1995, Table 3.5). We will return to the causes of the 1985 recession in Section 6.5 below.

6.3   THE BALANCE OF PAYMENTS

The Singapore balance of payments (BP) records all the economic transactions between Singapore residents and the rest of the world over a given time period. Annual BP accounts are published in the *Yearbook of Statistics Singapore* and quarterly figures in the *Economic Survey of Singapore*. Alternative tables, measured in US dollars, for comparison with other countries can be found in the monthly and annual *International Financial Statistics* compiled by the International Monetary Fund (IMF) and in the IMF's *Balance of Payments Statistics Yearbook*. Although the IMF adopts a standard format for the presentation of BP accounts, national tables do sometimes differ in their coverage and presentation. We will point out these differences for Singapore as we proceed.

Table 6.6 uses Singapore's published statistics to highlight the most important features of the Singapore BP in 1992, and on an average basis between 1960 and 1992, to take a longer view. 'Net' items use a single entry for an outflow and an inflow.

In 1992 the trade balance (sometimes called 'visibles') was in deficit since merchandise imports exceeded merchandise exports. The balance of services, however, was positive with (net) surpluses in investment income and travel,[12] so that the goods and services balance is in overall surplus. Taking the balance at this stage of goods and services and unrequited transfers gives a current account surplus of S$ 6.11 billion. The remaining entries in Table 6.6 refer to international transactions in capital assets, which affect national income in future periods. Capital transactions are highly heterogeneous and difficult to classify. In the IMF tables a distinction is made between long-term and short-term capital. Long-term capital flows are in turn subdivided into FDI, which is closely associated with MNCs setting up subsidiaries abroad, and portfolio investment, such as the purchase or sale of foreign bonds in primary and secondary domestic financial markets.[13] Short-term capital, on the other hand, includes such items as trade credit, or bank balances held in foreign countries. Unfortunately the

Singapore BP accounts do not make these distinctions clear. The private non-monetary sector in Table 6.6 makes no distinction between FDI and other non-monetary flows. Furthermore capital data are presented in the published accounts in net terms, so it is not possible to compare the inflow of capital with the outflow. With the 'second wing' policy of encouraging Singapore-registered firms to invest abroad, this distinction is becoming much more important than in the past. Nonetheless, in 1992, monetary outflows were more than covered by net non-monetary inflows, giving rise to a capital account surplus of over S$9 billion.

Table 6.6   The Singapore balance of payments 1960–92

	1960–69	1970–79	1980–87	1988–92	1992
	Annual average (S$ billions)				
Trade balance	–0.80	–4.57	–9.21	–6.67	–9.42
Balance of services	0.58	3.11	8.49	12.55	16.49
Investment income (net)	0.60	–0.08	0.11	2.05	2.54
Travel (net)	0.07	0.80	2.69	4.20	4.64
Goods and services (net)	–0.22	–1.46	–0.72	5.88	7.07
Unrequited transfers					
Private (net)	–0.04	–0.07	–0.38	–0.53	–0.66
Official (net)	0.00	0.01	–0.02	–0.24	–0.30
Current account	–0.26	–1.52	–1.12	5.11	6.11
Capital account	0.10	1.49	2.69	4.20	9.05
Non-monetary sector private (net)	0.08	1.27	2.64	5.13	10.24
Non-monetary sector official (net)	0.02	0.08	0.07	–0.05	–0.02
Monetary sector (net)	0.00	0.14	–0.02	–0.88	–1.17
Basic balance	—	1.38	1.86	9.36	14.12
Balancing item	0.34	0.96	0.66	–2.15	–5.20
Overall balance	0.18	0.93	2.23	7.16	9.96
Official reserves (net)	–0.18	–0.93	–2.23	–7.16	–9.96

Sources: Economic and Social Statistics 1960–82, Table 4.10; Yearbook of Statistics Singapore, various issues.

The basic balance measures the sum of the current account and long-term capital account. It is not a requirement of the IMF standard recording system but is often calculated by officials and economists to show the surplus or deficit in international transactions taking into account long-term capital flows and current account transactions, but excluding more volatile short-term capital items. If a country has a persistent deficit on its basic balance it may indicate underlying problems in its trade and payments. The long-term capital account is not given in the published data, so the basic balance cannot be calculated directly from Table 6.6. However, since both the current account and non-monetary capital account are in surplus in 1992, it is no surprise that the basic balance given in Table 6.6 is also in surplus, at S$14.12 billion.

The overall balance is obtained by adding the current account to the capital account and the balancing item (net errors and omissions in the IMF accounts). The latter ensures that the accounts add up in an accounting sense by allowing for unrecorded items (such as smuggling) or incorrectly recorded items. The overall balance is sometimes called the Official Settlements Balance because it represents the balance that must ultimately be financed or settled by a change in official reserves (discussed in Section 6.6 below). Since the overall balance for Singapore is in surplus in 1992 to the tune of S$9.96 billion, this *must* imply a net increase in official reserves in the next row of the same amount, but with the opposite sign.[14]

Looking at the Singapore BP over the longer run, a key feature between 1960 and 1987 is that the chronic trade deficit and small negative balance on unrequited transfers were not sufficiently offset by the surplus on services account. The result is current account deficits every year except in 1966. The negative trade balance is a direct consequence of the heavy import dependence discussed in Section 6.1. The capital account was in surplus over this period (except in 1986) largely as a result of substantial inflows of FDI.

The overall BP between 1960 and 1987 is in surplus every year except 1964 and 1965, resulting in a steady accumulation of official reserves, but the interpretation of the relationship between the current and capital accounts and items within the capital account itself is complicated by the large size of the balancing item. For many individual years between 1960 and 1976 when the overall BP registered a surplus, this was only because of the balancing item. This explains why the sum of the current and capital accounts in Table 6.6 using data averaged over 1960–69 and 1970–79 does not result in an overall surplus until the average balancing item is added. Interpretation of the capital account is also difficult, given the lack of decomposition referred to above.

From the mid-1980s onwards there is a significant change in the nature of the Singapore BP. The services surplus is now large enough to give a positive balance on goods and services from 1985 onwards and on current account from 1988 on. Important net surplus items here are travel receipts (tourism earnings), transport and services (ship repair, port services, bunker fuel for ships and aircraft) and investment income. The latter became positive in 1984 after persistent negative values between 1972 and 1983 (except in 1975), owing primarily to income earned by the official sector on public sector surpluses (budget surpluses, statutory board operating surpluses) lent abroad in earlier years by the Government Investment Corporation (GIC). Unfortunately no information has been made public on the magnitude of such investments and on their composition. In the national accounts (Chapter 1, Table 1.5) this explains the positive sign for net factor income from abroad and the reason why GNP exceeds GDP from 1989 onwards. Thus for 1988–92 the basic balance[15] and overall BP is strongly positive, resulting from both current account and capital account surpluses.

To introduce a comparative dimension to the Singapore BP, Table 6.7 shows some of the important BP aggregates in 1992 and averaged between 1988 and 1992 for selected countries, including Singapore, all measured in US dollars. By international standards Singapore has a strong BP. Her average annual surplus on overall balance for 1988–92 of US$4 billion is the highest of the countries listed. This allowed Singapore to accumulate by 1992 US$39.9 billion of official reserves, the highest per head (US$14 244) in the world. Does Singapore have a 'problem' with its BP?

Table 6.7   Singapore's balance of payments and international comparisons

	Overall balance 1988–92	Reserves 1992 US$ billions	Import coverage 1992 months
Singapore	4.0	39.9	5.7
Indonesia	1.2	11.5	3.4
Malaysia	2.1	18.0	4.5
Philippines	0.8	5.3	3.3
Thailand	3.7	21.2	5.2
Japan	−1.8	79.8	2.4
USA	−22.6	147.5	2.3
UK	−2.2	42.8	1.4
Australia	0.5	13.9	2.5

Source: *International Financial Statistics*, June 1994, *World Development Report 1994*, Table 17.

The BP must balance in an accounting sense because of the principle of double-entry bookkeeping and in an economic sense it must balance since a deficit (surplus) on current account must be matched by a surplus (deficit) on capital account or ultimately be financed by a change in official reserves. The conventional view is that whether a BP problem exists depends upon the extent to which the authorities are obliged to intervene to 'accommodate' an imbalance somewhere else in the accounts, for example when a persistent current account deficit is not covered by commercially motivated 'autonomous transactions' on capital account and results in the depletion of official reserves or official borrowing from agencies such as the IMF. If the exchange rate floats freely, 'accommodating transactions' such as these are not, in principle, necessary since the exchange rate will adjust the BP automatically. On the other hand, if the exchange rate is fixed, one can identify the problem directly from the overall balance and change in reserves, since the authorities must intervene in the forex market to maintain the fixed parity.

In the case of Singapore, where the exchange rate floats but is 'managed' within certain limits (discussed in Section 6.4 below) one can no longer strictly identify the 'problem' with the extent of accommodating action by authorities, but one would be hard pressed to identify a problem with respect to the BP, given the persistent overall surplus and negligible international debt. The negative trade balance is also a benign reflection of rapid growth and specialization in trade (discussed in Section 6.1 above) and is now offset by earnings from services, including investment income. Although it is not possible to tell whether the gross inflow of FDI exceeds gross outflows of FDI income from the data provided, it is likely that the BP impact of such capital flows is substantially positive, given the productive use to which foreign investment is put in Singapore's export-based activities.

Whether the BP constitutes a 'problem' also depends on the BP in the context of the domestic economy. An overall surplus does not necessarily imply no problem since it could spill over into domestic inflation, as in West Germany in the 1960s, or attract pressure from counterpart deficit countries to expand income and imports, as with Japan in the 1990s. An overall surplus might also only have been achieved at the expense of domestic recession and unemployment, since the latter will tend to reduce imports as income falls. For Singapore, internal balance has not been compromised in so far as it has an enviable record of low inflation and unemployment and surplus government budgets (see Chapter 2). However the overall BP surplus has tended to put pressure on the Singapore dollar to appreciate over time and this has important implications for government policy as it attempts to achieve internal balance (a low and stable inflation rate and high employment) while simultaneously maintaining the competitiveness of exports and a surplus on the BP. It is also debatable whether the accumulation of such a high level of official reserves is desirable from the social point of view. We will return to these issues in Sections 6.5 and 6.6 below.

6.4 EXCHANGE RATE POLICY

The foreign exchange market in Singapore is the means by which buyers and sellers of foreign exchange are linked. Before the 1970s this market was not very well developed (Tan Chwee Huat, 1992; Lee, 1990). A cartel association of banks determined exchange rates with fixed margins for commissions. After 1973, however, the banks were free to quote their own rates, and an inflow of foreign banks and specialized forex brokers increased competition in the market and reduced the spread between buying and selling rates. By 1993 the average daily turnover in the Singapore forex market was US$87.1 billion, making it the fourth highest in the world after London, New York and Tokyo (*Singapore 1994*). Trading takes place 'round-the-world, round-the-clock' to take advantage of Singapore's favourable time zone location. Dealing is particularly active in the German mark and Yen against the US dollar, but in recent years trade has increased in derivatives such as currency options and futures, as well as in interest rate swaps and forward rate agreements.

In the *Economic Survey of Singapore* and *Monthly Digest of Statistics*, bilateral exchange rates are given for a range of currencies defined as the Singapore dollar price of the currency concerned. These represent the cost of the foreign currency in terms of the Singapore dollar or the nominal Singapore dollar price of the currency concerned. A rise in the exchange rate in this case implies a depreciation of the local currency since it costs more to buy a unit of foreign exchange.

Sometimes it is more enlightening to look at the value of the Singapore dollar, not in terms of bilateral rates, but in terms of an average or 'basket' of currencies, each weighted in terms of the importance of the country concerned to Singapore's trade. Currencies with low weights would have to change by a large amount to influence this nominal effective exchange rate (NEER). An alternative 'basket' measure is the real effective exchange rate (REER). This adjusts the NEER for the price or cost of domestic goods and services relative to foreign, all measured in local currency. Although a variety of different cost indicators can be used (such as export prices or unit labour cost) to compile these rates, real exchange rates (RER) are designed to show changes in the home country's competitiveness in international trade.[16]

Figure 6.1 plots the nominal Singapore–US dollar exchange rate R and the ratio of the US CPI P^* to the Singapore CPI P between 1975 and 1993. Note that R is plotted as the reciprocal of S$/US$ so that a rise in R now signifies an appreciation of the Singapore dollar. Two observations can be made from Figure 6.1: R and the price ratio generally move together, and the long-run tendency is for the Singapore dollar to appreciate against the US dollar. Can these observations be explained?

According to the theory of purchasing power parity (PPP) the exchange rate between the Singapore dollar and another currency such as the US dollar should equal the ratio of the price levels in the two countries. This relationship is expected to hold in the longer run but need not hold in the short run. Figure 6.1 suggests that some sort of PPP relationship is at work for the Singapore dollar and US dollar. However, if PPP held exactly, the nominal exchange rate would adjust in relation to changes in P^* and P to ensure that the real exchange rate (RER) in Figure 6.2 was constant.[17] In fact there are times, such as between 1983–4 and 1985–6, when P fell in Singapore relative to P^*, yet the Singapore dollar deppreciated against the US dollar.

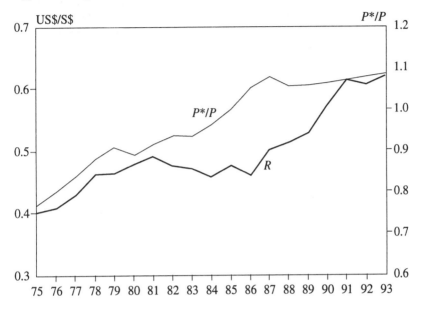

Source: IMF, *International Financial Statistics*, various issues.

Figure 6.1 The nominal Singapore–US exchange rate and relative consumer prices, 1975–93

Using a more formal statistical analysis, Abeysinghe and Lee (1992) found that the Singapore–US dollar exchange rate satisfied PPP, using data from the first quarter of 1975 to the third quarter of 1990, especially if an adjustment was made to remove short-run fluctuations. However the theory is not supported for the Singapore dollar in relation to the Malaysian ringgit, the pound sterling, Japanese yen or German mark.[18] In a more recent paper, Yip (1994) tested PPP on an annual basis between 1975 and 1994. The broader basket measure of the exchange rate NEER is used, defined in terms of a trade-weighted average of the Singapore dollar against ten major currencies. Figure 6.3 plots the Yip NEER and REER and an estimated *equilibrium* NEER based on long-run PPP equilibrium (PPP). A rise in NEER implies an appreciation of the Singapore dollar and a rise in REER a loss of competitiveness. NEER rises sharply between 1977 and 1984 and from 1988 to 1992. The key point, however, is that the actual

NEER is substantially overvalued (lies above PPP) from 1981 to 1985, and again
from 1990 onwards. From 1986 to 1989, on the other hand, it is undervalued.
If PPP is an accurate indicator of the equilibrium exchange rate, then overval-
uation may have serious consequences for export competitiveness and the
success of MAS policy in targeting its own NEER to contain domestic inflation.
We will return to these issues in Section 6.5 below, but before doing so we need
to examine what other factors, apart from PPP, might affect the exchange rate,
especially in the shorter run.

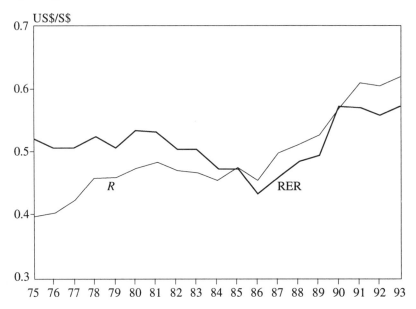

Source: IMF, *International Financial Statistics*, various issues.

Figure 6.2 The nominal and real Singapore–US exchange rate, 1975–93

One approach is to explain the exchange rate in terms of current account 'fundamentals'. A current account deficit, for example, implies excess demand for
forex and will lead under a flexible exchange rate system to a depreciation of
the currency. This will make exports cheaper to foreigners and imports more
expensive to domestic residents. If exports and imports are sufficiently own-
price elastic, the initial current account deficit will be corrected automatically.
The weakness of this approach is that it assumes that capital flows are essentially a passive means of financing temporary current account imbalances. For
Singapore this is especially misleading since both long-term and short-term capital
flows are essential to explain changes in the overall BP. Also the NEER has
increased steadily over time (appreciating currency) in Figure 6.3, while current

account deficits (surpluses from 1986) have fluctuated much more. Moreover, while the current account was improving in the 1980s, the NEER fell sharply between 1985 and 1987.

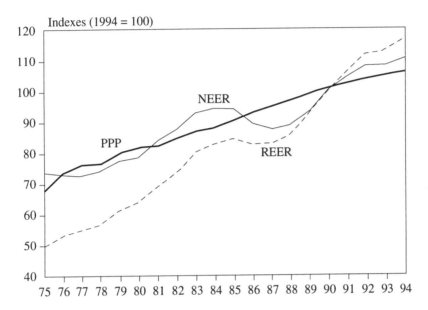

Source: adapted from Yip (1994).

Figure 6.3 Nominal and real effective exchange rates, 1975–94

For Singapore, capital flows have become increasingly important over time for the BP and the exchange rate, given virtually no controls on the inflow or outflow of currency funds by residents and foreigners. Movements in short- and medium-term exchange rates are dominated by capital market adjustments to changes in expected real returns from portfolios of financial assets denominated in different currencies. Capital flows are not passive but active and volatile. If foreign portfolio holders expect the real return on Singapore financial assets to increase, they will buy the Singapore dollar to buy the asset and thereby increase the demand for the Singapore dollar.

Table 6.8 shows that longer-term (non-monetary) flows (including a large but unknown quantity of FDI) dominate short-term (monetary) capital movements in terms of their absolute magnitude, but they are less volatile. FDI is motivated by the long-term profitability of production and exports in Singapore and may help to explain the steady appreciation of the Singapore dollar. Short-term capital flows (monetary movements), by contrast, are dominated by inter-bank borrowing and lending and are highly mobile, especially between offshore and onshore financial markets (see Section 6.7 below). These flows ensure that interest rates in Singapore are largely set by world markets. Changes in foreign interest rates, however, are not always passed through to domestic rates in Singapore. In 1994, for example, when US interest rates were rising, the three-month domestic inter-bank offer rate in Singapore (DIBOR) fell below the three-month Singapore inter-bank offer rate (SIBOR) in the offshore Asian Dollar Market, because the Singapore dollar was expected to appreciate against the US dollar.[19]

Table 6.8   Monetary and non-monetary capital flows, Singapore, 1980–93

	Non-monetary	Monetary
	S$ billions	
1980	3.09	0.29
1981	3.58	0.99
1982	4.22	0.72
1983	2.38	2.82
1984	1.77	1.60
1985	2.55	−1.02
1986	0.96	−3.79
1987	3.16	−1.81
1988	3.18	−1.99
1989	3.51	−2.62
1990	5.39	3.04
1991	3.28	−1.67
1992	10.23	−1.17
1993	10.68	4.59
Mean	4.14	0.001
Annual average change (%)	58.35	150.99

Sources: *Economic Survey of Singapore*, various issues.

The market-determined behaviour of the Singapore dollar thus results from a combination of forces.[20] In the longer run PPP requires that the NEER adjust in relation to Singapore's price level relative to the rest of the world. Current account fundamentals are important as long as the focus is on Singapore's strong export performance and associated inflow of FDI, rather than on the trade balance alone. In this sense the basic balance, which includes net long-term capital inflows, is a better indicator of the underlying strength of Singapore's trading position. Short-term capital flows, by contrast, are volatile and mainly monetary flows through the inter-bank market. Since the Singapore dollar is not an important international currency in the same sense as the US dollar or Japanese yen, and Singapore's domestic financial markets are not very 'deep' in the range of international financial assets traded, the Singapore dollar is relatively stable. In particular, it is less prone than the major currencies to speculative or other adjustments in international portfolios of financial assets, and gyrations in currency markets.

So far we have assumed that R or NEER respond entirely to market forces. In fact the Singapore dollar is not left to float freely in the market-place but has been 'managed' by the monetary authorities since 1975. From 1906 to 1967 the Singapore currency was fixed to the pound sterling. Although this ruled out any independent monetary policy or exchange rate policy, the system guaranteed a certain amount of financial and trading stability for Singapore. Singapore continued to fix to sterling under the post-Second World War Bretton Woods system when sterling was itself fixed to the US dollar, even after independence from Britain in 1959. But when sterling was devalued by 14.3 per cent against the US dollar in September 1967, the Singapore monetary authorities decided to peg to the stabler and more widely-used US dollar. Sterling was retained as the official intervention currency in view of Singapore's large pool of accumulated sterling reserves. The decision not to devalue at the same time as sterling was based on the expectation that this would lead to a significant rise in the price of imported food and entrepot goods from countries outside the sterling area, even though the decision not to devalue meant that Singapore exports now became less competitive against sterling area countries.

With the breakdown of the Bretton Woods system in the early 1970s and the floating of sterling in June 1972, Singapore adopted the US dollar as the official intervention currency. In May and June of 1973 the US dollar was very weak against the major currencies, generating inflationary pressures in Singapore and a large inflow of US dollars which the authorities were obliged to buy to support the fixed rate. Thus, in common with many other countries, Singapore moved to a floating exchange rate regime in June 1973. In September 1975 the Singapore dollar was managed in relation to an undisclosed basket of the currencies of its major trading partners. This policy of managed floating remains the forex regime for Singapore.

Under the system of managed floating the MAS, acting as a central bank, intervenes in the currency market to maintain the value of the Singapore dollar within an undisclosed target band, based on an unpublished NEER containing the currencies of Singapore's principal trading partners. Many countries adopt managed floating as a compromise between fixed and floating, but do not nec-essarily operate the system in quite the same way. Since 1981 managed floating in Singapore has been linked directly to a 'strong Singapore dollar' policy. The MAS, contrary to common belief, does not intervene in the currency markets simply to smooth out short-run fluctuations in the currency, but 'manages' the currency to keep it at a predetermined level in line with the government's economic objectives, more specifically to offset the effects of imported inflation. The NEER is thus an instrument of monetary policy to achieve low and stable domestic price inflation, consistent with a target for employment. If there is a sharp increase in import prices, the MAS will keep domestic prices from rising as fast by letting the Singapore dollar appreciate, but some imported inflation may be transmitted to the domestic economy, since the appreciation necessary to completely offset imported inflation may significantly decrease export competitiveness in the short run. Some countries, by contrast, find it to their advantage to keep their currencies at a slightly depreciated level in order to make their exports cheaper in foreign currency. This policy, known as 'dirty floating', is in essence a disguised form of protectionism.

Since managed floating constitutes only one of a number of possible forex systems or 'regimes' Singapore could choose, but is closer to the floating end of the spectrum than the fixed, is this particular regime the best choice for Singapore? (See Wilson, 1994b.) Economic theory (Heller, 1978) suggests that a country will be more likely to choose a fixed exchange rate if it displays the following characteristics: it is a price taker in international markets (small country), highly open in terms of exports and imports of goods and services in relation to its national income, is weakly integrated into international financial markets, its exports tend to be concentrated on one or a few commodities, and it is prone to domestic shocks such as a bad harvest or political unrest. The reasoning is that for such economies only small reductions in domestic income will be needed to reduce imports and improve the BP, without it being necessary to alter the exchange rate; and there will be less need for the exchange rate to change to 'insulate' the domestic economy from foreign shocks. Moreover, if the country produces only one or two major exports and sells them to one or two markets, it may be sensible to peg to the currency of the main trading partner to guarantee domestic price stability for a large proportion of its trade.

On the other hand, countries which are largely self-sufficient, have a more diversified economic structure, are financially integrated and are more susceptible to foreign shocks might prefer a more flexible exchange rate regime. This is also likely if the country consistently inflates at a substantially higher rate than its competitors, since allowing the currency to float down to compensate for the rise in the cost of its exports may be the only feasible way to remain competitive in international markets.

Although a relatively fixed rate probably made sense for pre-industrialized Singapore, when its trading structure was highly open, relatively narrow-based and trade with Britain and the sterling area countries was significant, the choice is not so clear-cut in later years. Applying the criteria above, a fixed rate is appropriate in so far as Singapore is a small, highly open economy, with low inflation relative to the rest of the world. On the other hand, a 'clean float' is feasible given its high degree of financial integration with the world economy, relatively diversified trade structure and susceptibility to foreign shocks. The Singapore dollar is not subject to significant speculative attacks, given Singapore's strong BP and high forex reserves, and any uncertainty generated by fluctuations in the exchange rate could be hedged through financial markets. The key to understanding the choice of managed floating, therefore, is the fact that the MAS believes that letting the currency float, but managing it by intervening in the forex market, is the most effective use of monetary policy to achieve its domestic inflation and employment targets, despite the negative effects which an appreciating currency might have on short-run export competitiveness. Has this policy been successful?

6.5 INTERNAL AND EXTERNAL BALANCE, 1980–93

Chapter 4 considered the macroeconomic issues which arise when an open economy attempts simultaneously to achieve a number of domestic and external goals. Domestic goals might include a low and stable rate of inflation consistent with a target for employment, whilst external goals might refer to a 'satisfactory' balance of payments position. This could take the form of an overall surplus BP or a deficit of a given size.[21] In Chapter 4 the framework used to analyse these problems was the *IS–LM–BP* model. When represented in two dimensions the slopes of the three curves were drawn to capture, as far as possible, the known characteristics of the Singapore economy, in particular a relatively steep *IS* curve and, crucially, a perfectly elastic *BP* curve. The latter emphasizes the very high degree of short-term capital mobility referred to in the previous section. Although Singapore also has a very high marginal propensity to import, characteristic of a VORE, which of itself would make the *BP* curve steeper, the effects of short-term capital flows are so overwhelming that they dominate the slope of the *BP* curve.

As well as being very open with respect to trade and capital flows, there are a number of other factors which lie behind Singapore's open economy macroeconomic policy which have also been discussed in earlier chapters. First, fiscal policy is relatively ineffective in Singapore as an instrument of demand management. It is well known that fiscal policy is relatively ineffective as a stabilization tool in open economies with flexible exchange rates and high capital mobility, compared to monetary policy,[22] but other factors also come into play in Singapore. In particular, the wealth effect of tax policy is reduced by CPF contributions; the fiscal crowding out of domestic investment is small since interest rates are set by the world market; and the very high marginal propensity to import reduces the multiplier effects on domestic income of any fiscal expansion or contraction. Tax reductions may, however, stimulate investment and output indirectly by increasing business optimism. The impressive growth of real GDP in 1994, for example, may have been helped by the cut in the corporate tax rate from 30 per cent to 27 per cent and the reduction in personal income taxes announced in the 1993 budget.

Second, as pointed out in Chapter 5, a large proportion of changes in the money supply in Singapore are due to net flows from abroad via external sector net foreign assets. Controlling M1 is possible in principle but is too narrow to have any effect on an ultimate target such as inflation. M2 and M3, on the other hand, are not stable or controllable by the MAS, since they are affected by international money markets. Interest rates in Singapore cannot be used as effective instruments since they are tied to international rates. If the MAS tried to fix interest rates above world rates, and the currency was left to float, funds would flow in and the currency would appreciate and shift the *IS* curve to the left as the current account worsened. Even if the MAS decided to use monetary policy for domestic goals, the effectiveness of open market operations is reduced by the small domestic secondary market for government securities.

Third, Singapore's high dependence on imports means that increases in import prices have a significant effect on domestic prices. According to Low (1994) a 1 per cent increase in the import price index leads to a proportionate increase in wholesale prices and an approximate 0.7 per cent increase in the CPI within two years. The monetarist link between the money supply and the aggregate price level is, therefore, less important than the link through import prices.

The MAS therefore assigns external monetary policy (it targets the exchange rate) to achieve its domestic objectives with respect to inflation and unemployment, because it believes this is the most effective way to achieve these objectives (Teh and Shanmugaratnam, 1992). In principle, the MAS can use exchange rate policy to offset any pressures, domestic or foreign, for inflation to rise beyond its target level. A 1 per cent rise in import prices could be neutralized by an appropriate appreciation of the currency. However, once the exchange rate is the target, the money supply becomes a by-product of this policy. For example, if MAS were to intervene to push up the Singapore dollar by selling US dollars from its official reserves and buying the Singapore dollar on the open market, the money supply would automatically decrease.

Monetary policy is also relatively free to focus on domestic inflation and unemployment because there is no conflict with fiscal policy. In many countries the priority for internal monetary policy is to finance government budget deficits, by extending credit or printing money. The result is high interest rates, crowding out of private investment and limited possibilities for tight monetary policy to be used to tackle inflation instead. In Singapore, however, the government runs a budget surplus so the MAS actually receives funds from the government.

The high domestic savings rate in Singapore, largely due to CPF and public sector surpluses, tends to drain liquidity from the domestic banking sector. By itself this would be deflationary and put pressure on the Singapore dollar to appreciate. At the same time, the net foreign capital inflow, especially FDI associated with export-led growth, increases the net foreign assets of the monetary sector and increases the domestic money supply. The combined effects of the savings-induced liquidity drain and the strong BP on the Singapore dollar could, if left to themselves, undermine export competitiveness. This is why, in the past, the MAS has intervened in the forex market to stop the Singapore dollar from appreciating too fast by buying US dollars and selling the Singapore currency. This simultaneously increases domestic liquidity and official forex reserves.

Since 1981, however, the use of a strong Singapore dollar policy to contain domestic inflation means that, if the MAS forecasts that inflation is going to exceed its target, it will let the currency appreciate in order to lower import prices and subsequently domestic costs and prices, in which case domestic liquidity is automatically reduced. The money supply, BP, exchange rate and official reserves are thus intimately related to each other.

Table 6.9 presents percentage changes (U is in level terms) in some key economic indicators affecting Singapore between 1980 and 1993. The lagged effects of the second oil shock in 1979 resulted in slower OECD income growth and higher global inflationary pressures in the early 1980s. The spillover effects were felt in Singapore through increased inflation (through rising import prices) in 1980 and 1981, and slower export growth in 1981 and 1982. These unfavourable developments in the international arena coincided with booming home demand, especially in construction, and low unemployment. Unit labour costs rose sharply from 1980 to 1982 owing to a combination of high domestic demand and the pass-through of inflationary expectations into wage bargains. The high wage policy after 1979 and the steady rise in employer CPF contribution rates in the early 1980s (to a peak of 25 per cent by 1985) also raised unit business costs. This domestic loss of competitiveness was translated into a higher REER in the early 1980s (see Figure 6.3), but the story is complicated by the managed appreciation by the MAS after 1981 to reduce the effects of imported inflation. Indeed inflation and the rise in *ULC* did slow by 1983. Note that real non-oil domestic exports grew fast in 1983 and 1984.

In 1985 OECD income growth slowed and Singapore export growth was negative. Although external demand (YOECD) was still quite buoyant, it is argued that Singapore was particularly affected by a fall in foreign demand for electronic goods, ship repair and oil refining, and that this coincided with a fall in regional tourism and entrepot trade. Unfortunately for Singapore, this also coincided with a sharp fall in domestic demand, especially in construction. The official view of the recession is that it was the result of a coincidental cyclical downturn in both domestic and external demand in areas which mattered most to Singapore. This part of the story is consistent with our earlier discussion of the 1985 recession in Section 6.2 using value-added data. The loss of competitiveness due to the rise in NEER and REER, which was itself partly due to the strong dollar policy, made matters worse, but it is suggested that other Asian NICs also suffered a slowdown in export demand in 1984 and 1985; yet REER fell for Malaysia and Thailand in the early 1980s (Teh and Shanmugaratnam, 1992).

Table 6.9   Selected macroeconomic indicators, 1980–93

	YOECD	POECD	Y	CPI	X	U	MAN	CON	ULC
	Annual change (per cent)								
1980	1.5	13.5	9.7	8.5	19.8	3.5	10.0	11.0	8.8
1981	1.6	10.8	9.6	8.2	3.0	2.9	9.3	17.6	10.8
1982	–0.8	8.0	6.9	3.9	–5.2	2.6	–3.5	36.4	15.1
1983	2.9	5.6	8.2	1.2	16.9	3.2	2.8	29.3	7.6
1984	5.2	5.6	8.3	2.6	25.9	2.7	7.5	15.5	3.9
1985	3.8	4.9	–1.6	0.5	–4.1	4.1	–7.3	–15.4	1.0
1986	2.9	3.0	1.8	–1.4	23.2	6.5	8.4	–22.4	–11.2
1987	3.4	3.6	9.4	0.5	35.4	4.9	17.3	–9.8	–4.1
1988	4.5	4.3	11.1	1.5	40.7	3.3	18.0	–3.9	3.4
1989	3.2	5.4	9.2	2.4	11.6	2.2	9.8	1.5	8.9
1990	2.3	5.8	8.3	3.4	12.5	1.7	9.5	7.2	8.5
1991	0.8	5.2	6.7	3.4	11.9	1.9	5.4	21.0	7.0
1992	1.6	4.1	6.0	2.3	15.0	2.7	2.5	20.0	2.5
1993	1.3	3.6	10.1	2.4	17.0	2.7	9.8	8.0	–0.5

Note: YOECD is real OECD GDP; POECD is the consumer price index for OECD; Y is real GDP Singapore; CPI is the consumer price index for Singapore; X is real non-oil domestic exports in Singapore; U is the unemployment rate in Singapore (not a growth rate); MAN is real manufacturing output in Singapore; CON is real construction output in Singapore; ULC is unit labour cost in Singapore.

Sources: OECD, *Main Economic Indicators*, various issues; *Statistical Yearbook Singapore*, various issues.

Singapore recovered rapidly from the 1985 recession as the result of a combination of favourable external and internal factors. OECD incomes rose, imported inflation fell and exports grew fast from 1986 to 1988. At the same time domestic manufacturing demand increased and competitiveness improved as ULC and inflation fell (helped by lower employer CPF contributions and wage restraint). The result was a fall in NEER in 1985–7 and in REER in 1985–6 (constant in 1986–7).

Between 1988 and 1993 the international environment displayed steady but not spectacular growth (slower in 1991–3) and moderate inflation, but Singapore exports and GDP growth were impressive. Unemployment reached a historic low at the beginning of the 1990s despite moderate inflation. This strong performance took place even though there was a sharp rise in both NEER and REER after 1988. The MAS argues that the rise in NEER (helped by managed appreciation) was necessary to keep ULC and inflation low to maintain long-run competitiveness and that this outweighed the possible negative effects on exports from the rise in the foreign currency price of exports. Simulating a 1 per cent slower rate of appreciation of the NEER starting in the first quarter of 1988, using the MAS (unpublished) macroeconometric model, increases output and exports in the short run, but given the high import content of Singapore's exports, the effective subsidy is low and is quickly offset in the longer run by a rise in wages in response to both the tighter labour market and the rise in the CPI. The mechanics of the MAS model are analysed in more detail in Chapter 8.

Yip (1994), however, takes issue with the MAS view of events since 1981. In his opinion, the NEER was substantially overvalued compared to his own long-run estimate of PPP (Figure 6.3) from 1981 to 1985, undervalued from 1986 to 1989 and overvalued again from after 1990 onwards. This, he suggests, played an important part in the recession of 1985–6 and has significantly reduced Singapore's export competitiveness in the 1990s, leaving it vulnerable to the same unfavourable circumstances as occurred in the mid-1980s. Since the export competitiveness issue is central to an assessment of government policy, it is worth considering it in more detail.

There is a conventional wisdom that the costs of doing business in Singapore are rising over time and compared to major competitors, and that this is adversely affecting exports and the inflow of FDI. In 1994 Siemens announced it was relocating to China and India, and Thomson relocated TV production to Bangkok and Batam (Indonesia). Yet foreign investment commitments in manufacturing grew by an average of 18 per cent between 1989 and 1993 and real non-oil export growth remained buoyant at 14.1 per cent on average over the same period (Table 6.9 and *Economic Survey of Singapore 1993*, Table A7.5). Moreover a Swiss-based annual competitiveness report, using 381 criteria, consistently places Singapore close to the top of the country rankings, especially with respect to government policies.[23]

One difficulty stems from the choice of REER. If PPP is measured solely in terms of the Singapore dollar–US dollar bilateral exchange rate and the relative movements in their CPI, as depicted in Figure 6.1, the strong Singapore dollar policy may not have created a disequilibrium exchange rate (Abeysinghe and Lee, 1992). Using the REER compiled by the Asian Development Bank confirms the sharp increase in Singapore's REER between 1988 and 1991 compared to Malaysia and Thailand (Figure 6.4), but the competitive picture with respect to the Asian NICs in Figure 6.5 is not so clear.

A study by DBS Bank in 1992 (DBS, 1992) also casts doubt on the view that exchange rate movements have adversely affected the competitiveness of Singapore's exports. In fact Singapore seems to have *improved* its position compared to Hong Kong, Korea, Taiwan, Malaysia and Thailand in both the US and Japanese markets by squeezing profits to maintain export prices.

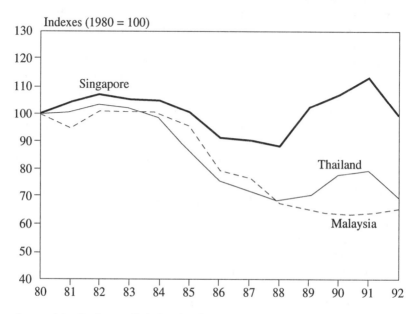

Source: Asian Development Outlook, various issues.

Figure 6.4 Real effective exchange rates, Singapore, Malaysia and Thailand, 1980–92

One way to help resolve this debate would be to disaggregate exports and see how different industries or firms react to changes in cost components, including imported inputs, when setting export prices. Given Singapore's very high import content of manufactured exports, her traditional entrepot exports and increasingly sophisticated service sector (also with high import content), the net effect of a rise in NEER may not be as detrimental to export growth as was once thought, especially where non-price factors are important in determining sales. There is an interesting parallel here with the long-term appreciation of the yen against the US dollar. Although the US trade deficit with Japan has improved since 1987, low-technology products account for most of the gains. The imbalance in high-technology industries actually increased between 1987 and 1990, despite the appreciation of the yen after 1985 (Tyson, 1995). The experience of currency appreciation may even act as an incentive to reduce costs and improve quality and to rationalize production within the global perspective of the MNC by shifting labour-intensive production overseas and purchasing cheaper components from abroad. There is also scope for Singapore to improve its competitive position by increasing research and development. According to DBS (1992, Exhibit 10), Singapore allocated only 0.9 per cent of its GDP to R&D in 1990, compared to 1.3 per cent in Taiwan, 1.8 per cent in South Korea and 2.9 per cent in Japan.

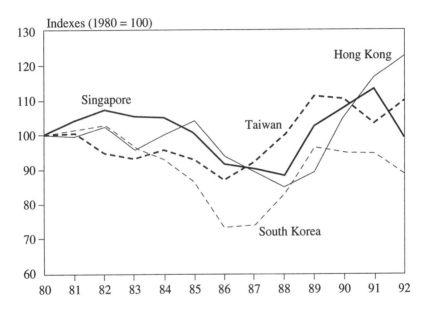

Source: Asian Development Outlook, various issues.

Figure 6.5 Real effective exchange rates, Singapore and East Asian NICs, 1980–92

6.6 SINGAPORE'S INTERNATIONAL RESERVES

All central banks hold official reserves comprising a mixture of stocks of convertible foreign currencies, commodities such as gold, and special drawing rights (SDRs) issued by the IMF.[24] A country may also hold a positive net balance of reserve assets at the IMF.[25] Table 6.10 shows Singapore's total official reserves in 1992 to be US$39.9 billion. Of these, 99.44 per cent are foreign exchange holdings (including gold), with negligible amounts of SDRs (0.17 per cent) and reserves at the IMF (0.39 per cent) (*International Financial Statistics*, June 1994). The amount of reserves declared to the IMF includes those liquid foreign assets such as bank deposits, treasury bills or other government securities available for official foreign exchange intervention, or to finance a balance of payments deficit. The assets of the MAS, however, include such items as the deposits which financial institutions in Singapore are required to hold at the MAS as reserves in exchange for government debt, and savings from the government and statutory boards. This makes it difficult to unravel the flow of funds into Singapore's official reserves from the different public and private sources, including the CPF and the unpublished foreign investment income generated by the Government Investment Corporation (Low and Toh, 1989). The official view is that the MAS has its own funds primarily to 'manage' the Singapore dollar, while the GIC acts as a resource bank to 'manage' the reserves. The primary objective of the GIC is thus to safeguard public funds, largely through hedging, rather than to make money in the forex market by speculating.

Table 6.10   Singapore's official international reserves

	1963–69	1970–79	1980–87	1988–93	1963–93
	Average annual growth (%)				
Singapore	15	18	12	17	15
1992	Reserves (US$ billions)	Per capita		Months of imports	
Singapore	39.9	14 244		5.7	
Switzerland	61.0	8 841		6.7	
Taiwan	86.8	4 341		11.5	
UAE	6.0	3 516		—	
Norway	12.3	2 868		3.1	

Note: Reserves are gross official end of year total reserves; UAE is United Arab Emirates.

Sources: *Yearbook of Statistics Singapore*; *World Development Report 1994*, Table 17; *Asian Development Outlook* (1993).

It is somewhat easier to interpret the relationship between changes in Singapore's overall BP and changes in reserve assets, since an increase in the BP surplus is translated into a counterpart rise in reserve assets. In 1992, for example, Singapore recorded an overall BP surplus of US$6.1 billion in the IMF accounts and a corresponding rise in reserve assets of the same amount (with an opposite sign). Reserves and related items thus came to the same thing. By contrast, in the same year, Nigeria experienced a BP deficit of US$5.638 billion, which was financed by a fall in reserve assets of US$3.727 billion and 'exceptional financing' from the IMF to the tune of US$1.911 billion.[26] Thus Nigerian reserves and related items fell by US$5.638 billion dollars but only 3.727 billion of this was due to a fall in reserves.

Although Singapore does not have the highest absolute reserves in the world in 1992 (US reserves are 148 billion), according to Table 6.10 it does have the highest per capita, at US$14 244, well above its nearest rivals (Switzerland and Taiwan). Are the reserves too high?

Central banks hold reserves of liquid assets to transact from day to day in the forex market, as a precaution against unexpected BP deficits, or to lend to other central banks. Although central banks are not generally motivated to make profits by taking large risks with their portfolios of reserve assets, they will nonetheless alter their portfolios in line with changing expectations about the risk and return characteristics of the assets they hold, and they will have a certain attitude towards the amount of risk they are willing to take. The quantity of reserves must be sufficient to be able to finance trade and payments without liquidity crises or a loss of confidence in the currency, and the composition of the reserves portfolio will depend on expectations about the risk and return characteristics of the assets available, together with a subjective preference with respect to risk and return. Objectively countries which are very open to trade and investment flows, which experience relatively high volatility in such flows, or whose currency is subject to frequent speculative activity, will tend to hold higher reserves. Certainly Singapore is a very open economy with potentially volatile trade and investment flows, but the fact that the Singapore dollar is not a truly international currency held in large quantities by non-residents or other central banks means that speculative activity in the Singapore dollar is relatively small.

The official view is that the current level of reserves is necessary, given Singapore's high import dependence, to instil stability and confidence in Singapore as an international monetary centre, and to keep the Singapore dollar 'strong' to combat inflation, when necessary, through the policy of managed floating. They are also required as a 'shock absorber' against unexpected capital outflows. A common international criterion is for reserves to be sufficient to finance about three to four months of imports. The data in Table 6.10 show that, on this score, Singapore has less import coverage than Switzerland or Taiwan. But if entrepot trade is excluded, on the grounds that there is no need to buy imports for re-export, but only for domestic consumption and for intermediate use in production, the figure rises from 5.7 to 9.8.[27] According to the World Bank classification (*World Development Report 1994*, Table 17), the average import requirements for all 20 high-income countries, including Singapore, in

1992 is 2.8. This rises to 3.2 if Taiwan and South Korea are added (Hong Kong data are not available). This further rises to 3.7 if we add 36 upper-middle-income countries.[28] Of course one can always justify any level of reserves or savings according to a doomsday scenario, or on the grounds of extreme vulnerability to external political threat (Taiwan), but it is not good economics. Singapore has substantial in-built stabilizers to deal with export shocks and a low risk rating for borrowing in international markets. Prudent government budgetary policies and financial credibility are all-important, but the analogy with households in debt or businesses going bankrupt is a false one in international finance. Sovereign governments cannot go bankrupt and the international financial system has shown itself in the past to be quite capable of dealing with temporary crises affecting individual countries.

A more subtle justification for a high level of reserves in Singapore is the need for the reserves to grow in line with increased population and living standards, to provide a 'nest-egg' to cover future liabilities to CPF holders within the context of an ageing population. The reserves have certainly played an integral part in Singapore's development strategy over the last three decades as forced savings through the CPF mechanism have been used to provide development infrastructure, such as roads and buildings, while, at the same time, some of these domestic assets have been converted into a diversified portfolio of foreign assets at the MAS and GIC. Indeed, as discussed in the previous section, the liquidity drain which public savings have generated has a direct counterpart in the accumulation of official forex reserves whenever the MAS intervenes to buy US dollars in exchange for Singapore dollars through managed floating. The high savings rate in Singapore has thus enabled Singapore to finance development in a non-inflationary fashion without recourse to deficit financing, foreign aid or commercial foreign debt, while at the same time achieving export-led growth based upon an inflow of FDI (Sandilands, 1992). The latter is especially efficient since the scarce inputs needed for export-led growth (technology, specialized capital inputs, marketing outlets and managerial expertise) do not have to be purchased separately from the global market but come already 'wrapped up' in a package in the form of the MNCs. But there are, of course, opportunity costs to high savings and reserve accumulation through the constraint on domestic consumption and the alternative real returns which might be earned on public sector surpluses, both domestically and as foreign assets. The returns on public savings and reserve holdings are not public information but according to *The Economist* (Financial Indicators, 8 September 1994) the real return on pension funds in Singapore between 1983 and 1993 of 2.3 per cent per annum is the lowest of the 18 countries cited.

There is an expectation in Singapore that, as the magnitude of the surplus savings required for basic development falls, the reserves will reach a plateau. At the same time, public sector funds with the MAS will fall as citizens are given more freedom over the use of CPF funds in their portfolio decisions, financial institutions are required to hold less government debt and government bodies begin to rely more on commercial risk management services. It is also possible that more details of the nations's wealth, including the fixed assets of the GIC, will be made available and the flow of funds between the various government and non-government bodies will be made more transparent. The figures in Table 6.10, however, give no indication of a slowdown in the growth of the official reserves in the 1990s. In an interview with *Euromoney* in February 1995, Finance Minister Richard Hu reiterated the government's policy of 'encouraging people not to spend too much on consumption' and to 'put aside every dollar we can lay our hands on'. The size of the reserves and the responsibility for managing them will continue to be an important political issue in Singapore. Indeed one of the reasons for the appointment of an elected President of the Republic since 1993 is to act as a protector of the national reserves to prevent a future elected government squandering the national wealth (Low and Toh, 1989).

6.7 SINGAPORE AS AN INTERNATIONAL FINANCIAL CENTRE

Singapore satisfies many of the essential requirements for an international financial centre (Tan Chwee Huat, 1992; Luckett *et al.*, 1994). It has a strong domestic economy, a stable currency and a strategic location, both in terms of physical sea and air trade routes, and overlapping financial market time zones. It also boasts a substantial foreign presence in terms of banks and other financial institutions and a long history of commercial trading in the region. These are important reasons why Singapore has the fourth largest forex market in the world measured by average daily turnover. On the other hand, domestic financial markets are still relatively underdeveloped with respect to secondary markets for government bonds and securities and risk management services. Also the Singapore dollar is not internationalized in the same way as the US dollar or the yen and the government continues to take steps to prevent its further internationalization.

Unlike other major financial centres, such as New York and London, which developed in a largely spontaneous fashion to service the demand for financial services, the former enhanced by its role as a headquarters for MNCs after the Second World War and the latter through the commercial network associated with the British Empire and Commonwealth, the development of Singapore as a financial centre has been more the result of conscious government initiative. Good examples of this are the development of offshore financial markets based in Singapore, including the Asian Currency Market (ACM) and the Asian Dollar Bond Market (ADBM).

The ACM began operating in Singapore in 1968 when the Singapore branch of the Bank of America was given a licence to set up an Asian Currency Unit (ACU) to deal in US dollars or other hard currencies. This is equivalent to the Eurodollar Market, except that ACUs are located in Asia. The decision to set up ACUs was taken primarily to attract non-resident Asian deposits to lend to foreign corporations or government agencies for development in the region, to further Singapore's ambition to develop as a regional financial centre and to diversify away from manufacturing into services. The intention was to keep the offshore market separate from the onshore financial system so they would not compete with each other. Tax exemptions on offshore income applied only to non-residents and, until recently, residents could not deposit or borrow to finance trade and investment.

Although the turnover in the ADM (Asian Dollar Market) is still small compared to the Eurodollar market, the number of ACUs had reached 198 by 1991, with assets/liabilities amounting to US$355 billion by 1992. These assets are mostly short-term (maturity of less than three months) and are predominantly lent and borrowed between banks.[29] The market is attractive because ACUs are exempt from the usual reserve requirements imposed on domestic banks and favourable tax treatment is offered for the ACU units themselves and non-resident depositors. Competitive rates are offered for borrowers as well as opportunities for portfolio diversification.

The ADBM is the equivalent in Asia of the Eurobond Market. It takes the form of buying and selling, in primary and secondary domestic capital markets, of bonds denominated in a foreign hard currency, usually the US dollar. It is a market for long-term and medium-term funds, involving financial institutions in Singapore, and the bonds are listed on the local stock exchange. The market began in Singapore in 1971 when the Development Bank of Singapore (largely government-owned) floated bonds worth US$10 million for redemption in 1982, guaranteed by the Singapore government. Further issues by Singapore Airlines (1976) and Keppel Shipyards (1975–7) followed. Japanese banks and corporations tended to dominate the market in the mid-1970s, but over time the market has attracted a wide range of international interest. By 1991 the cumulative total of issues amounted to 111 (Tan Chwee Huat, 1992, Table 10.1).

In 1985 the Economic Committee, set up to re-examine economic policy in the light of the 1985 recession, recommended that Singapore should take steps to develop itself into a risk management centre based upon a range of money market and capital market activities. To stimulate the development of fund management activities the Committee suggested various fiscal reforms to remove existing obstacles to the development of domestic fund management services and changes in the funding practices of government ministries and statutory boards. A key step was the announcement in 1994 that from January 1995 CPF funds could be used to invest in overseas stocks, initially on the Stock

Exchange of Singapore, but subsequently on regional markets (by January 1999). This further frees the use of CPF funds for approved investment purposes, a process which has gathered momentum in the 1990s, to stimulate the use of risk management services by households and increase the returns on CPF funds. Government-linked companies and statutory boards will also have to use capital markets for funding instead of relying on POSBank and savings banks. This includes the GIC, which will be investing with fund management companies operating in Singapore rather than directly through Tokyo or New York. The hope is that this will lead to an increased volume of funds in the hands of professional fund managers in Singapore.

Although the Singapore government has encouraged the development of offshore financial markets, such as the ADM and the ADBM, it has preferred to keep these markets separate from the onshore financial system to insulate the domestic monetary system and prevent the offshore market impeding the development of the domestic financial system. Similarly, although steps have been taken to promote Singapore as an international financial centre, the government is not anxious to internationalize the Singapore dollar by encouraging the creation of a market for depositing and lending the Singapore dollar outside Singapore. Singapore's Finance Minister, Dr Richard Hu, emphasized the government's cautious stance with respect to the further internationalization of the Singapore dollar in an interview for *Euromoney* in February 1995.

Internationalization would involve non-residents holding Singapore dollar deposits in Singapore, banks located in Singapore would lend to non-residents in Singapore dollars, non-residents would hold Singapore government securities and corporate bonds, and foreign central banks could hold the Singapore dollar as a reserve asset and use it as an intervention currency in the forex market. At present none of these activities is encouraged. ACUs are not allowed to trade in the Singapore dollar, domestic bank lending to non-residents in Singapore dollars is restricted, unless the end-use is within Singapore – for trade financing or manufacturing investment or for housing development. The holding of Singapore government securities and corporate bonds by non-residents is also made unattractive by a withholding tax. In February 1995 the MAS issued a warning to the banks in Singapore to stop the practice known as 'roundtripping' by which the banks arrange with their non-bank customers in Singapore to place Singapore dollar deposits with their sister branches or subsidiaries outside Singapore to earn a higher return and to circumvent MAS reserve requirements.

There are certain advantages from allowing a currency to become internationalized. Singapore exporters and importers would no longer face forex risk if payments and receipts are made in Singapore dollar. This would also apply to Singapore companies investing abroad. The volume and depth of the financial market in Singapore may be expected to increase as Singapore dollar-denominated assets are increasingly traded in the region (especially in Singapore), and

Singapore trade and investment may be stimulated if regional trade and investment flows are facilitated by being financed in Singapore dollars. Singapore would also be in a position to earn 'seignorage' by issuing international money, in the same way as the USA does at present, as long as the rest of the world is prepared to accept Singapore dollars in exchange for goods, services and assets.[30]

The MAS view is that further internationalization should proceed at a controlled pace to ameliorate the increased vulnerability of Singapore to the speculative monetary and capital flows which internationalization may bring with it. The gains from seignorage and the reduction of forex risk may be relatively small in magnitude and adequate liquidity for regional trade and payments is available from the existing ADM and ADBM. The increased vulnerability to speculative monetary and capital flows would constitute a serious problem for a highly open economy such as Singapore. Moreover the increase in the pool of Singapore dollars outside Singapore would imply a further loss of control by the MAS over monetary policy. Simulation exercises using a macro-econometric model based at the National University of Singapore in 1992 (Econometric Studies Unit, 1992) appear to confirm these worst fears. An explosive growth in the money supply and related fall in domestic interest rates generates a domestic boom, with negative feedback effects on investment and output, and a loss of monetary control by the MAS. For reasons discussed in Chapter 8, this may be an overly dramatic interpretation of the likely effects of a sudden internationalization, but internationalization would certainly make it more difficult for MAS to implement its anti-inflationary policy through external monetary policy. At present the MAS is confident that it has sufficient resources to deal with a speculative attack as it did during the 1985 recession.

There is, of course, nothing to stop the autonomous internationalization of the Singapore dollar. It has already become acceptable de facto in settlement for tourism services in neighbouring Johor (Malaysia) and the Riau islands (Indonesia).[31] There is also a leakage of Singapore dollars offshore as Singapore companies increase their investment overseas. The allocation of Singapore dollars to which foreign banks are allowed access has also been raised, in line with economic growth, to S$100 million by 1995. In this sense, the MAS is engaged in a rearguard action. There will be increasing pressures to remove the restrictions on internationalization as Singapore develops as an international financial centre from, for example, foreign companies wishing to list on the Singapore Stock Exchange in Singapore dollars to remove currency risk. These pressures are likely to increase as Singapore competes with other emerging financial centres, especially in the rapidly growing derivatives market. On the other hand, the process of internationalization is likely to be slow. In spite of the weakness of the US economy since the late 1960s and the rise of 'strong' currency rivals such as the yen and the German mark (at least until the unification of Germany), and attempts to expand the use of the SDR and European Currency Unit (ECU) between central banks, over half of world trade and 51 per cent of world foreign exchange reserves in 1991 were still denominated in US dollars (*The Economist*, 9 September 1991). The nearest rival is the German mark, with 19 per cent of world forex reserves.

SUGGESTIONS FOR FURTHER READING

For some background on the structure of trade in Singapore, the evolution of trade policy and the role of foreigners and foreign resources, see Lim and associates (1988) and Koh (1987). The interpretation of Singapore as a VORE is based on Lloyd and Sandilands (1986). Tan Chwee Huat (1992) and Lee (1990) provide useful detail on the financial system in Singapore, including the forex market and offshore capital markets. The MAS view of monetary and fiscal policy in the context of exchange rate targeting, together with an assessment of its policies since 1980, can be found in Teh and Shanmugaratnam (1992).

NOTES

1. The import penetration ratio for Singapore in Table 6.1 exceeds 100, implying that exports exceed production, because entrepot exports are included.
2. The growth of intra-industry trade, especially for developed countries and the newly industrializing countries, such as Singapore, has had important repercussions on trade theory. For a review, see Greenaway and Milner (1986).
3. See Lloyd and Sandilands (1986), Woon (1991) and Tan (1995).
4. This means the trade to GDP ratio in Table 6.1 is exaggerated, since it includes both officially defined entrepot exports, including oil, and intermediate inputs used in export production.
5. The structural changes experienced by Singapore over this period are similar to those of other countries undergoing a process of rapid industrialization. See Chenery (1960), Chenery *et al.* (1986) and, for an application of this analysis to Singapore, Tan (1995).
6. Singapore–Australia trade is also more important than in the past, accounting for 2.3 per cent of Singapore's exports and 1.7 per cent of her imports. Saudi Arabia supplies 3.9 per cent of Singapore's imports but almost exclusively in the form of crude oil for refining and export.
7. These contributions are even higher if you add the indirect effects of export expansion on domestic demand and import substitution through its stimulatory effect on GDP itself. See Tan (1995).
8. Earlier discussions of trade policy in Singapore can be found in Tan (1984), Lim and associates (1988) and Koh (1987).
9. It has been surprisingly difficult to determine the pattern of Singapore's comparative advantage, largely because of the distortions introduced into factor intensities by the high import content of exports. When adjustments are made, however, the facts are broadly in line with an extended Heckscher–Ohlin framework. See Tan (1984), Wong (1984) and Sandilands and Tan (1986).
10. For an assessment of the achievements of ASEAN, see Wong (1988). More recent developments in ASEAN economic integration, including AFTA and growth triangles, are discussed in Ariff (1994) and Chia (1994b).
11. The five founding countries – Indonesia, Malaysia, Singapore, Thailand and the Philippines – were joined by Brunei in 1984 and Vietnam in 1995.

12. Note that other service items such as shipment are not shown in Table 6.6 but are still counted in the overall service balance. In the IMF accounts investment income is called 'income'. Service items together with unrequited transfers are often called 'invisibles'.

13. With FDI the MNC owns and controls the income-generating assets (factories, hotels). Portfolio investment, on the other hand, implies certain rights over the income from holding a financial asset such as a bond, but the bondholder does not become directly involved in the process which generates the income.

14. The IMF entry directly below the overall balance is called 'official reserves and related items' and a separate entry is made afterwards for official reserves on their own. For Singapore these related items are zero, so this distinction is not made.

15. The basic balance is not published for earlier years but is approximated in Table 6.6 as the sum of the current account and non-monetary capital account. The figure for 1992, however, is the published figure.

16. The IMF regularly publishes the NEER for most countries in the world, and the REER for developed industrial countries, in its *International Financial Statistics*. The Asian Development Bank also publishes the NEER and the REER for its members, including Singapore, in its annual *Asian Development Outlook*.

17. If $R = P/P^*$ then $RER = RP^*/P$ will equal unity and $\log RER = \log R - \log(P/P^*)$ will equal zero.

18. The testing of PPP assumes that R is an equilibrium rate. If, as is the case for Singapore, R is a managed or official rate, a deviation of R from PPP need not imply that PPP is incorrect (Abeysinghe and Lee, 1992).

19. If capital and currency markets are efficient, profit-motivated arbitrage will quickly eliminate differences in real risk-adjusted interest rates between countries. Remaining differences will reflect forex risk. The relationship between interest rates and spot and forward exchange rates is based upon the theory of covered interest arbitrage (Caves *et al.*, 1993).

20. There is also a monetary approach to the determination of exchange rates, often linked to PPP, based upon the process of equilibrating the supply and demand for money (currency) in each country. Since the difficulties associated with the identification of stable causal monetary flows has been emphasized in Chapter 5, this approach is not discussed further here.

21. In international economics these issues are discussed in the context of the attempt to achieve simultaneous internal and external balance by 'assigning' various policy instruments to domestic and foreign economic objectives (Caves *et al.*, 1993).

22. A fiscal expansion will raise interest rates and attract short-term foreign capital. This, in turn, leads to a currency appreciation, a worsening of the current account and the shifting of the *IS* curve to the left until *IS–LM–BP* equilibrium is restored (Caves *et al.*, 1993, chap. 22).

23. In 1994 Singapore was second overall out of 41 countries and first in terms of government policies. The report is discussed in *The Economist*, 9 October 1994.

24. SDRs were first issued to member countries in the early 1970s to increase international liquidity. They take the form of accounting entries at the IMF which can be used by central banks to settle debts among themselves or to intervene in the forex market. The value of the SDR is currently based upon a basket of currencies. Although SDRs constituted only about 2 per cent of total international reserves in 1993, the SDR is the official unit of account at the IMF and is also a reference point for some commercial financial assets.

25. A country's net reserve position at the IMF will be positive if its reserve tranche exceeds any credit it may be receiving under the IMF's various borrowing facilities. The reserve tranche is a deposit of reserves made by a country according to its quota allocation. If the IMF is a net user of the member's currency, this reserve deposit will also increase.

26. The data for Singapore and Nigeria are from the IMF *International Financial Statistics*, June 1994. BP and reserve data are published here for each member country on a monthly and annual basis, together with world aggregates.

27. Import requirements are calculated by dividing total reserves by one-twelfth of the value of imports in the same year. Retained imports for Singapore were approximated by total imports less entrepot exports. The latter are used as a proxy for entrepot imports in the absence of alternative data.

28. Botswana was excluded from the upper-middle-income category since it appears to have an import coverage figure of 18!
29. According to the *Economic Survey of Singapore 1993*, Table A8.6, inter-bank loans constituted 55 per cent of assets and 79 per cent of liabilities in 1992.
30. 'Seignorage' comes from the French word for a mediaeval lord or seigneur who had the right to put his stamp on coins. Seignorage is the benefit given to the first issuer of an international currency, based on the difference between its cost of issue (negligible for the Singapore dollar) and the value of the goods, services and assets it buys in international trade. Once it has been spent it takes on the characteristics of conventional money.
31. For details on the gradual internationalization of the Singapore dollar since 1978, in terms of non-resident holdings and payments, see Hewson, in Tan and Kapur (1986).

7. Growth and cycles

In this chapter we summarize the research that has tried to account quantitatively for Singapore's high growth rates and then review the nature of the cyclical fluctuations in Singapore's growth path in the light of some of the insights we gained from Chapters 3 and 4.

7.1 ACCOUNTING FOR GROWTH

Long-term growth in any country depends on the growth of the quantities of the factors of production available and the efficiency with which they are used. We can capture the nature of this by using a form of the aggregate production function that appeared first in Chapter 3:

$$Y = A(K^d N^{(1-d)})$$

The notation is the same. Here we have presented a specific form of the production function: one with constant returns to scale as the sum of the exponents of the capital term and labour term have been set equal to unity. This is the most common form of this function used in empirical work concerning growth in Singapore. If we assume profit maximization, competition and consumer equilibrium then, together with constant returns to scale, the exponents d and $(1-d)$ represent the share of total income accruing to capital and labour, respectively. This is a useful assumption as it makes estimates of relative importance of different factors contributing to growth possible. Here we have added another term represented by the term A. This factor, known as total factor productivity (TFP), is non-observable and is assumed to grow over time. The evidence from developed countries is that it does. We can see that

$$A = Y/(K^d N^{(1-d)})$$

In principle we could estimate A for each year if we had the relevant data but most studies are more concerned with the rate at which A grows as we can see that growth in A can increase output without there being any increase in the capital input, K, or the labour input, N.

The purpose of growth accounting is to try to estimate the relative importance of three factors contributing to growth: growth in TFP, growth in the capital input and growth in the labour input. We can derive the required framework easily. Take logarithms and differentiate with respect to time and we obtain the relationship in terms of growth rates:

$$y = a + dk + (1-d)n$$

which means that output growth is the sum of TFP growth (a) plus the growth rate of the capital input weighted by its share in output plus labour input growth weighted by its share of income. Estimates of the variables y, k and n can, in principle, be derived from statistical sources and so the term a is estimated as a residual. Some studies further decompose the inputs into different types of capital, perhaps add land as an input and use different types of labour input. There are many significant data problems in applying this technique in any economy and they are probably more serious for the case of Singapore. There are no official capital stock figures, so this series has to be estimated using a guess of the capital stock in some early year of the study and then adding gross investment minus some reasonable estimate for depreciation. The data on the share of income going to labour and capital are crude.

7.2   GROWTH ACCOUNTING FOR SINGAPORE

One of the first applications of this technique to Singapore's early growth experience was Tsao (1986) which examined the period 1966–80. This pioneering work clearly recognized the huge data problems and made several sets of estimates using different assumptions about the possible rate of depreciation and the factor shares in output. The period under study was 1966–80 but it was only possible to calculate the required data for the single year 1966 and for each year from 1972 to 1980 inclusive, so the average growth rates for the period 1966–72 were based on the end points whereas those for 1972–80 could be calculated from a full annual series. Estimates of the capital and labour series were based on three indices for each. The results showed that for the period 1966–72 capital grew at an average annual rate of 16.7 per cent and labour by 6.0 per cent per annum. After 1972 capital grew by 10.9 per cent per annum and labour by 5.5 per cent. This shows that capital grew faster in the earlier period but the average labour growth rate was roughly the same. The estimates of the sources of output growth were very interesting and are summarized in Table 7.1.

Tsao performed sensitivity analysis using different assumptions necessary to generate the data, but the picture remained very much the same. These results showed that all of Singapore's output growth could be explained in terms of increases in the quantities of factors of production used, particularly capital, and that there had been no TFP growth. Studies in developed countries suggest that anything from one-third to one-half of observed growth is due to productivity growth, so this was a remarkable finding for Singapore. Tsao (1985) had also looked at productivity growth in 28 manufacturing industries for the period 1970–79. There was virtually no TFP growth for the average of all industries and it was negative for 17 of them. There was no correlation between output growth and TFP growth across industries. In South Korea and Japan productivity growth had accounted for 21 and 18 per cent of actual growth, respectively, for a similar period, whereas in Singapore it contributed just less than 10 per cent. No wonder this paper was entitled 'Growth without productivity'.

Table 7.1   Estimates of the sources of output growth, 1966–80 (per cent per annum)

	Output growth	Contribution of		
	y	Capital	Labour	TFP
1966–72	12.5	9.3	2.7	0.6
1972–80	8.0	6.8	2.1	–0.9

Source: Adapted from Tsao (1986, Table 2.5).

Tsao (1986) offered some reasons for this state of affairs. Unlike the situation in developing economies, Singapore did not have a large agricultural sector from which labour could be transferred to higher-productivity manufacturing jobs. Government manpower policies of the 1970s could have restrained TFP growth as they allowed a large increase in the foreign labour force after the first oil shock and wage increases were restrained. This was thought to be a deterrent to efforts aimed at increasing productivity (Tsao, 1986, p.30).

Tsao did see some evidence that in the later years of her sample, 1977–80, TFP growth rates did become positive and she thought this might be a consequence of the 'corrective high wage policy of 1979–81'. She hoped that this was an indication of further increases in productivity (Tsao, 1986, pp.30–31).

An early reaction to Tsao's 1986 paper was that of Lim (1986) who noted that her 'explanation of the low rate of TFP growth does not appear to be completely impeccable' and 'it is extremely difficult to disprove her main conclusion of the low rate of TFP growth unless one goes through the whole process of her definitions, methodology and computation oneself' (Lim, 1986, pp.5–6). Lim's main comment was: 'if a country can raise its standard of living so spectacularly with a very low TFP growth, does it then matter whether TFP growth is low?' This comment misses the point and does so in a way that is common in Singapore. Economists are used to looking at and comparing the costs and benefits of any activity. Here Lim is just looking at the benefit, increasing living standards resulting from high growth, and ignoring the cost of achieving such a growth rate. This point was brought out more vividly in the work of Alwyn Young, which we will review shortly, but it was already apparent in the estimate of Tsao. Singapore was growing at a rate similar to that of Hong Kong, but this was accompanied by a much higher rate of investment and capital accumulation in Singapore compared with Hong Kong (Peebles, 1988, pp.61,77). The cost to the economy was a low rate of consumption, the lowest rate in the world. That is why it matters.

Young's initial work compared the growth performance of Singapore and Hong Kong using a similar accounting framework. Table 7.2 reports his major findings. Again different estimates were made on the basis of different assumptions to check the sensitivity of the results to the basic assumptions necessary for generating any estimates. The estimates imply, for example, that of the 51 per cent increase in output over the period 1966–70, 14 per cent was due to extra labour, 64 per cent to more capital and 23 per cent to TFP growth. This is the highest estimate for TFP growth for any sub-period. For other periods TFP growth was negative or virtually zero and for the entire period its contribution was minus 8 per cent of recorded growth. In other words, the increase in quantities of labour and capital accounted for 108 per cent of growth. The largest factor causing growth was capital stock growth. In Hong Kong, TFP growth contributed significantly to output growth, explaining on average 30–50 per cent of output growth.

Table 7.2 Contributions to growth, 1966–90

	Output growth	Contribution of		
		Labour	Capital	TFP
1966–70	0.507	0.14	0.64	0.23
1970–75	0.454	0.31	1.05	−0.36
1975–80	0.408	0.32	0.63	0.05
1980–85	0.300	0.42	0.78	−0.20
1970–90	1.545	0.25	0.83	−0.08

Source: Adapted from Young (1992, Tables 5 and 6).

In response to Tsao's hope that TFP growth would rise in the 1980s we can see that Young's estimates imply that it was negative over the period 1980–85 and 120 per cent of that period's growth could be explained solely in terms of increases in quantities of capital and labour.

Young's explanation of this remarkable difference focuses on the low education level of Singaporean workers in the 1940s and 1950s compared with those in Hong Kong and the nature of Singapore's growth policies. He argues that the government's policies of industrial transformation have pushed production from one sector to another (textiles to electronics and refining then to clothing and electronics and banking services) too rapidly for there to be enough time for higher productivity rates to be achieved. A quantitative estimate of structural transformation in manufacturing suggests that the extent of transformation in Singapore has been twice that in Korea and two-and-a-half times that in Hong Kong (Young, 1992, pp.28–9).

Young (1994a; 1994b) returns to these comparisons on a much broader scale, making estimates for a few East Asian countries in Young (1994a). Some of his estimates for Singapore were able to benefit from access to unpublished data from the Singapore government. His theme is that, with the exception of Hong Kong which does seem to have achieved high productivity growth, the experience of the Asian NICs shows that they have achieved growth, not through 'unusually rapid productivity growth in manufactures but, rather, that they have successfully expanded investment and employment in manufactures, hence the title: industrializing' (Young, 1994b, p.972).

Young (1994b) offers some interesting rankings of the high-performing Asian NICs, including Singapore. In terms of growth of per capita output over the period 1960–85, the six fastest growing economies, in order out of a sample of 118, were Botswana, Taiwan, Hong Kong, Singapore, South Korea and Japan. However, if we look at the growth of output per worker, which is a better indicator of productivity growth, Taiwan fell to fourth place, South Korea to seventh, Hong Kong to eighth and Singapore to fourteenth. In terms of TFP growth over the period 1970–85, out of 66 countries Hong Kong is sixth fastest growing and Singapore 63rd, with an average rate of 0.1 per cent per annum, not much different from the numbers implied by the earlier estimates. Last is Switzerland, with zero TFP growth. As it is the richest country in the world, in terms of GNP per capita, this resurrects the question: what does it matter if TFP growth is low or zero? The answer is that Switzerland, Singapore's chosen role model, *is* the richest country in the world, has GNP per capita growing at about 1.4 per cent per year, only invests about 24 per cent of its GDP at home and its private consumption is 59 per cent of GDP.

Young's work is now being cited in standard macroeconomic textbooks such as Dornbusch and Fischer (1994, p.251) and we expect to see these comparisons become more common in macroeconomic textbooks as they take a more comparative stance and include information on the Asian growth miracle.

It would be an exaggeration to say that Young's claims became the hot topic of conversation of the *kopi tiam* (coffee shops) of Singapore, but they did generate some debate that tended to concentrate on two points. One was similar to Lim's earlier response that it did not matter what the possibly inaccurate estimates of an unobservable theoretical concept implied. The evidence was before everyone's eyes: Singapore had progressed without TFP growth, so it did not matter. The second argument pointed out that much of Singapore's investment has been in infrastructure, especially in public housing, and this could not be expected to contribute directly to productivity growth. There is a supporting hypothesis that could have been cited which argues that it is investment in equipment that contributes to output growth (De Long and Summers, 1991). The World Bank study, *The East Asian Miracle*, did use this in its regressions, in place of the cruder ratio of total investment to GDP, and found that it was a significant factor in explaining growth differences in a smaller sample of 54 countries. If tests were done using only investment in machinery, or if directly non-productive investments were given a lower weight in the calculation of the capital index, this might reduce Singapore's 'investment' to GDP ratio to something similar to that of Hong Kong and suggest that there was not a massive amount of capital accumulation that was not being use efficiently. Our estimates of A might now be larger as our estimate of K would be lower. However, if we were to use the growth accounting approach, we might get the same results because the growth rate of this new 'investment' concept might be the same as that calculated for K so there would be no difference in capital's contribution to output growth (k^d).

Apart from these informal reactions there have been two technical papers challenging Young's findings. One 'would like to dispel the pessimism implied by negative TFP estimated for Singapore and its relatively higher usage of capital but lower returns from capital compared to Hong Kong's experience' (Toh and Low, 1994, p.2). The authors constructed their own capital series for the period 1970–92 on the basis of regression analysis and it implied a growth in the capital–output ratio from 1.67 in 1970 to 3.03 in 1992. Using this capital stock series, growth accounting estimates were made to explain the growth of GDP using different assumptions about the share of labour in output. The estimates implied a virtually zero TFP growth contribution over the entire period 1971–92 but the rate was higher after 1981, contributing either 0.51 or 1.87 percentage points of the observed 7 per cent output growth after 1981.

The other paper looked at TFP growth in manufacturing in the 1980s. This was thought to be a direct way of challenging Young's claims as he 'argued that the low TFP growth can be traced to the Singapore government's "industrial targeting" policy which, by rapidly encouraging new industries, tends to shift the technological frontiers of these industries far beyond the learning capability of the labour force' (Wong and Gan, 1994, p.178 – the first author being a senior economist at the MAS). They examined TFP growth in 27 manufacturing industries during the 1980s and drew comparisons with those in Tsao (1985). Their claim is that their estimates show that from 1981 to 1990 overall TFP growth contributed 1.6 percentage points (24 per cent) of the observed 6.7 per cent average growth in gross manufacturing output. Over the period 1981–5 TFP growth was negative but after 1986 it rose, contributing four percentage points (33 per cent) to the observed 12.05 per cent per annum increase in manufacturing gross output. The authors of the second paper see this as showing that 'TFP had been a significant contribution to output growth in the Singapore manufacturing sector during the 1980s' (Wong and Gan, 1994, pp.180–81). However, of their 27 industries, we can observe that, for the entire decade of the 1980s, 16 showed negative TFP growth offset by positive growth in 11 industries. After 1986 TFP growth was negative in 12 industries, offset by large positive estimates in a few sectors such as tobacco products (17.04 per cent per annum TFP growth), non-ferrous metal products (11.59 per cent per annum), non-metallic mineral products (15.14 per cent per annum), food (7.70 per cent per annum) and transport equipment (7.60 per cent per annum). These high figures for certain sectors could be contributing to the higher average figure for TFP growth after 1986 and the authors do comment that 'the fact that a large number of industries experienced low or negative average TFP growth during the decade [1980s] remains an issue of concern' (ibid., p.192).

7.3 CROSS-SECTION EVIDENCE ON GROWTH

Recently another approach to identifying the main factors contributing to growth has become more common and has been used by the World Bank in its study, *The East Asian Miracle* (1993). The approach uses cross-section regression over a large sample of countries. It uses common sense to suggest which variables should be included and then tries to assess their relative importance. Barro (1991) is an example of this approach. The World Bank's study presents a number of such regressions, one based on the experiences of 113 countries over the period 1960–85. Average annual per capita GDP growth is the variable to be explained.

We cite one such equation in Table 7.3, which shows that the high-performing Asian economies (HPAEs) grew nearly 2 per cent faster than all the others in the sample, whereas those of Latin America and Sub-Saharan Africa grew about 1 per cent more slowly. The main factors behind growth were differences in the relative level of GDP from that of the USA in 1960. The lower this ratio, the faster the country grew after 1960. This represents a form of catching up due to the fact that many of these countries were mainly agricultural and so could shift labour into manufacturing. This is not likely to have been a factor behind

Singapore's growth, as we shall see in a moment. The finding also shows that the main factor behind growth was the extent of school enrolment in 1960, especially in primary schools. In most of the other regressions the ratio of investment to GDP was a significant explanation of growth differences.

Table 7.3   Determinants of growth: regression results

Intercept	−0.0042
GDP relative to USA, 1960	−0.0320**
Primary enrolment, 1960	0.0272**
Secondary enrolment, 1960	0.0069
Growth of population, 1960–85	0.0998
Average investment/GDP, 1960–85	0.0285*
HPAEs	0.0171**
Latin America	−0.0131**
Sub-Saharan Africa	−0.0099*
N = 113	
Adjusted R^2	0.428

Note: ** statistically significant at the 0.01 level; * statistically significant at the 0.05 level.

Source: *The East Asian Miracle*, Table 1.8.

The World Bank then took the predicted growth rate for each country and calculated the contribution of each of these factors. The results for Singapore are shown in Table 7.4. Here we can see that the main factors behind Singapore's growth are its high primary school enrolment and its high average investment ratio. These two factors alone account for 118 per cent of predicted growth. As suspected, Singapore's relative backwardness compared to the USA plays no role in explaining its growth. In short, the factors responsible for growth were high investment in human capital in the 1960s and then in physical capital. Young (1992) based his explanation of Singapore's low TFP growth on the low educational level of Singaporean workers in the 1940s and 1950s. In 1960, however, school enrolment figures were very high. These pupils would have become workers in the late 1960s and early 1970s, educated and able to handle the new technology that was being introduced by the MNCs on which Singapore based its growth strategy. In 1960, for example, primary school enrolment in Singapore was 111 per cent of the primary school age group (the ratio can exceed 100 per cent as pupils outside the official primary school age limits often go to these schools) compared to 87 per cent in Hong Kong, 96 per cent in Malaysia, 92 per cent in the UK and 118 per cent in the USA (*World Development Report 1980*, Table 23).

Table 7.4   Contributions to growth, Singapore

	Percentage of predicted growth
Intercept	−18
GDP relative to USA, 1960	−27
Primary enrolment, 1960	75
Secondary enrolment, 1960	22
Growth of population, 1960–85	5
Average investment/GDP, 1960–85	43

Source: Adapted from *The East Asian Miracle*, Table 1.9.

The World Bank also made its own estimates of TFP growth for the period 1960–89. It produced a figure of 1.19 per cent per annum (after rounding the figures from four decimal places) for Singapore, compared to 3.65 per cent for Hong Kong, 3.48 per cent for Japan and 3.76 for Taiwan, to mention the highest figures they found.

TFP is estimated as a residual and many people are prepared to call it an unknown as it reflects a great many factors that could increase productivity: better management, greater worker enthusiasm and morale, higher levels of education and hence less loss of time in training workers, higher productivity brought about by using the latest technology and so on. The World Bank team tried to split its TFP estimates into two components: that due to technical progress and that due to improvements in technical efficiency.

Think of a country having the best technology available for its kind of production and call this 'best practice'. Apart from increasing its inputs it can only increase its output by increasing its productivity using that best technique. That is technical progress. Other countries that do not have the best technique can improve their performance, given their inputs, by adopting the best practice techniques. Moving from average practice to best practice is called positive technical efficiency change. Observed TFP growth consists of productivity growth, based on best practice, and technical efficiency growth, moving to best practice. It is thought that in developed countries, where the best practice technology is likely to have been developed and implemented first, there are few opportunities for benefiting from technical efficiency. In backward countries that are catching up, TFP growth could be much higher than in developed countries as it could consist of a high element of positive technical efficiency change. TFP growth will be negative if technical efficiency change is negative and greater than the rate of technical progress. The World Bank made estimates of technical efficiency change for the HPAEs and their estimate for Singapore was *minus* 3.45 compared to plus 1.97 for Hong Kong, plus 0.99 for Japan and *minus* 1.78 for Malaysia (*The East Asian Miracle*, p.69).

Other recent research has also tried to identify factors that contribute to high TFP. Unsurprisingly, it has been found that the greater a country's expenditure on research and development (R&D) the higher its TFP. One study found that a 1 per cent increase in the R&D stock of the Group of Seven countries increased their TFP by 0.22 per cent. A more interesting finding was that R&D spending in the USA has a significant spillover effect on the TFP of other countries. The smaller the country, the greater was the spillover effect of US R&D expenditure. Over the period 1985–90 a 1 per cent rise in US R&D stock increased TFP in 77 countries by an average of 0.04 per cent, but the impact on Singapore was to increase its TFP by 0.22 per cent.[1] The suggested mechanism by which small countries benefited from US R&D expenditure was through their importing American high-technology goods which improved the efficiency of their industries and through the chance it gave them to copy the technology developed by other countries.[2] In the case of Singapore it is much more likely that there is a direct route through the fact that many MNCs in Singapore are American and thus directly apply the technological developments made in their research laboratories to their production in Singapore. Whether this development spills over to indigenous Singapore firms is an interesting issue for future research, as is the question why Singapore's TFP growth remains so low, given the fact that there are many advanced MNCs located there. The above finding also explains why Singapore's expenditure on R&D seems so low: most of it is being conducted in Japan and the USA and transferred to Singapore through the MNCs.

7.4   FORECASTING GROWTH TRENDS

Forecasting long-term growth trends obviously requires considering the supply-side factors we have identified above: labour force growth, the rate of capital accumulation and likely rate of productivity growth. Short-term forecasts for the next year or so concentrate on demand-side factors such as the rate of growth in important markets, likely growth in domestic demand, changes in government fiscal and monetary policy and movements in the exchange rate, or use a technique of leading indicators, which will be discussed below. Here we will just indicate the difficulties involved in trying to predict changes in growth trends by means of an interesting example.

In 1987, as a response to the downturn of 1985, a team of three academics, working with information provided by government ministries and the MAS, prepared a report on the state of the Singapore economy. One of their conclusions was that 'the potential growth rate of Singapore for the rest of the 1980s is about 4–6%. It will be a banner year in which 7 per cent growth is achieved'

(Krause *et al.*, 1987, p.228). In fact since 1987 the real annual growth rates of GDP, in percentages, have been 11.1, 9.2, 8.8, 6.7, 6.0 and 9.9 (for 1993), averaging nearly 8 per cent per annum. Every year after 1987 posted a growth rate of at least 6 per cent and two-thirds of them were well above the 'banner' rate of 7 per cent. In other words, according to the official data, the predicted slowdown of the growth trend to 4–6 per cent has just not happened. This shows how difficult it is to predict something as general as the changing trend in growth. Many commentators have taken the view, however, that the sustainable long-run growth rate of the economy is about 4–6 per cent and this is reflected in statements by the Minister of Finance, Dr Richard Hu. He sees the main constraints as labour shortages and high wages, both of which can be moderated by relaxing 'restrictions on entry of foreign workers for selective labour industries, such as the shipyard and construction sectors, to ease rising wages' (*Business Times*, 21 November 1994, interview for Reuters). The MAS believes that the potential rate of output growth over the period 1994–8 is 6–7 per cent per annum (*Monetary Authority of Singapore Annual Report 1993/94*, p.15).

7.5   THE BUSINESS CYCLE

The business cycle is the seemingly regular recurring alternation of booms and slumps in the economy, or periods of rapid growth and periods of slower growth or falling output, in which certain key macroeconomic variables tend to move in tandem either procyclically or countercyclically. Business cycles have been studied extensively, especially in the USA, and most macroeconomic theories are aimed at explaining the regularities found there or in developed industrialized economies. There are strong similarities across countries which share the same market-based economic system. Keynes (1936, chap. 22) applied his general theory to explaining the nature and key features of the business cycle, then generally called the trade cycle, as it was understood at that time. Subsequent theories have had longer periods to study, during which time many more data and cheaper and more accessible computer technology have become available to help analyse the properties of cyclical movements in key variables.

Let us review what a typical but very good macroeconomics textbook presents as the essential features of the cyclical nature of the main macroeconomic variables, based on American experience, as summarized by the Bureau of Economic Analysis (Abel and Bernanke, 1995, p.301). A procyclical variable is one that moves in the same direction as aggregate economic activity. Countercyclical variables move in the opposite direction, and an acyclical variable shows no relationship with changes in general economic activity. A leading variable is one that moves in advance of the change in general economic activity, a lagging variable follows the change in general economic activity and a coincident one changes at the same time.

- *The main procyclical and leading variables* are residential investment, inventory investment, average labour productivity, real wage (procyclical, but no timing identified), money growth and stock prices.
- *The main procyclical and lagging variables* are inflation and nominal interest rates (real interest rates are acyclical).
- *The main procyclical and coincident variables* are consumption, business fixed investment and employment.
- *The main countercyclical variable* is unemployment (with no timing clear).

The identification of a number of variables that lead the cycle inspired a research programme that collected and combined these indicators statistically to produce an index that would forecast business cycle turning-points, periods of higher or lower than usual economic activity or even the future rate of growth of GDP.

7.6   CYCLES IN SINGAPORE

As Koh (1992a, p.24) notes, the study of the business cycle in Asian countries is in its infancy and interest in the Singapore business cycle started only in the 1980s, possibly as a consequence of the recession of 1985–6. One indication of this interest is the official construction of an index of leading indicators of the cycle. This is the Composite Leading Index (CLI) constructed using quarterly data by the Department of Statistics, Singapore, with the help of the Center for International Business Cycle Research at Columbia University which, in 1986, suggested the components, using a methodology developed by the National Bureau of Economic Research of the United States (Chow, 1993, p.26). The composition of the index has been revised since then and now comprises nine indicators which are thought to be the leading ones: new orders, money supply (M2), stock (share) prices, stocks of finished goods, company formation, the inverted CPF default rates for the manufacturing sector, business forecasts for wholesale trade, the wholesale price index for manufactured goods and inverted real unit labour costs. The index is used to predict the changes in economic activity about three quarters in the future. Analysis of the index's progress with that of GDP shows reasonably close movement, but there are some periods, such as mid-1990, when the index fell but GDP continued to grow strongly (*Economic Survey of Singapore 1993*, Chart 7.1). Chow (1993) subjected the index to detailed scrutiny, finding that some components, such as unit labour cost and the CPF default rate, were more like lagging variables, not leading ones, although the

CLI 'displayed a leading quality over GDP' and was useful for short-term projections of economic growth (ibid., p.33). Another leading indicator is compiled by Chow Kit Boey (Chow, 1988) on the basis of leading sectors in the economy, not macroeconomic variables. Informal leading indicators exist, of course. A few that are often featured in the press are the rate of money growth, the rate of growth of bank loans to the private sector and the number of outgoing international telephone calls.

On the basis of joint research between the Institute of Developing Economies in Tokyo and the National University of Singapore, it is argued that there have been 'six complete business cycles since 1960' (Chow, 1988, p.86). These are identified with differences in growth rates and, apart from the first and last, are referred to as 'growth rather than classical cycles'. As we have seen, real GDP has only fallen in Singapore in 1964 and 1985. These studies are forced into 'heavy dependence on the GDP series for the reference points' as 'variables similar to those selected in industrial countries for measuring business cycles are either unavailable or of doubtful coverage' (ibid., pp.86–7).

The six periods identified in Chow (1988) are:

1960–1965: slow growth (5.9 per cent per annum);
1966–1973: rapid growth (12.7 per cent per annum);
1974–1977: slow growth (6.4 per cent per annum);
1978–1984: moderate growth (8.7 per cent per annum);
1985–1987: Very slow growth (2.9 per cent per annum);
1988–1989: Moderate growth (10.1 per cent per annum).

We can add that the growth rates since 1989 have remained reasonably high, falling to 6 per cent in 1992 but averaging 7.4 per cent. Note that these studies are prepared to refer to 10 per cent annual real growth as 'moderate'. The periodicity varies significantly for these periods, from seven years for 1978–84 to just three for 1985–87. Other attempts at dating cycles have used quarterly and monthly data, available from the early 1970s. Table 7.5 summarizes one set of such findings.

These periods are based on the behaviour of a diffusion index which summarizes the changes in a number of variables. We can see from these periods that the cycles vary considerably in length. Although the average length of expansions is 24 months, one expansionary period lasted only 14 months and another 35. It is remarked with respect to the Singapore cycle that it is closely related to the American economy, and of Asian economies Singapore and Thailand show the closest relationship between turning-points (Mori, 1991, p.155).

Let us now turn to the nature of the relationship between the main sectors and macroeconomic variables during different phases of growth. Koh (1990) is the pioneering study in this field. She uses visual inspection of time series graphs and correlation analysis between relevant variables and detrended GDP for the period 1960–1988. Her main finding concerning the length of the cycles in GDP is that expansions and contractions last about four years each and there have been three main cycles over the period 1960–88. Sectors that showed greater amplitude were construction, manufacturing, commerce and transport. Utilities, services and finance showed much smaller amplitude in their fluctuations. Of the three components of domestic demand studied, gross fixed capital formation was much more unstable than both private and government consumption expenditure. All of these three 'demand components', as they are called in this study, are procyclical, with private consumption expenditure being most closely correlated with movements in GDP, and gross fixed capital formation also being significantly correlated. Government consumption expenditure was weakly procyclical (Koh, 1990, pp.188–9).

Table 7.5   Cycles in Singapore

			Duration (months)		
Trough	Peak	Trough	Expansion	Contraction	Total
Apr. 1975	Mar. 1977	May 1978	23	14	37
May 1978	Apr. 1981	Feb. 1983	35	22	57
Feb. 1983	Apr. 1984	Mar. 1986	14	23	37
Average			24	19.6	43.6

Source: Osada and Hiratsuka (1991, p.16).

The general findings about the relationships between major macroeconomic variables and the changes in general economic activity, as indicated by deviations from its trend, tended to 'conform with empirical features of business cycles elsewhere' (Koh, 1990, p.197). Correlation analysis showed that the following were significantly procyclical: consumer price index (wholesale prices were insignificantly negatively correlated), M1; velocity of M2 (its growth rate, judging from the scatter diagram evidence) and three-, six- and 12-month interest rates. The significantly countercyclical variables were the trade balance, the current account and unemployment. That is, booms in the economy led to a worsening of the trade and current accounts. None of these results is surprising. Singapore, however, did stand out from the general pattern with respect to price movements found for the Asian NICS, in which prices were countercyclical, as they were in the OECD countries (Koh, 1990, p.170). In Singapore, however, consumer prices were 'strongly and significantly procyclical' (ibid., p.191). There seems little prospect for a revisionist New Classical interpretation of the cyclical nature of price movements in Singapore.

We can illustrate the important cyclical relationship between unemployment and fluctuations in output growth in Singapore. We concentrate on the period 1970–93 because of data availability. We have calculated the deviation from its trend for this period of real GDP. Koh (ibid., p.161) argued that using the simple exponential trend is the most appropriate method for the Asian NICs and we have done this here, though we show deviations from trend as the number of percentage points by which GDP in any year differs from this trend value. Figure 7.1 is a scatter diagram showing the relationship between unemployment (*U*) on the vertical axis and the deviation of GDP from trend, *X*, on

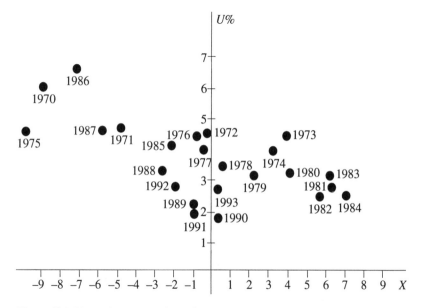

Figure 7.1 Unemployment and the deviation of output from trend, 1970–93

the horizontal axis. Some interesting features can be discerned. First, there is a clear inverse relationship. Despite the existence of foreign workers who can be used to bear the brunt of unemployment when output falls, unemployment tends to be high when output is below trend, and vice versa. The boom of the early 1980s is clearly shown, with output being well above trend. The recession years of 1985 and 1986 stand out clearly and the movement from 1984 to 1986 clearly shows the inverse relationship. The regression equation linking unemployment (*U*) to the deviation of output from trend (*X*) is:

$$U = 3.64 - 0.148\,X \qquad R^2 = 0.333$$
$$(17.7) \quad (-3.32) \qquad n = 24$$

This implies that, when output was at its trend value, unemployment was, on average for the period 1970–93, about 3.6 per cent. This could be taken as a crude estimate of the natural rate of unemployment. We will examine another estimate of this rate in the next chapter. We can see from Figure 7.1 that, when output was near trend in such years as 1972, 1976, 1977 and 1978, unemployment was higher than in years such as 1989, 1990 and 1993, when output was similarly near trend. In 1992, when output was below trend by the same extent as in 1985, unemployment was lower than in 1985. This suggests that since 1970 the rate of unemployment associated with output being at trend has fallen, the opposite picture from that found in European countries where, until the late 1980s, it seemed that the level of unemployment observed at the natural rate had risen considerably. The correlation coefficient between the two variables is minus 0.577, significant at the 5 per cent level for this number of observations, and it compares well with Koh's correlation coefficient for the period 1960–88 of minus 0.476 (Koh, 1990, p.190).

In this chapter we have described some of the relationships between major macroeconomic variables as they occurred over the business cycle. In the next chapter we look at the way in which economists have tried to quantify some of the behavioural relationships that we studied in Chapter 3, such as the consumption and investment functions, using actual historical data and put them together in the form of an econometric model.

SUGGESTIONS FOR FURTHER READING

For studies of aspects of growth and development in East Asia we recommend *The East Asian Miracle: Economic Growth and Public Policy* by the World Bank (1993) and Young (1992; 1994b).

On cycles: good textbooks that feature business cycles include Abel and Bernanke (1995) based on American evidence and Parkin and Bade (1986) using British evidence. For Singapore, see Koh (1990; 1992b)

NOTES

1. These results are emerging from continuing and unpublished research. We have taken this information from *The Economist*, 18 March 1995, p.90. Most of the results are from work by David Coe and Elhanan Helpman.
2. This was one of the benefits of international trade identified by David Hume and has played a role in the technological development of such countries as Japan and South Korea.

8. Modelling the economy

In contrast to earlier chapters in this book, which present 'stylized' relationships between macroeconomic variables but make no attempt to measure the strengths of these relationships, in this chapter we focus on macroeconometric models which try to quantify the relationships among such variables as output, employment, government spending, interest rates and exchange rates. By representing the economy as a mathematical model and quantifying its key relationships using actual data, these models hope both to provide a realistic description of the macroeconomic behaviour of the economy in the past and to forecast its likely behaviour in the future.

8.1 EARLY MODELS OF THE SINGAPORE ECONOMY

It is generally accepted that macroeconometric modelling began with Jan Tinbergen's 1936 empirical model of the Dutch economy and Lawrence Klein's pioneering work on the US economy after the Second World War.[1] The first UK model was produced by Klein, Ball and Vandome in 1961. At the present time there are a multitude of national models, for both developed and developing countries, as well as multi-country models linking together a series of country models or groups of countries.

Experimentation with simple macroeconometric models in Singapore began in the early 1970s under the auspices of the Ministry of Finance (MOF) and the Ministry of Trade and Industry (MTI).[2] The primary purpose of such models was to calculate the likely export–import and investment–savings resource gaps which would result from given targets for GDP growth. In 1976 a revised version of a model developed by Norman Hicks was used for policy analysis by the Economic Activation Committee, which had been set up in the aftermath of the 1974/5 world recession. In particular, the model was used to calculate projections for GDP growth and sectoral value-added growth rates for computing manpower needs. Although this model was subsequently revised, model-building efforts at the MOF and MTI were superseded in the 1980s by work on a macroeconometric model at the Monetary Authority of Singapore (MAS), which has tended to take over responsibility for macroeconometric modelling. This was the genesis of the present official MAS model. At the same time, the Econometric Studies Unit (ESU) was established at the National University of Singapore in 1981 to undertake applied work in econometrics.

Until the mid-1980s there had been very little independent academic work in applied macroeconomic modelling for Singapore (see Table 8.1). The models were small, used simple estimation techniques and validation procedures, and were designed for simple structural analysis or policy analysis rather than for forecasting. Exceptions were the models by Tang (1985) and Ezaki (1985). The Tang model focused on short-term macroeconomic stabilization policy as an exercise in optimal control theory, while the Ezaki model was used to calculate the multiplier effects on major macroeconomic aggregates of changes in government consumption spending, domestic and entrepot exports and the monetary base. We will look at some of these multipliers in Section 8.2 below. The Ezaki model was an offshoot of the early MAS model, and was relatively large compared to its predecessors.

Table 8.1   Macroeconometric models of Singapore

Model	Period	Equations	Estimation	Public domain	Special features
Wong (1974)	1960–69 annual	5 + 3	OLS		Structural analysis
Ostby (1977)	1971–75 annual	4 + 0	OLS		Structural analysis
Toh (1984)	1970–81 annual	8 + 2	OLS		Integrated input–output model Forecasting output, manpower
Toida (1984)	1971–82 annual	6 + 2	OLS		Link model for Project ELSA
Tang (1985)	1965–84 annual	11 + 2	TSLS	Listing Data	Short-term stabilization policy using optimal control theory
Ezaki (1985)	1969–81 annual	21 + 16	OLS	Listing	Generic basis in early MAS model Link model for Asian Link Project
ESU86	1960–85 annual	12 + 12	OLS	Listing	Structural analysis, policy analysis, counterfactuals, twice-yearly forecasts
Toh and Low (1990a)	1960–88 annual	25 + 36	OLS	Listing Data	Link model for Project Link
Toh and Ramstetter (1994)	1973–89 annual	22 + 10	OLS	Listing Data	Link model for Asian Link Project
ESU94	1960–93 annual	32 + 37	OLS	Listing Data	Structural analysis, policy analysis, twice-yearly forecasts
MAS94	1980–94 quarterly	80 + 190	OLS		Structural analysis, policy analysis, official forecasting

Note: The estimation and/or simulation periods may be shorter than the data period cited here; the number of equations includes behavioural equations plus identities; ESU94 incorporates quarterly forecasts for GDP and sectoral growth from separate ARIMA models.

The first serious attempt to build a non-official continuing macroeconometric model of the Singapore economy was initiated in the Department of Economics and Statistics at the National University of Singapore in 1986, in conjunction with the publication of a book on the Singapore economy by Lim and associates (1988).[3] Since the publication of its first forecasts in this book, the 'prototype' ESU86 model has been extensively revised and now gives half-yearly public forecasts. The current (1994) version is discussed in more detail in Section 8.3.

Overall there is a relative paucity of independent macroeconometric models of the Singapore economy compared to other countries, including those in the East Asian region. This is surprising given its level of economic development and the sophistication of its statistical sources. Although there are well-known data problems for Singapore,[4] such as the absence of published trade data with Indonesia, these problems are no more intractable than for other countries in the region. The problem seems to be that the authoritative models on Singapore, such as the early models of the MOF and MTI, and later MAS model, were not available to the public. By contrast, the more recent models by Toh and Low (1990a) and Toh and Ramstetter (1994), summarized in Table 8.1, are accompanied by a list of the model's equations and the data sufficient for a third party to replicate them.[5] While not all model-builders wish to have their models copied and modified, especially those from official bodies or commercial forecasting agencies, the 'open' approach has been an important catalyst in the development of macroeconometric modelling as an academic subject, increasing both the range and the quality of national and global models.[6]

8.2   THE RATIONALE BEHIND MACROECONOMETRIC MODELLING

Although macroeconometric models are designed with different purposes in mind, they are usually constructed according to a similar series of steps.[7] We will illustrate these steps using the 'prototype' ESU86 model. Although this model has been significantly improved over the years, its simplicity and published results in Lim and associates (1988) make it very convenient for our purposes, and a good basis for comparisons with later models.

The first step in building a macroeconometric model is to specify a mathematical model which contains 'behavioural equations' describing the aggregate behaviour of groups such as consumers (consumption function) or investors (investment function), together with 'accounting identities' defining exact relationships which hold at all points in time, such as the components of final expenditure. The real GDP identity, together with behavioural equations for consumption, the Consumer Price Index and level of employment from ESU86, are listed below.[8]

$$Y = C + I + G + X - M \tag{8.1}$$
$$C = 574.7 + 0.5226 \, Ct - 1 + 0.3084 \, Yd + 0.0135 \, M3 \tag{8.2}$$
$$CPI = 0.56 + 0.2957 \, Pm + 0.0382 \, ULCt - 1 \tag{8.3}$$
$$N = 532.4 - 3.1832 \, W/P + 0.0583 \, Y \tag{8.4}$$

Equation (8.2) explains real consumer expenditure in terms of real disposable income Yd (allowing for taxes and CPF contributions), a measure of liquidity (real M3), and consumption one year ago to capture time delays in the adjustment of consumers to Yd and M3. Equation (8.3) determines the Consumer Price Index in terms of an index of import prices Pm and real unit labour costs one year ago. Finally, equation (8.4) relates employment N (in thousands) to the real average weekly wage rate (W/P), where P is the GDP price deflator, and real GDP.

Y, C, CPI and N are examples of endogenous variables whose values are determined within the model; exogenous variables determined outside the model are G, X and M3. Note that, although other variables such as I and M are not explained in equations (8.1) to (8.4), they are in fact endogenous in the full model. The numerical values contained in equations (8.2) to (8.4) were estimated from data using ordinary least squares (OLS).[9]

The next step is to solve the full model numerically on a computer using a simulation program. The model is solved in this way since many relationships in economics are non-linear and are best represented in log-linear form or include ratios of variables such as W/P in equation (8.4) above. To solve the equations in any other way would be very difficult.[10]

At this point the simulation model would be 'evaluated' to see how well it replicates or 'tracks' the known endogenous variables within the data sample period, including plots of simulated against actual. Table 8.2 evaluates the tracking performance of equations (8.1) to (8.4) in terms of two popular summary statistics: R-squared between actual and simulated and the percentage root mean square error.[11] There are no absolute criteria for assessing the performance of a simulation model, and a good 'fit' for individual equations is no guarantee that the model as a whole will perform well, but the high R-squared values and relatively low PRMSEs would suggest that these particular equations were satisfactory.

One of the most useful functions of macroeconometric simulation is to shed light on the way the economy works: for example, to compare the relative effectiveness of monetary and fiscal policy on aggregate variables such as income and the price level, including the magnitude of 'crowding out', as well as the effects of external shocks, such as a rise in the price of oil, or a recession in industrial countries.

Table 8.2   Simulation performance of the ESU86 model

	PRMSE	R^2	Forecast	1984 Levels Actual	PE	1987 Growth rates Forecast	Actual
Y	2.9	0.99	18 333	18 262	0.4	5.1	9.4
C	1.9	0.99	9 352	9 380	0.3	3.5	9.7
CPI	4.8	0.89	2.054	2.245	8.5	12.0	0.5
N	1.9	0.98	1 280	1 156	10.8	4.5	4.3

Note: PRMSE is the percentage root mean square error, R^2 is the R-squared between actual and simulated; PE is the per cent forecast error, Y and C are measured in millions of 1968 Singapore dollars; *N* is in thousands, *CPI* is in index form (1968=100).

Sources: Adapted from Lim and associates (1988); actual growth rates for 1987 are from the *Yearbook of Statistics 1993*.

Table 8.3 presents a selection of unit multipliers from ESU86 and Ezaki (1985). These multipliers measure the change in real GDP from a unit increase in selected exogenous variables, such as real government spending, using the initial solution of the model as the 'base' from which to measure the changes. They are analogous to the multipliers calculated algebraically from the theoretical models in earlier chapters but are based on the more complex numerical solution of a (non-linear) macroeconometric model.

The results in Table 8.3 suggest that fiscal policy has only a small effect on real GDP: a one Singapore dollar increase in *G* leads to only a 65 to 78 cents increase in *Y*. This is a direct reflection of relatively large income leakages in Singapore, by international standards, through CPF, imports and so on. Monetary policy (a change in *Ms*) also has negligible effects in the ESU86 model and small effects in Ezaki. However this is not surprising since the only channel for *Ms* to work through in both models is its impact on *C*, as in equation (8.2) above. Although there are good grounds for thinking that monetary policy is ineffective in Singapore (as discussed in Chapter 5), neither simulation model contains enough equations to capture possible interactions between real and monetary variables to test this hypothesis adequately. The weak or negligible impact on *Y* from shocks to exports (*X*) or foreign income (*YF*) also partly stems from the construction of the two models. In the ESU86 model exports are entirely exogenous, so *YF* has no effect on exports and the export multiplier is similar to a change in exogenous *G*. The only channel for *YF* to work through is a weak stimulus to investment. The endogenization of *X* in the Ezaki model and later ESU94 models is more realistic in this respect.

Table 8.3   Multipliers and elasticities from the Singapore simulation models

Change in:	Unit multipliers unit impact on Y	
	ESU86	Ezaki
G	0.78	0.65
Ms	0.00	0.27
X	0.70	0.38
YF	0.00	—

	Elasticities					
	Y		N		P	
	Ezaki	T&R	Ezaki	T&R	Ezaki	T&R
G	0.064	0.050	0.040	0.021	0.010	0.010
MS	0.034	—	0.016	—	0.040	—
W	—	0.000	—	0.245	—	0.174
X	0.250	—	0.150	—	0.025	—
XE	0.106	—	0.066	—	0.018	—
YF	—	1.950	—	0.850	—	0.450
YFA	—	0.340	—	0.140	—	0.090
FDI	—	2.450	—	1.050	—	0.560
REER	—	0.144	—	0.064	—	0.034

Notes: G is real government consumption, MS is real M3 in ESU86 and the monetary base in Ezaki; X is real goods exports in ESU86 and real domestic goods exports in Ezaki; YF is nominal GNP of OECD countries in ESU86 and real *GNP* of OECD in T&R, Y is real GDP; N is employment; P is the GDP deflator; W is the average nominal weekly wage rate; XE is real entrepot exports; YFA is real GNP of the ASEAN4; FDI is the ratio of real cumulative direct foreign investment to cumulative real private investment; REER is the real effective exchange rate; the unit multipliers from ESU86 are impulse multipliers summed over the simulation period, for Ezaki they are averaged over the period from sustained shocks; the elasticities are based on averages from sustained shocks.

Sources: Adapted from Lim and associates (1988); Ezaki (1985); Toh and Ramstetter (1994).

Although multipliers are routinely calculated in macroeconometric models they are not always measured in the same way. This makes comparability difficult. Table 8.3 compares the effects of different domestic and foreign shocks on *Y*, *N*, and *P* (as defined above) by interpreting the multipliers in Ezaki (1985) and Toh and Ramstetter (1994) as elasticities. These indicate the proportional change in the endogenous variable from its base value resulting from a proportional or percentage change in the exogenous variable. The result is a pure number measure of the relative strength of the relationship concerned, so the multipliers can be compared with each other.

The relatively small effects of monetary and fiscal policy are confirmed in Table 8.3. A 1 per cent increase in G, for example, leads to only a 0.05 to 0.064 of a percentage point increase in Y. In the T&R model both the money supply and interest rates are left exogenous so there is no effective channel to simulate monetary policy. Some attempt is made to endogenize the money supply in the Ezaki model but the author admits that most monetary variables are left exogenous. Nonetheless fiscal policy is found to be more effective than monetary policy on Y and N. The effects of monetary and fiscal policy on employment are smaller than on Y since wage and price adjustment cushions the effects on N. There are negligible effects on the GDP deflator P (and thus CPI) since prices are largely determined by import prices and unit labour costs (as in equation 8.3 above). A rise in the autonomous component of the nominal wage W has negligible effects on real Y (as opposed to nominal Y) since P rises and employment falls.

In proportional terms shocks emanating from the external sector are more important than fiscal or monetary shocks, given the high export to GDP ratio in Singapore, although, as one would expect, changes in entrepot exports XE are less important than changes in domestic exports X. Changes in foreign income YF and YFA are also important now (compared to ESU86) since they directly affect exports in the T&R model. Note that a shock of an equal relative size (for example 1 per cent) in real income of the ASEAN4 countries (YFA) is much less important to Singapore than a shock to OECD real income (YF), since YFA constitutes only 2–4 per cent of YF. Depreciation of the Singapore dollar by increasing the real effective exchange rate REER[12] also has important effects on domestic exports in the T&R model, but the effects on Y and N are cushioned as wages rise and induced imports increase leakages (service exports are not related to REER in this model). Note the strong effects on Y, N and P in the T&R model from an exogenous rise in ratio of cumulative foreign direct investment to cumulative private investment FDI as manufacturing and service export capacity increases and raises aggregate demand.

A second function of simulation analysis is to carry out counterfactual exercises to see how the economy might have behaved in the past if some alternative policies had been implemented, or the exogenous environment had been different. The base solution to the model is used as an approximation to what actually happened and a second run is used to represent the alternative scenario.

A good example of counterfactual analysis is provided by the ESU86 model. Using this model, Lim and associates (1988) found that, if the anti-recessionary measures actually adopted in 1986 by the Singapore government had been implemented in 1984, prior to the recession of 1985–6, there would still have been a recession in 1985, but real GDP would have fallen by only –0.5 per cent instead of the actual –1.8 per cent. Similarly, if public construction had fallen steadily between 1981 and 1986 instead of falling sharply from 1985 onwards, there would still have been negative growth in real GDP of 0.9 per cent in 1985, suggesting that a fall in external demand played a crucial role in the recession. This was confirmed in the third counterfactual experiment when real exports were allowed to grow at 7 per cent per annum from 1980 to 1986 and the total level of investment was kept at its average 1983/4 level in 1985 and 1986. The simulated path for GDP indicates a growth cycle: slower growth at 5.5 per cent but no recession. In view of the simplicity of the prototype ESU86 model, it would be interesting to repeat these exercises with the later ESU94 model or any of the subsequent models listed in Table 8.1.

A third role for simulation is to engage in forecasting. Despite much criticism over the years about the accuracy of macroeconometric forecasts, it is still a popular activity for government departments, international organizations, private forecasting agencies and academics. It is defended on the grounds that it contributes to broader forecasting judgement, helps evaluate alternative scenarios, directs attention to key empirical issues and helps economists to monitor current government strategy. *Ex post* forecasting is used to evaluate the performance of a macroeconometric model over a period of time when the data for all the variables are available, so the actual outcomes are known at the time of the forecast. Table 8.2 compares the forecast and actual levels of Y, C, CPI (in index form) and N for the ESU86 model for 1984. The percentage forecast errors for Y and C are not too bad, but are noticeably worse for the CPI and N.

An altogether more risky exercise is to carry out *ex ante* forecasting to predict the endogenous variables over a period of time when both the endogenous and exogenous variables are unknown. The exogenous variables must be projected into the future in order to solve the model, although in practice they are often assumed to remain unchanged at their existing levels or projected to grow at a constant rate based on their recent behaviour. Of course the results of the forecast cannot be assessed until the data become available. Table 8.2 reproduces the *ex ante* forecasts for growth in Y, C, CPI and N for 1987 from ESU86 and compares them with the actual outcomes (supplied by the present authors). The errors are much larger, especially for the growth in CPI (inflation rate). In practice, forecasts are constantly revised as the prediction date approaches and more information becomes available and usually the mechanical predictions of the model are adjusted in some way according to the 'judgement' of the forecaster. Thus different forecasts can be made from the same underlying model.

8.3 THE ESU AND MAS MODELS

Table 8.4 summarizes the basic structural features of the 1994 versions of the Econometric Studies Unit (ESU) and Monetary Authority of Singapore macroeconometric models.[13] The classification used is similar to that of Whitley (1994, Table 2.1) so interested parties can compare these two Singapore models with six major models for the UK.

Table 8.4   Structural characteristics of the Singapore models

	ESU94	MAS94
Disaggregation	Value-added by sector	By spending categories
Main features	Keynesian demand-driven Short- to medium-term Largely eclectic	Keynesian demand-driven Short- to medium-term Official view of the links between monetary policy, the exchange rate and inflation/unemployment
Expectations	Implicit	Implicit
Demand		
Consumption	Real disposable income	Real disposable wage and property income, dependency ratio
Domestic investment	Foreign investment, exports, factor prices, material prices	GDP growth, factor prices, CPF balances, real exchange rate, corporate tax rate
Exports	World demand, relative prices, real exchange rate, capacity	World demand, unemployment rate, capacity, real exchange rate
Imports	Domestic investment or demand, relative prices	Domestic demand, export demand, relative prices
Government revenue	Time trend, employment, wage rate, contribution rate	Employment, wage rate, tax schedule, dependency ratio
Government spending	Exogenous	Exogenous
Supply		
Production technology	Not explicit	Not explicit
Employment	Domestic demand, real wage	Domestic demand, labour productivity
Wage formation	Real wage depends on domestic spending, productivity	Unemployment, inflation, labour productivity
Prices	Import prices, wage costs, money supply (M2)	Import prices, wage costs
Interest rates	Exogenous	Exogenous
Exchange rate	Exogenous	Policy variable
Money supply	Domestic income, interest rate	Domestic income, interest rate

The ESU94 model is an annual model but its half-yearly forecasts are now supplemented by quarterly forecasts for real GDP and sectoral growth aggregates from separate ARIMA time-series models. The use of time series models to help improve forecasting performance is now common practice in macroeconometric modelling and it is recognized that 'structural' macroeconometric models have limitations when it comes to *ex ante* forecasting. We return to this issue below. The last detailed discussion of the model's theoretical underpinnings, with some validation statistics on *ex post* tracking performance in 1970–89 were published in ESU (1990). The most recent public listing of the model (without data) was in ESU (1993).

Although the model has undergone significant changes from the prototype ESU86 version,[14] it is largely ad hoc and eclectic in nature, rather than being derived from any specific stream of macroeconomic theory. It is based upon a consensus view about the way the Singapore economy works, together with some earlier theoretical insights derived from Kapur (1983). This consensus views Singapore as a small open economy susceptible to external shocks and heavily reliant on foreign direct investment. It is also a price taker in international markets with strong links between import prices and the domestic CPI. In the absence of capital controls, and given the high mobility of international short-term capital, domestic interest rates are set in international markets and are left exogenous in the model. Although the money supply (M2) is seen predominantly as a by-product of external monetary policy and of volatile movements in net short-term capital flows, it is, in fact, endogenized in the model with respect to real GDP and the minimum lending rate. M2, in turn, enters as an explanatory variable in the equations for the GDP deflator and CPI. Consumption is constrained by the reduction in disposable income due to CPF contributions, and distinctions are made in the model between entrepot and domestic exports and entrepot and retained imports.

The ESU94 model is essentially a demand-driven real sector model embodying many of the features of the Singapore economy described in this book. However the model does have its limitations. There is no explicit production function or labour supply constraint, despite recognition of the importance of the latter since the late 1970s. Unfortunately there are no published data on the magnitude, composition or employment destination of foreign workers coming to Singapore, yet their contribution to employment and output is substantial. In 1994, for instance, employment grew at approximately 4.5 per cent, while domestic labour force projections were between 1 and 2 per cent (ESU, 1995).

Although the model captures the transmission mechanism from import prices to domestic inflation, there is no explicit model for the inflation–unemployment trade-off in the ESU94 model. With interest rates and the nominal exchange rate taken to be exogenous, the model contains little by way of a financial system or links between the financial sector and real variables, such as the effects of private sector wealth or liquidity on consumption. Yet the spillover effects of asset price inflation, and the substantial increase in the prices of COEs and private residential property in 1994, must have had important repercussions on consumer wealth. The model is also unable to make the connections between the foreign assets of the monetary authorities and the balance of payments, or between government deposits at MAS and the budget, discussed in Chapters 5 and 6.

Table 8.5 assesses the *ex ante* forecasting performance of the ESU94 model between July 1991 and August 1994, focusing on six key variables. Although there are no hard-and-fast criteria for evaluating the performance of a forecasting model of this type, the size of the mean absolute errors suggests that, in a forecasting context, the model could be improved. Forecasts for the next year are significantly worse than for the same year in which the forecast is made. The average difference between the actual and the forecast for GDP growth, for instance, is 3.81. The actual value might be 10 per cent, while the forecast value is 6.19 per cent! Similarly the inflation forecast might be 3 per cent but the actual rate only 2.24. The forecasts are especially pessimistic about GDP growth in 1993 and 1994, yet the inflation rate is consistently overestimated. The inflation forecast for 1994 was complicated, however, by the introduction of a new value-added tax, in the form of a 3 per cent Goods and Services Tax (GST). As it turned out, a combination of a large appreciation of the Singapore dollar and the absorption of GST by domestic retailers kept the inflation rate down to 3.6 per cent. Moreover the failure to predict high real GDP growth in 1993 and 1994 is not confined to this model. We return to this issue in Section 8.5 below.

Table 8.5   The ex ante forecasting performance of the ESU model, July 1991 to August 1994

	Forecast mean absolute error		
	Same year	Next year	Both
Consumer expenditure	1.78	1.64	1.72
Private investment	6.05	5.48	5.79
Exports of domestic goods	5.06	9.29	6.83
Imports of goods	5.13	8.37	6.48
GDP	1.41	3.81	2.69
Consumer price inflation	0.79	0.76	0.78

Note: All variables are in real terms (1985=100), the forecast mean absolute error $=\Sigma |yi - \hat{y}i|/n$, where yi is the actual growth rate, $\hat{y}i$ is the forecast growth rate and n is the number of forecasts for the variable; the same year forecasts are the February and August forecasts for the same year; next year forecasts are for the following year; both combines same year and following year.

Sources: The forecasts are taken directly from the half-yearly publications of the Econometric Studies Unit; actual outcomes are from the *Economic Survey of Singapore* various issues.

The ESU also includes regular policy simulations of topical interest with its half-yearly forecasts. ESU (1991), for example, considered the National Productivity Board point of view that wage increases should lag behind productivity increases, in order to ensure that firms have sufficient resources to increase investment and to maintain international competitiveness. Compared to the base simulation, where real wage increases exceed productivity growth, if real wage increases were less than or the same as productivity growth there were positive effects on real investment, real income and real exports (largely due to a fall in unit labour costs), with only a slight increase in inflation. However, the ESU notes that the sharp increase in employment might be untenable in the longer run, given a tight labour market, if the supply of foreign workers remained constant.

ESU (1992) examined the implications of the liquidity drain arising from the placement of government budgetary surpluses and statutory board deposits with the MAS. The share of Government and Statutory Board Deposits (GSBD) as a proportion of total deposits was assumed to continue to rise at the same rate as in the late 1980s (12 per cent) up to 1995. The simulated output resulted in slower economic growth owing to crowding out in the financial and business sector as the liquidity drain reduced the money multiplier and the inflation rate fell. The ESU concluded that the slower output growth might be justified by the 'strong' Singapore dollar policy to keep inflation low.

ESU (1992) also addressed the controversial issue of the internationalization of the Singapore dollar, discussed in Chapter 6. The simulation assumed that the Singapore dollar would undergo a once-and-for-all appreciation of 8 per cent after internationalization with correspondingly sharp falls in domestic interest rates and an increase in the money supply. The simulated appreciation is taken to be a conservative estimation of what would happen, based on the assumption that the Singapore dollar is currently undervalued and that internationalization would result in a substantial increase in foreign demand for it. The results supported the MAS case: there would be a boom in output, especially in business and financial services, a loss of control by the MAS over monetary policy, and unstable feedback effects from the boom over time. Predictably, if the MAS is now assumed to intervene in the forex market to prevent the Singapore dollar appreciating too fast (by selling the Singapore dollar), the negative effects are the same, but are smaller in magnitude. As noted earlier, the ESU94 model is not very well equipped to deal with this type of financial scenario, but it does at least focus empirical attention on an important policy issue.

In contrast to the ESU94 model, the MAS94 model summarized in Table 8.4 is considerably larger, and is quarterly. Although it is used for official purposes, it is not used in collaboration with the Ministry of Trade and Industry for the latter's published quarterly forecasts of real GDP growth in the *Economic Survey of Singapore*. A brief description of the structure of the model and its ethos, including a simplified schematic flow chart is available in Low (1994). The model is based on the same 'stylized' facts for Singapore as the ESU94 model above, but it contains a much more explicit MAS view as to how the economy works, especially as regards the transmission mechanisms through which monetary and fiscal policy have operated since 1981. Central to this view is the assumption that domestic monetary and fiscal policies are relatively powerless as macro stabilization tools.

The perception of Singapore as a price taker in world markets and the very strong links between changes in import prices and domestic prices are also emphasized in the construction of the model. The price of consumer imports is first determined on the basis of an exchange rate adjustment of the foreign non-oil price index. The CPI is then made a function of the price of consumer imports, domestic unit labour costs and oil prices. The estimated coefficients imply that a 1 per cent rise in the price of consumer imports feeds through to a 0.7 per cent increase in the CPI within two years.

A key ingredient of the MAS model is the inclusion of an augmented Phillips curve relationship to determine nominal wage growth ($\Delta W/W$) on the basis of price inflation ($\Delta P/P$), the unemployment rate (U) and labour productivity growth ($\Delta L/L$).[15]

$$\Delta W/W = 8.6 - 2.7\,U + 1.0\,(\Delta P/P) + 1.0\,(\Delta L/L) \qquad (8.5)$$

Using the above simplified coefficients provided by Low (1994), the implication is that wages are very responsive to labour market conditions. A one percentage point increase in the unemployment rate leads to a 2.7 percentage point fall in the rate of growth of wages and the dynamics in the MAS model suggest that price changes are fully passed on to wages within two years. This is close to the classical flexible wage adjustment assumption with no money illusion. In addition, labour productivity gains are reflected in wage growth since wage bargaining in Singapore explicitly takes productivity change into account. We may rearrange equation (8.5) into:

$$\Delta W/W - 1.0\,(\Delta P/P) - 1.0\,(\Delta L/L) = 8.6 - 2.7\,U \qquad (8.6)$$

So for real wage growth to match productivity change:

$$0 = 8.6 - 2.7\,U \qquad (8.7)$$

so $U^* \cong 8.6/2.7 = 3$ per cent, where U^* is the natural rate of unemployment. The policy implication is that, if wage growth exceeds productivity growth, there will be a loss of competitiveness for Singapore since actual U will lie below the natural rate U^*. However, an automatic stabilizer will operate since a persistent $U < U^*$ will raise unit labour costs and dampen exports and GDP growth, thus reducing labour demand and bringing U back to the natural rate.

The MAS model also embodies the MAS philosophy discussed in Chapter 6 that targeting the exchange rate is the most effective way of maintaining domestic price stability in Singapore, which in turn ensures the continued inflow of foreign capital, long-run export competitiveness and sustainable economic growth. Since conventional monetary and fiscal policies are viewed as ineffective instruments for domestic inflation control, targeting the NEER (which is an exogenous policy variable in the model) to neutralize imported inflation works through the more effective transmission mechanism linking import prices to the CPI and through the augmented Phillips curve to wages and employment.

The rapid adjustment of wages to changes in prices, labour productivity and the unemployment rate also lies behind the MAS view that a weaker Singapore dollar will not help export competitiveness in the longer run. Simulating a slower rate of appreciation of the Singapore dollar than the base run improves competitiveness in the short run by lowering the REER and increasing exports and output (which further increases productivity). But in the longer run the rise in import prices passes through to the CPI, and the combined effects of higher domestic prices and a tighter labour market lead to higher wages through the augmented Phillips curve mechanism described above. The initial gains in competitiveness from the manipulation of the NEER are thus offset by higher wages and prices, so that there is no long-run trade-off between inflation and unemployment in Singapore. The speed of adjustment is, of course, crucial here. MAS simulations, summarized in Low (1994), suggest that the period over which external monetary policy can have some effect on real variables such as unem-ployment and output is about three years. After that point 'classical' price and wage adjustment will ensure that exchange rate policy leads only to nominal rises in wages and prices.

The July ESU (1991) also simulates a 'weak dollar' policy by comparing a base run from 1991–5 with the import price index constant, to approximate the policy of neutralizing foreign inflationary pressures, with an alternative scenario in which the import price index rises by 5 per cent each year to represent a weak dollar scenario. In the absence of a Phillips curve relationship to determine nominal wages in the ESU94 model, the inflationary effects of the weak dollar work through by lowering *real* wages and unit labour costs, stimulating a significant growth in employment, but with relatively small effects on real output. Although total exports increase as a result of the weaker dollar, possibly owing to the effects of a rise in tourism spending on service exports, domestic exports of goods do not increase as a result of the depreciation. The ESU94 results are similar, in spirit, therefore, to the MAS model (but based on an annual model), but a more detailed comparison of the transmission mechanisms involved is not possible without the full simulated results from the MAS model, or a similarly constructed equivalent. This emphasizes the need for more independent quarterly models for Singapore.

8.4 MULTI-COUNTRY MACROECONOMETRIC MODELS

A logical extension of the process of building macroeconometric models for individual countries is to link them together through a trade sub-system. One can then analyse how a given country, such as Singapore, or a bloc of countries such as ASEAN, are affected by other countries or blocs of countries, and investigate the interdependence of members of a bloc. Usually this means simplifying the individual country models and modifying them to focus on the objectives of the project, as well as establishing consistent link equations through a trade matrix.[16]

Three multi-country studies have incorporated a model from Singapore. The first is included in Ichimura and Ezaki (1985). This was the original Asian Link Project for East and South-East Asia and contains country models for Japan, the USA, Korea, Taiwan, Hong Kong, China, the Philippines, Malaysia, Singapore, Indonesia and Thailand, together with regional blocs for the rest of the world. The Singapore model is the Ezaki model summarized in Table 8.1. The sequel to this study is Ichimura and Matsumoto (1994) which adds models for Canada, Australia and the European Economic Community. The Singapore national model is the Toh and Ramstetter model in Table 8.1.

Particularly relevant to Singapore's membership of ASEAN is the multi-country study by Yap and Nakamura (1990), linking together country models for Singapore, Malaysia, Indonesia, Thailand and the Philippines. Although it is recognized that intra-ASEAN trade accounts for only a small percentage of any member's total trade, and is dominated by bilateral trade between Singapore and Malaysia (see Section 6.1), the authors nonetheless conclude that significant gains could be achieved by all members from simulations of trade liberalization. They also point to important interdependencies between the ASEAN countries, with Singapore playing an important role. For example, in their chapter 8 they utilize a simple Keynesian multi-country income expenditure framework developed by Toh and Low to examine these interdependencies between 1974 and 1981 and between 1981 and 1986. Although an exogenous increase in final expenditure in Singapore generates a relatively small multiplier feedback effect on its *own* real national income compared to the other ASEAN members, because of Singapore's high marginal propensity to import, it is interesting that Singapore has the strongest multiplier effects of the group on *other* member countries' national incomes, especially on Malaysia and Indonesia.

As expected, Malaysia has the greatest impact on Singapore's national income as compared with the other ASEAN countries. Other kinds of interdependency are also explored, including the calculation of trade multipliers, and policy scenarios assuming closer trading ties between the member countries.

8.5   ALTERNATIVE APPROACHES TO FORECASTING

Rather than building a structural macroeconometric model of the Singapore economy, which may involve heavy fixed costs and extensive revisions and updating (especially if the model is large), why not use a simpler and less costly time-series model? A time-series model attempts to forecast variables such as real GDP using information contained in its own past behaviour or the past behaviour of related variables, instead of on the basis of a set of variables in a causal macroeconomic framework.[17]

One approach is to extract cyclical patterns from the data and to identify 'leading indicators', whose behaviour (especially turning-points) consistently lead the cycle. These can then be combined into an index with a common base year and used to forecast economic activity some quarters ahead. Since most relevant macroeconomic time-series contain strong trends, in practice this cyclical behaviour is a growth cycle and deviations are measured from this trend.

The only published leading indicator for Singapore is the official Composite Leading Index (CLI) published quarterly since 1978 by the Department of Statistics in the *Economic Survey of Singapore*. This predicts economic activity up to three quarters ahead. Table 8.6 lists the nine leading indicators currently used in the CLI, together with a brief description of the reason for their selection. Notice that the manufacturing sector is heavily represented and the last three indicators are measures of business expectations taken from survey data. Business expectations are often a good short-term guide to future activity and are published for one quarter ahead in the *Economic Survey of Singapore*, with separate entries for manufacturing, commerce, transport and storage, business services, real estate and financial services.

Figure 8.1 plots the CLI and an index of real GDP between the first quarter of 1990 and the fourth quarter of 1993. In the fourth quarter of 1993 the CLI grew by 3.4 per cent, up strongly from 1.5 per cent in the third quarter of 1993. Only two components of the index, the wholesale price index for manufactured goods and the (inverted) real unit labour cost, recorded declines during the fourth quarter of 1993. This, together with optimistic expectations by industrialists and businessmen for January to June 1994, influenced the official forecast for real GDP growth in 1994. The forecast, published in the November 1993 *Economic Survey*, was for between 6 and 8 per cent growth in real GDP. This implied a slowdown from the 1993 provisional growth rate of 9.9 per cent (later revised to 10.1) as the boom in the electronics industry was expected to subside, and the unusually high volume of transactions in the stock market in 1993 was not expected to be repeated. In fact this turned out to be too pessimistic, as actual growth in real GDP in 1994 was 10.1 per cent.

Table 8.6   Components of Singapore's Composite Leading Index

Leading indicator	Interpretation
1. Money supply (M2)	Indicates monetary stance
2. Real unit labour costs (manufacturing)	Business costs
3. CPF default rates (manufacturing)	Business costs
4. New company formations per month	Business activity
5. Index of stock prices (SES All Share Price Index)	Business confidence
6. Wholesale price index (manufacturing)	Supply costs
7. Stocks of finished goods	Manufacturing business expectations
8. New orders	Manufacturing business expectations
9. Business forecasts of wholesale trade	Wholesale business expectations

Note: 2 and 3 are inverted before being added to the CLI since they are expected to move inversely with real GDP.

Source: *Economic Survey of Singapore 1993.*

An independent approach to monitoring and forecasting the business cycle for several Asian countries, including Singapore, has been under way since 1984 as part of a regional project initiated and financed by the Japanese Institute of Developing Economies.[18] A series of leading, lagging and coincident indicators has been identified from time-series data and each group of indicators is combined into a 'Diffusion Index' (DI). This measures the proportion of the individual indices showing an increase in value over a previous period.[19] If over half the indicators show a higher value the DI will be above 50 per cent, and vice versa. An expansionary (contractionary) phase is identified if DI is positive (negative) for at least two quarters. This is especially useful for looking at turning points in the business cycle, since troughs and peaks are clearly indicated whenever the DI crosses the 50 per cent threshold and remains on one side for at least two quarters.

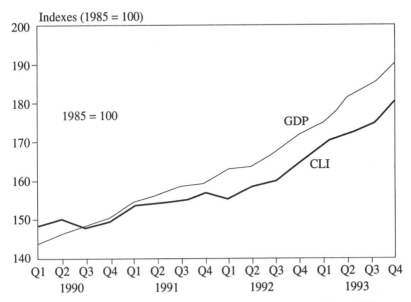

Source: *Yearbook of Statistics Singapore*, various issues; *Economic Survey*, February 1994, Table A1.2.

Figure 8.1 The Composite Leading Index and real GDP, 1990–93

When the diffusion indexes are plotted in Chow Kit Boey (1992) the coincident DI identifies contractionary phases of the growth cycle (slowing down in economic activity) for Singapore from the first quarter of 1977 to the third quarter of 1977, and from the fourth quarter of 1981 to the first quarter 1983, but a 'classical' business cycle (absolute downturn) between the last quarter of 1984 and the last quarter of 1985. The leading DI also gave early warnings of the 1981–3 slowdown and 1985 recession, and the lagging DI confirmed in 1986 the start of the 1985 recession.

How good is the CLI as a forward-looking indicator? Chow (1993) uses time-series statistical techniques to evaluate the CLI, both in terms of the strength of the relationships between the leading indicators and actual GDP, and of the accuracy of the CLI as a forecaster of future GDP. Between the first quarter of 1978 and the second quarter of 1991 the CLI does generally lead GDP but the lead time is very short.[20] The three expectation variables listed in Table 8.6 (7–9) perform well but real unit labour costs in manufacturing (2) and CPF default rates (3) were found to be better as *lagging* indicators, and the index of stock prices (5) was coincident (and very volatile). A solution is to replace these indicators with other leading indicators, but this is hampered by a shortage of suitable variables with a long enough time-series.

To test the forecasting accuracy of the CLI Chow (1993) fitted a simple time-series model to quarterly GDP data from the first quarter of 1978 to the second quarter of 1991, and lagged values of the CLI ranging from one to six quarters were added to the model to see if it improved upon the 'fit'. It turns out that the CLI significantly improves the model up to three periods ahead, which therefore makes it suitable for short-term forecasting, but its contribution falls off sharply after the first quarter. When the time-series model with CLI included is used to forecast two years beyond the sample it performs better than the time-series model alone when the CLI is lagged up to three periods.[21] At present, therefore, the CLI is only useful for forecasting up to three quarters; longer-run predictions will require either an alternative time-series model or a structural model such as the ESU94 or MAS94 macroeconometric models. But would a simple time-series model forecast better than the structural ESU model?

Abeysinghe (1992) compared the forecasting performance of the ESU model between 1988 and 1992 for real GDP with his own small quarterly time-series model.[22] This model uses only past data for real GDP and current and past data for two exogenous variables: the Malaysian industrial production index (to capture regional activity) and the OECD industrial production index (to capture growth in the rest of the world). The coefficients of the model estimated between 1975 and 1988 suggest that quarterly growth in GDP can be explained by 90 per cent of the quarterly growth of GDP of the same quarter in the previous year plus some fractional contribution from growth in the Malaysian and OECD industrial indexes. The exogenous variables only contribute positively to GDP growth if they grow by more than 90 per cent of their growth over the same quarter of the previous year.

Table 8.7 shows that the simple time-series model forecasts remarkably well, both in absolute terms and compared to its much bigger rival! The author concludes that, if the objective is purely to forecast, then you might as well use the smaller model, which is less expensive to compute, and make the same sort of judgemental adjustments to this model as you would to the larger structural model. In fact, the quarterly GDP forecasts from the ESU since August 1994 have been based on both the structural ESU94 model and additional time-series models.

Although time-series models have been increasingly used to supplement or replace macroeconometric models as forecasting tools, there is no real alternative to the all-round capability of a structural macroeconometric model (Whitley, 1994). In fact, the use of time-series models for forecasting would free the ESU94 model for more experimentation, since the size of the tracking errors would be less important than the capacity of the model to embody currently missing features of the Singapore economy. The ESU is currently attempting to build a quarterly structural model for Singapore.

Table 8.7   The ESU and Abeysinghe forecasts for real GDP growth, 1988–94 (per cent)

Year	ESU	Abeysinghe	Actual
1988	—	11.05	11.10
1989	8.10	9.29	9.20
1990	8.75	8.56	8.80
1991	7.49	6.69	6.70
1992	4.70	5.86	6.00
1993	8.12	8.10	10.10
1994	9.90	10.00	10.10

Note: The actual figures are revised figures from the *Economic Survey of Singapore 1994*, not the figures from Abeysinghe (1992); the ESU forecasts are from the July publication of the same year, the Abeysinghe model uses data available up to the fourth quarter of the previous year, except for 1994, which is based on data up to the third quarter of 1993.

Sources: Abeysinghe (1992) and subsequent updates.

8.6   FORECASTING SINGAPORE'S GDP

Table 8.8 lists a range of *ex ante* forecasts, both official and independent, of Singapore's real GDP growth in 1993, 1994 and 1995, together with the actual figures for 1993 and 1994. The forecasts come from a range of approaches including structural macroeconometric models such as ESU (before August 1994), a mixture of structural and time-series analysis, such as the MTI (including the CLI) and the Institute of Developing Economies (IDE), as well as more ad hoc judgemental forecasts based on a mixture of information sources, such as those contained in the survey by the *Business Times* on 7 October 1994.

Although it is not possible to compare these forecasts in any formal sense, since they appear at different time intervals and later figures are often revised to take into account what has happened since the earlier forecasts were published, the message from Table 8.8 is that both official and independent forecasters underestimated growth in both 1993 (10.1 per cent) and 1994 (10.1 per cent). Not one forecast exceeded the actual! Even more surprising is that there does not seem to be any learning process! The predictions for 1994 were substantially below the actual even though it was common knowledge that the forecasts for the previous year were far too pessimistic and the quarterly figures which became available during the year were well above expectations. The reader will be able to judge whether this will be repeated for 1995, when the data become available after the publication of this book.

*Table 8.8   Independent and official forecasts of real GDP growth, 1993–5
          (per cent)*

Forecaster	Date of forecast	1993	1994	1995
Ministry of Trade and Industry, Singapore (MTI)	November 1992	5–6		
	May 1993	6–7		
	August 1993	7.5–8		
	November 1993		6–8	
	February 1994		6–8	
	May 1994		6–8	
	August 1994		9–10	
	November 1994		8–9	
	February 1995			7.5–8.5
Econometric Studies Unit, National University, Singapore	February 1993	6.4	4.1	5.2
	August 1993	8.1	6.3	5.3
	February 1994		8.5	7.5
	August 1994		9.9	8.3
	February 1995			8.1
Abeysinghe (1992)	February 1993	8.1		
	August 1993		10.0	
Economics Intelligence Unit, London (EIU)	March 1993	6.7	6.3	
National Research Institute (NRI)	September 1993	7.7	6.7	
Institute of Developing Economies, Tokyo (IDE)	November 1993	9.0	6.5–7	
Business Times, Singapore	October 1994		9.4	7.7–8
Actual	Annual	10.1	10.1	
	First quarter	7.5	11.9	
	Second quarter	11.1	9.5	
	Third quarter	10.3	10.9	
	Fourth quarter	10.7	8.3	

Note: MTI forecasts are given in the quarterly *Economic Survey of Singapore*; the real GDP forecasts from the Econometrics Studies Unit beginning in August 1994 are supplemented by time-series models related to Abeysinghe (1992); the *Business Times's* forecasts are based on an average of 20 forecasters from banking houses, banks and research institutes compiled in the *Business Times*, 7 October 1994, the IDE, EIU and NRI forecasts are reproduced from Toida and Hiratsuka (1994).

Especially interesting here is the reluctance of the MTI to revise its original forecasts for 1994 in spite of buoyant growth throughout the year. The May 1994 forecast retained the February estimate of 6–8 per cent (but with stress on the upper limit) despite first quarter growth of 11 per cent (later revised to 11.9). Only in August was this forecast revised up to 9–10 per cent. The view seemed to be that growth in 1993 was unusually high and that, although 1994 was also expected to be a good year (based on an upward trend for the CLI and optimistic business expectations discussed above), growth would be lower than in the previous year: over the long run Singapore growth would settle down to a steady and sustainable 4–6 per cent. Whether the formal models used by the MTI are performing badly or conservatism is entering at the judgemental stage is, of course, impossible to say, since the information is not made public.

This pessimistic attitude seems to have been shared by independent forecasters. There is a perception in Singapore that independent forecasters are overly influenced by the official forecasts and that, given Singapore's status as a leading financial centre, it ought to have a wider range of 'authoritative' independent forecasts (*Straits Times*, 12 September 1994). It is heartening to learn that the Economic Society of Singapore has launched an 'Economic Forecast of the Year Award' to stimulate the further development of economic forecasting in Singapore.

SUGGESTIONS FOR FURTHER READING

For a recent review of the history of macroeconometric modelling, 'warts and all', see Bodkin *et al.* (1991). Research specifically on East and South-East Asia is reviewed in Ichimura and Matsumoto (1994). Whitley (1994) provides an excellent introduction to macroeconometric modelling and forecasting, including a comparison between the major UK, US and European models. A non-technical explanation of attempts to identify business cycles for Singapore is contained in Chow Kit Boey (1988).

NOTES

1. For a review of the history of macroeconometric modelling, see Bodkin *et al.* (1991).
2. Further details on the evolution of macroeconometric modelling in Singapore can be found in Toh (1990).
3. The ESU86 model should, strictly speaking, be regarded as quasi-official, since in Singapore University staff are regarded as public employees.
4. These problems have been extensively discussed in Soon Teck Wong *et el.* (1990). For an official guide to the sources of the data on Singapore, see *Statistics Singapore: An Official Guide* (1994).
5. A listing of the equations of the ESU model is contained in the February ESU (1991) but without the data. We have been assured, however, that these data are available for public use.

6. The relative shortage in the supply of macroeconometric models for the Singapore economy is noted in the comprehensive reviews of model-building in East and South-East Asia by Ichimura and Ezaki (1985) and Ichimura and Matsumoto (1994).

7. For an excellent introduction to macroeconometric modelling and forecasting, including a comparative discussion of the major UK, US and European models, see Whitley (1994).

8. A term for statistical discrepancies is omitted from equation (8.1) for simplicity, as is a dummy variable from the original employment equation.

9. t-statistics and adjusted R^2 are supplied for all estimated equations in Lim and associates (1988).

10. The principles of simulation, including simulations of macroeconometric models, together with plenty of useful examples, can be found in Pindyck and Rubinfield (1991).

11. R-squared measures the correlation between actual and simulated. The higher the correlation, the closer the simulated series matches the actual data. PRMSE measures the deviation of the simulated variable from actual in percentage terms. The lower the PRMSE, the better the tracking performance of the simulated variable.

12. A rise in REER here implies an improvement in competitiveness. In Chapter 6 we inverted this to facilitate interpretation when graphed.

13. Although the MAS model is not available for public use, we are grateful to the MAS for providing us with the necessary information to complete Tables 8.1 and 8.4, and to facilitate the discussion of the model in the text.

14. Equations are now included for Singapore's investment abroad, net factor income from abroad, and private investment in construction and works. Allowance is also made for the corporate tax rate and changes in regional GNP.

15. The CPF contribution rate is also included in the equation but is omitted here to simplify the exposition.

16. Multi-country trade models are reviewed by Hickman (1991). See also the review by Klein (1994) of current and projected work on Project Link in the Asia–Pacific region.

17. For a discussion of time-series models and how they compare with other forecasting models, including macroeconometric simulation models, see Pindyck and Rubinfield (1991).

18. See Chow Kit Boey (1988, 1992).

19. $DI = [(\Sigma +) + 1/2 (\Sigma 0)]/N$; where + indicates a higher value of an indicator over a previous period, 0 implies no change, and N is the total number of indicators.

20. If a component of the CLI leads GDP, the cross-correlation coefficients between the two should be more significant at the positive leads, while more significant spikes at the negative leads would suggest that the indicator is lagging GDP.

21. Chow and Chan have also developed a set of leading indicators for monitoring and forecasting Singapore's inflation rate. For further details, see ESU (1995).

22. Updated figures were supplied subsequently by Dr Abeysinghe.

9. In place of a conclusion

In this chapter we present a few issues that are currently being discussed in Singapore. We attempt no predictions of likely outcomes, nor do we attempt to offer answers to these questions. Interested readers will be able to discover whether they do become important issues in the near future and what effect they have on the economy through their own observations.

9.1 THE 'SECOND WING' POLICY AND 'HOLLOWING OUT'

We have seen how keen the government is to encourage Singaporean firms to invest in the developing and liberalizing countries of the region. Many GLCs have taken this up and Singapore is involved in several regional economies in different forms of activity. Prominent initiatives include town planning and development in Suzhou in China, and building industrial parks in India and a new port in Vietnam. The budget for FY95 gave further incentives to Singaporean firms to continue this trend (*Business Times*, 2 March 1995).

One possible consequence of this policy that has given rise to concern is the 'hollowing out' of the economy. This term is used in regard to the possibility that Singaporean manufacturing firms might relocate to cheaper neighbouring countries, thus 'exporting jobs', as it is sometimes put, and reduce the manufacturing 'core' of the economy. This issue is based on the 'sandwich problem' discussed in Chapter 6, derived from the view that Singapore will eventually lose its comparative advantage in the production of low-skill labour-intensive goods and some capital-intensive goods to other NICs and emerging NICS before it has reached the stage at which it can compete with advanced industrial countries in technology and skill-intensive goods. The shift to service provision, such as providing conference facilities and tourism and servicing the high value-added manufacturing that would remain in Singapore, would not be a problem as long as the service sector grows to absorb the growing and retrenched labour force.

A good example of an economy that has exported its manufacturing sector is Hong Kong where, from the early 1980s, its entrepreneurs were able to relocate their manufacturing activities to places in the Pearl River delta. Sometimes the 'capital' was exported in visible and physical form as businessmen closed down their factories on a Saturday, sent their machinery and equipment across the border and started work again the following week employing Chinese workers. In Hong Kong the manufacturing sector's share of GDP has fallen from 29 per cent in 1970 to 16 per cent in the early 1990s, whereas in Singapore, over the same period, manufacturing has risen from 20 per cent to 28 per cent of GDP. As it is the government's view that manufacturing must be retained at this proportion of output, there might be a problem. The fear is that the Singaporean workforce might not be able to adapt to the loss of manufacturing jobs and switch to those activities that would service the overseas manufacturing base, such as design and marketing services and the provision of insuring, banking and transport services. Many of Singapore's exports come from foreign firms which brought with them their own marketing skills, markets and connections, so there is not much indigenous talent in these areas. Hong Kong has been able to achieve this restructuring probably because of its better educated and flexible workforce and their skills in the areas of design and marketing, and also because of its continuing role as China's main port and thus entrepot for the goods that are being manufactured in China. Singapore does not have a reputation equal to that of Hong Kong for its design and marketing skills.

Some Singaporean leaders stress the need to retain manufacturing at its present level. In late 1994, when he was in Australia, the Prime Minister announced that Singapore would, however, emphasize financial services and information technology in its next stage of development (*Business Times*, 19 September 1994, p.1).[1] This will be connected with the recently announced new policy direction of making Singapore 'grow its own multinationals' as announced by the Prime Minister (*Business Times*, 25–6 March 1995, p.1). He noted that these need not be wholly Singaporean-owned MNCs but could tie up with foreign partners so that 'we add on to the vast contributions of the foreign MNCs'. The aim is to build up about a dozen into major firms in the region and this must be done systematically. The plan is for the Economic Development Board to use about S$1 billion to 'nurture 100 promising local enterprises (PLEs) over the next 10 years'. Many of these PLEs are likely to be associated with Singapore's 'targeted industry clusters, such as electronics, precision engineering, heavy engineering and chemicals'. The Prime Minister summarized by noting:

> MNCs and borrowed technology have helped us rapidly leap from a poor trading village to an NIE, and in time to come to a developed economy.
>
> Foreign MNCs will continue to play a dominant part in our development. But to break through to the next level of development, we have to increasingly develop our homegrown talent and our own MNCs. (*Business Times*, 25–6 March 1995, p.1)

9.2 WHAT IF THE MNCs MOVED OUT?

This is a question sometimes asked in Singapore. If it is profitable and desirable for Singaporean firms and GLCs to relocate some activities to neighbouring countries could this also apply to the MNCs already in Singapore? Announcements of further investment plans by MNCs in Singapore are given prominent press coverage and those of decisions to relocate some activities abroad or not to expand in Singapore are also covered. Even the Prime Minister has expressed his worry, each time an important MNC has announced investment outside Singapore, that it might be the beginning of a trend: 'PM's fear: Siemens' move to China might be followed by other MNCs' (*The Straits Times*, 9 November 1994, p.1) so this issue cannot be labelled 'scaremongering'. As a PAP member of parliament, Koo Tsai Kee, put it, 'At present a significant proportion of our GDP is non-indigenous, meaning that our technological base is weak' (*The Straits Times*, 4 March 1995, p.34). Not only is the technological base weak but there is the problem of labour shortages, especially of skilled and tertiary-educated workers, resulting in employers pushing for larger quotas for foreign workers. Population growth is now slower and participation rates are high. As we have seen, Singapore's growth has been mainly based on the growth of the labour force and the capital stock rather than through significant productivity growth.

This dependence on MNCs has been recently stressed by Richardson (1994) in his assessment of the possible position of Singapore in the early twentieth century. Richardson's overall conclusion is that Singapore will be 'first-world' in terms of income and wealth and will have a 'first-world' economic structure, with a highly developed services sector and more specialized manufacturing (p.96). He continues, however:

> But Singapore will remain economically vulnerable in a way that 'first-world' countries are not. The predominance of foreign-owned firms in its manufacturing base will continue and a substantial proportion of these will remain US-owned. These firms have no underlying reasons to remain in Singapore and if economic or political circumstances forced them elsewhere, Singapore would find it difficult to fill the void. Singapore will continue to have little influence on international events. While it may become a substantial investor in some Asia-Pacific countries, it is unlikely ever to gain such a presence that the host government can be pressured to accede to its wishes. In international arenas Singapore's tiny size, and the authoritarian nature of its government, will make it difficult for it to exert much influence. (Richardson, 1994, p.97)

Of the various senses in which the Singapore economy is described as being 'vulnerable', the possibility of highly volatile movements in both short-term and long-term capital flows, including the very important foreign direct investment component, is perhaps the most important. Traditional arguments about export instability, as applied to developing countries, may not be so applicable to Singapore. Although there have been significant fluctuations in export earnings, this has not prevented Singapore from achieving high and stable long-run growth with low inflation. Export fluctuations have caused no obvious balance of payments difficulties given overall balance of payments surpluses and growing official foreign reserves. Moreover the income multiplier effects generated by external shocks are heavily damped by leakages from the circular flow of income. As we saw in Chapter 2, 1994 saw a huge increase in net exports and there have been no obvious adverse effects on the economy.

9.3   PUBLIC AND PRIVATE ACTIVITIES AND OVERSPECIALIZATION

Despite the government's plans to privatize some of its activities and to encourage the indigenous private sector, it is felt by some that the public sector still dominates the economy with harmful effects on both economic and social life (Chee, 1994, pp.101–12). The government continues to lay down the direction the economy must take, sometimes bringing local firms into its plans. We have also seen a few examples of this in Chapter 1 in the area of computer technology and the recent view that financial services and information technology should be encouraged and that PLEs need to be 'nurtured' to MNC status. We have seen that this policy of continually pushing the economy into new areas of endeavour is blamed by Young (1992) for Singapore's very poor performance in increasing its total factor productivity (Chapter 7) and that this thus requires a very high ratio of investment to GDP to achieve its high GDP growth rates. As we saw in Chapter 1, the structure of the manufacturing sector has been shifting more and more towards electronic products and components, petroleum products and paint, pharmaceuticals and other chemical products. Academic economists, as well as politicians, have expressed concern (Chee, 1994, p.109; *The Straits Times* 4 March 1995, p.34).

The recent reconsideration of the question of whether Singapore is a developed country and the nature of its problems seems to have been inspired by the Economist Intelligence Unit report, *Singapore 2003: Aspiring to the First World,* by Graham Richardson (1994) mentioned above. Richardson thinks the average real GDP growth for the period 1994–8 will be 7.7 per cent, before settling down to an average 4.8 per cent per annum during the period 1999–2003, mainly owing to a fall in the competitiveness of the manufacturing sector caused by rising real wages and other costs and the drift of banking and other services to other regional centres as fears about Hong Kong's future ease, and because of a poorly performing Singapore stock market (Richardson, 1994, p.95).

A PAP member of parliament, Koo Tsai Kee, has ben quoted as saying he 'dismissed as "absurd" the idea that Singapore was a developed country' (*The Straits Times*, 4 March 1995, p.34).

9.4 CONSUMPTION, INVESTMENT AND GROWTH

Singapore maintains a very high ratio of investment to GDP and thus has to have a very low ratio of consumption to GDP, given its low rate of productivity growth. The government keeps current consumption low through the CPF scheme and through limits on bank lending for consumption purposes. This has produced continuing complaints that the quality of life is just not improving in Singapore. Why should people work harder in order to maintain a high growth rate for Singapore Inc. and not see their lives improve? The government's reaction is, in the words of the Prime Minister:

> Singaporeans' lives get tougher because ... they're spending more. They are buying homes, buying cars. They are asset-rich but cash-tight. That's the problem we are facing. (*Business Times*, 25–6 February 1995, p.2, reporting on his interview with the *Financial Times*. Omission is in this source.)

The Deputy Prime Minister, BG (NS) Lee Hsien Loong, attributes the dissatisfaction of Singaporeans with current circumstances to rising, and possibly unsustainable, expectations:

> One reason for high expectations is our smooth and apparently effortless success – no recessions, no disasters. Dr Albert Winsemius, who was here, pointed out to MTI that it has been quite long since we had a recession; perhaps it is time to organise one. (*The Straits Times*, 14 February 1995, p.28 reporting his address at the Nanyang Technological University.)[2]

The most common explanation the government offers for the low standard of living is the very size of Singapore, which limits the possibility of providing more recreational facilities, opportunities for travel within the country and so on. Singapore provides just 220 square metres of land per person compared to 17 000 for each Malaysian and 9500 for each Indonesian. This comparison was offered by Dr Richard Hu in parliament to justify the government's preoccupation with building up cash reserves as 'All we have is cash reserves and nothing else' (*The Straits Times*, 16 March 1995, p.1).

Economic progress is nearly always identified with the growth rate of real GDP, to the exclusion of all else except the government's reminder about the increase in household ownership of cars and consumer durables. It is admitted that in Singapore things might not be perfect today but they will be better in the future. The Prime Minister has said that now is not the time for political liberalization, but perhaps in 20, or even ten, years' time things will be freer. In the schools the children are taught to sing, 'Tomorrow it will be better' (*Mingtian hui geng hao*).

The continued rapid growth of Singapore Inc. has become an obsession and it is usually identified with the growth rate of GDP. Civil servants' bonuses are based on this rate and it is the main indicator used in announcements of economic progress. As soon as last year's growth rate is announced projections for the next year appear and people do their informal planning on the basis of these forecasts.[3] Recently it has been suggested that a better yardstick should be found to replace reliance on this single GDP growth rate. A Singaporean academic, Associate Professor Basant Kapur, has suggested compiling a weighted average of Indigenous Gross National Product (IGNP) and some index that reflects the change in the distribution of income. The weights to be used, in Singaporean fashion, 'could be determined through discussion and consensus' (*The Straits Times* 25 February 1995, p.46). However anyone is free to construct such an index using their own approach, or any other index, and see whether it commands general consensus in the market-place of ideas.

We have reviewed the easily available data of IGNP in Chapter 1 and have shown that it is more relevant for identifying the incomes of Singaporeans. It would be more useful if we were to use the per capita measure which is calculated for us by the statisticians. This measure includes income from all sources and only relates to Singaporeans' incomes. Its growth rate would thus show how, on average, a Singaporean benefited from economic growth in terms of income from all sources. In the three years 1991–3 real IGNP grew by 6.2, 5.4 and 8.4 per cent when real GDP grew by 6.7, 6.0 and 9.9 per cent, respectively. The per capita IGNP growth rates were 4.0, 3.3 and 6.3 per cent, a more interesting measure. Perhaps wider knowledge of this lower growth rate would moderate Singaporeans' expectations when they hear that 'the economy grew 10.1 per cent this year', as it did in 1994.

Combining the growth of IGNP with a measure of income distribution would provide an index that reflected how the distribution of this IGNP changed from year to year. We guess that the proposer would design the index so that an increase in the degree of equality of income was thought to be a good thing, but he did not actually say this, so his audience does not know. The resulting index might be rather difficult to understand as it combines two different types of information and we would want to know why it changed at a certain rate in a given year; was it the IGNP growth that dominated or was there a big change in income distribution? Perhaps a simple 'report card' approach would be clearer, with a number of indicators being featured for the current and a few previous years so we could see their change. For example, we could list the following: GDP growth rate, GNP growth rate, IGNP level and its growth rate both in aggregate and per capita terms, Singapore's IGNP per capita as a proportion of that of Switzerland, perhaps, the unemployment rate and the rate of inflation, an index of the distribution of income, the suicide rate, the number of people who have emigrated each year, the serious crime rate and other social indicators.

9.5 COMPETITIVENESS

In early 1995 the main focus of the concern about Singapore's competitiveness relates to the exchange value of the Singapore dollar. The local currency continued to appreciate against the US dollar as the latter continued to depreciate against nearly all other major currencies, particularly against the Japanese yen. By 17 March 1995 the US dollar bought only S$1.402. For companies in Singapore exporting to the USA, Singapore's largest market for domestic exports, a continuation of this trend would erode the value of their export earnings. One benefit of an appreciating Japanese yen would be that Japanese MNCs would be more willing to expand production in their factories located outside Japan. Many of these factories buy their inputs from the USA and then export the finished goods back to that country. One Japanese company, NEC, has stated that it will extend its production outside Japan, including its activities in Singapore. Those Japanese MNCs located in Singapore that import their inputs from Japan and then export to the USA would feel the effect of the increasing costs of inputs and the falling value of export sales. The general manager of Hitachi Consumer Products (Singapore) Pte has announced that profits are falling and he believes that, 'If this situation continues, most manufacturers may have to relocate from Singapore' (*The Straits Times*, 7 March 1995, p.40).

The MAS is aware of this issue and as a 'monetary officer' put it:

> We are well aware that we must try to keep the S$ at a level where it does not have an adverse effect on economic performance, especially on exports. At the same time, we operate an open system and cannot stop large amounts of foreign funds parking in S$s. (*Financial Times,* 'Survey on Singapore', 24 February 1995,p.II)

Whether the MAS's exchange rate policy has adversely affected export competitiveness will continue to be a hotly debated issue in the near future. Opinions differ according to the exchange rate examined and the theory used to try to identify the equilibrium exchange rate. Some economists such as Yip (1994) believe that the NEER was substantially overvalued in terms of its long-run purchasing power value between 1981 and 1986 and again after 1990, with important implications for export competitiveness and the success of the MAS's policy in targeting its own NEER to contain inflation. Others, such as the DBS report (DBS, 1992), are less sure that Singapore's competitiveness is so far out of line with that of other countries in East Asia or that exchange rate movements have adversely affected the competitiveness of Singapore's exports in the late 1980s. In fact, Singapore may have improved its position compared to Hong Kong, Korea, Taiwan, Malaysia and Thailand in both the American and Japanese markets by squeezing profits to maintain export prices. This is an important empirical issue that requires further research to disaggregate exports to see how different industries or firms reacted to changes in cost components including imported inputs when setting prices. It may be the case, as is sometimes argued with respect to Japan, that currency appreciation might even act as an incentive to reduce costs and improve quality, an argument sometimes heard in Singapore.

Much discussion about competitiveness likens countries to companies that are competing in the same market where the gains to one company, in terms of larger market share for example, are the losses to its rivals. The fear that a country can 'go bankrupt' is derived from this analogy, which can be taken too far as it fails to recognize that countries are not like competing firms and that international trade allows all parties to gain. Specialization allows gains, but for the gains to be realized there must be full opportunities to trade in open markets. Firms in Singapore have the advantage of having access to these open markets and can, if allowed, adapt to the changing world environment. What Singapore needs is rich and developing neighbours. Furthermore identifying 'competitiveness' with an overall index such as labour costs is misleading since at any given time there will be some sectors that are finding things difficult while there will be other sectors that are able to produce profitably and expand.

9.6   INTERNATIONALIZATION OF THE SINGAPORE DOLLAR

Although the Singapore government is keen to promote Singapore as an important international financial centre, it continues to adopt a cautious stance with respect to the further internationalization of the Singapore dollar. This was clearly revealed in Dr Richard Hu's interview in *Euromoney,* in February 1995. On the one hand, policy since 1986 has been directed towards developing Singapore into a risk management centre based upon a range of money market and capital market activities. The further liberalization of the CPF scheme in 1994 is part of the policy of encouraging fund managers to locate in Singapore. On the other hand, the incentives given to the development of offshore financial markets such as the ADM and the ADBM have been balanced by the determination to keep these markets separate from the onshore financial system to insulate the domestic monetary system and prevent the offshore market from impeding the development of the domestic financial system. This has become increasingly difficult as the amounts of equities foreigners are allowed to buy have increased and the quota of Singapore dollars allocated to foreign banks has been progressively raised to the current level of S$100 million. There is also a 'leakage' of Singapore dollars abroad as Singapore companies are encouraged to invest abroad.

In view of these factors, the policy of not encouraging the internationalization of the Singapore dollar by creating a market for depositing and lending the dollar outside Singapore is a 'rearguard action' (*Euromoney*, February 1995). Financial development in Singapore requires some flexibility in allowing banks to deal in the Singapore dollar but this makes the economy vulnerable to the movement of dollar assets outside Singapore. In February 1995 the MAS issued a warning to the banks in Singapore to stop the practice known as 'roundtripping' through which the banks arrange with their non-bank customers in Singapore to place Singapore dollar deposits with their sister branches or subsidiaries outside Singapore to earn a higher return and to circumvent MAS reserve requirements.

The MAS view is that the further internationalization should proceed at a controlled pace to prevent the increased vulnerability to speculative monetary and capital flows which internationalization would bring with it. Moreover the increasing pool of Singapore dollars outside Singapore would imply a further loss of control by the MAS over monetary policy. At present the MAS is confident it has sufficient resources to deal with any speculative attack. There will, however, be increasing pressure on the MAS to remove its restrictions on internationalization as Singapore develops as an international financial centre from, for example, foreign companies wishing to list on the Singapore stock exchange in Singapore dollars to remove currency risk.

9.7   HONG KONG AND '1997'

How Hong Kong's economy will develop after it returns to Chinese sovereignty at midnight on 30 June 1997 is still unknown and continues to be subject to speculation. The official Singapore view is that Hong Kong and Singapore are complementary economies, and so what is bad for Hong Kong is bad for Singapore, and that Singapore could not benefit from any harmful impact on Hong Kong's economy before or after 1997. In Singapore it is expected that there will be a smooth transition. Singapore has, however, taken advantage of worries and uncertainties that have arisen in Hong Kong during its long transition period. For example, in 1989, after the impact of the killings in and around Tiananmen Square in Peking in June, the Singapore government stepped up its recruitment programme for skilled workers in Hong Kong. Special recruitment booths were set up and the promise of permanent residence or citizenship were dangled in front of up to 25 000 Hong Kong citizens and their families. It seems that the response has been disappointing (Richardson, 1994, p.47). Singapore continues to send recruitment teams abroad and recently attention has been paid to the countries of central and eastern Europe and the former Soviet Union in the search for specialists in computing and electronics.

The further liberalization of the CFP scheme in late 1994 and the new policy of making statutory boards and GLCs issue bonds and use fund managers in Singapore are seen by some as aimed at attracting fund managers from Hong Kong to Singapore.

9.8   INFORMATION AND ECONOMIC DATA

Research on the Singapore economy is hampered by the lack of official data in some areas. Singaporean economists frequently bemoan the lack of data about the foreign workforce, which makes it difficult to analyse questions of income distribution and productivity. Data on the nature of people who choose to leave Singapore are not readily available and they are hardly ever discussed and analysed in the media in the way in which they are in Hong Kong, for example. The effect emigration has had on the workforce is hard to assess.

Recently *The Straits Times*'s editorial (7 March 1995) called upon the CPF to release more data on investments by members who have withdrawn funds for their own investment purposes in order for us to assess whether private investors have been able to obtain a better return on their funds than the CPF offers. There is also the question of whether the liberalization of the use of CPF funds and the development of Singapore as a financial centre will result in greater transparency about the nation's wealth, including the fixed assets of the GIC and the flows of funds between the various government and non-government bodies. As privatization proceeds, questions might be asked about the returns being earned on public sector surpluses both domestically and abroad. The accumulation of large amounts of foreign exchange reserves remains an important priority for Singapore, as Dr Richard Hu confirmed in *Euromoney,* in February 1995.

There is an insufficient supply of independent macroeconometric models in Singapore compared to the situation in other countries, including those in the region. This is despite Singapore's level of economic development and the sophistication of its data base. This has led to an overreliance by forecasters on official forecasts and a lack of a constructive framework for assessing government policy. The construction of rival models based on open access to the listings of the models' equations and data has been an important catalyst in the development of macroeconometric modelling in other countries and this has increased both the range and quality of their models. The development of quarterly models along the lines of the MAS model would be especially useful since it would enable independent researchers to evaluate critical government policy assumptions such as the augmented Phillips curve relationship and the mechanisms linking managed floating of the exchange rate to inflation and export performance. There are important differences of opinion here which simulation analysis may be able to clarify. This would also facilitate more comparative work on the magnitude of important multipliers and structural relationships of the economy and allow the much-needed extension of real sector models, such as the ESU model, to include supply-side constraints and financial variables.

In Chapter 8 we noted that the Economic Society of Singapore has established an annual award for the 'Economic Forecast of the Year'. The first winners were announced in March 1995. There were seven participant teams who had to provide forecasts for 1994 in the third quarter of 1994 itself. The variables that had to be forecast included real GDP growth, growth rates for sectors of the economy, the inflation rate, the exchange rate of the Singapore dollar and the stock market index, and participants had to explain how they arrived at their forecasts. The best set of forecasts was by Mr Kaan Quan Hon of DBS Investment Research. The forecasts themselves and how close they were to the actual outcomes for 1994 were not revealed. DBS Securities does not use a full-fledged econometric model and the forecasts were based on 'an eclectic approach'. (*The Straits Times,* 29 March 1995, p.38). The winner also predicted real GDP growth for 1995 to be about 8 per cent.

SUGGESTIONS FOR FURTHER READING

We cannot provide footnote references for all of the above statements as they are derived from our experience of living and working in Singapore. Our suggested readings must be the sources from which we have derived these points and impressions: that is, the Singapore press, the non-Singapore press, Singaporeans and discussions about Singapore found on the discussion group soc.culture.singapore available to some people through the Internet computer network. We provide some information about electronic sources of information about Singapore in the references to this book.

Richardson (1994) is well worth consulting, as is Tremewan (1994).

NOTES

1. This is a very common feature of Singapore government policy announcements: they are often made by the leaders when they are outside Singapore, showing that they probably think they are more relevant to foreign investors than to Singaporeans.
2. Dr Albert Winsemius was the head of a United Nations Survey Mission which wrote a report, 'A Proposed Industrialisation Programme for the State of Singapore', in June 1961. 'The First Development Plan, 1960 to 1964, extended later to 1965, prepared by the Economic Planning Unit under the Prime Minister's Office drew considerable guidance from this unpublished UN

document' (Low, 1993a, p.33). 'Dr Winsemius stayed on as the government's economic adviser until 1984' (Low, 1993b, p.85).

3.   Consider what would happen if the rate of growth of GDP fell. Recently 10 per cent annual growth has provided a bonus of two or two-and-a-quarter months' salary for civil servants in the last few years. If growth fell to 6 per cent and it was felt that bonuses should only be one month's salary then total annual income would fall from 15 months' basic salary (civil servants usually get 13 months' basic salary) to 14 months, that is by 7 per cent. The economy would still be growing but salaries would fall. This is an accelerator principle linking a level (incomes) to a rate of change. If no bonuses were paid then annual income would fall by about 14 per cent. Perhaps this is why some people want to maintain high growth rates of GDP.

Bibliography

STATISTICAL SOURCES AND REPORTS

Annual Report and Accounts of the Board of Commissioners of Currency, Singapore, Singapore: Board of Commissioners of Currency, various years.

Asian Development Outlook, Manila: Asian Development Bank, various years.

Asian Development Report 1993, Manila: Oxford University Press for the Asia Development Bank.

Balance of Payments Statistics Yearbook, Washington D.C.: International Monetary Fund, various years.

Bank Negara Malaysia: Annual Report 1992, Kuala Lumpur, Bank Negara Malaysia, 1993.

Competitive Salaries for Competent & Honest Government: Benchmarks for Ministers & Senior Public Officers, White Paper, Command 13 of 1994, Prime Minister's Office, Republic of Singapore.

Digest of Singapore Labour Market Statistics 1991, Singapore: Singapore Institute of Labour Studies.

Direction of Trade Statistics, Washington, D.C.: International Monetary Fund, June 1994.

Economic and Social Statistics Singapore 1960–1982, Singapore: Department of Statistics Singapore, 1983.

Economic Survey of Singapore, Singapore: Ministry of Trade and Industry, Republic of Singapore, various years.

Economic Survey of Singapore, Singapore: Ministry of Trade and Industry, Republic of Singapore, various quarterly issues.

Efficiency of Singapore Companies: A Study of the Return to Assets Ratios, Singapore: Department of Statistics, Occasional Paper in Financial Statistics, 1992.

Estimates of Gross Domestic Product 1966 to 1983, Hong Kong: Census and Statistics Department, 1984.

Financial Highlights of Companies on the Stock Exchange of Singapore 1983–1992, Singapore: Prentice-Hall.

First Development Plan 1961–1964: Review of Progress for the Three Years ending 31st December, 1963, Singapore: Economic Planning Unit, Prime Minister's Office, 1964.

International Financial Statistics, various *Yearbook*s and monthly issues, Washington, D.C.: International Monetary Fund.

Main Economic Indicators, Organization for Economic Cooperation and Development, various years.

Monetary Authority of Singapore: *Annual Report 1993/94*, Singapore: Monetary Authority of Singapore (and earlier issues).

Monthly Digest of Statistics, Singapore: Department of Statistics, various issues.

Parliamentary Debates Singapore: *Official Report*, Singapore: Government Printer.

Post Office Savings Bank of Singapore Annual Report 1993, Singapore: POSBank, 1994.

Report of the Cost Review Committee, Singapore: SNP Publishers, 1993.

Report on the Census of Industrial Production 1992, Singapore: Research and Statistics Unit, Economic Development Board, n.d.

Report on the Labour Force Survey of Singapore 1993, Singapore: Research and Statistics Department, Ministry of Labour, n.d.

Report on Wages in Singapore 1993, Singapore: Research and Statistics Department, Ministry of Labour, May 1994.

Singapore 1994, Singapore: Ministry of Information and the Arts.

Singapore Census of Population 1990: *Economic Characteristics*, Singapore: Department of Statistics, 1993.

Singapore: Facts and Pictures 1994, Singapore: Ministry of Information and the Arts, 1994.

Singapore National Accounts 1987, Singapore: Department of Statistics, March 1988.

Singapore Trade Division Annual Report 1961–66, Singapore: Department of Statistics.

Singapore's Corporate Sector: *Size, Composition and Financial Structure*, Singapore: Department of Statistics, June 1992.

Statistics Singapore: An Official Guide, by Dr Paul Cheung, Singapore: Department of Statistics, October 1994.

Survey of Current Business, Washington, D.C.: US Department of Commerce, July 1993.

The Singapore Economy: *New Directions* (Report of the Economic Committee), Singapore: Ministry of Trade and Industry, February 1986.

Times Directory of Foreign Business in Singapore 1988/1989, Singapore: Times Trade Directories Ltd.

United Kingdom National Accounts 1993, London: HMSO, 1993.

World Development Report, Washington, D.C.: Oxford University Press for the World Bank, various years.

World Tourism Organization Yearbook of Tourism Statistics 1988, Madrid: World Tourism Organization.

Yearbook of Statistics Singapore, Singapore: Department of Statistics, Republic of Singapore, various years.

BOOKS AND ARTICLES

Abel, Andrew B. and Ben S. Bernanke (1995), *Macroeconomics*, 2nd edn, Reading, Mass.: Addison-Wesley.

Abeysinghe, Tilak (1992), 'A small-scale model to forecast GDP of Singapore', in Yadolah Dodge and Joe Whittaker (eds), *Computational Statistics*, Heidelberg: Physica-Verlag.

—— and Lee K.H. (1992), 'Singapore's strong dollar policy and purchasing power parity', *Singapore Economic Review*, 37.

——, Tilak, Ng Hock Guan and Phang Sock Yong (1995), 'Outlook for the Singapore economy', paper presented at the Workshop on 'Economic Outlook for Singapore and the Region', 24 February, Econometric Studies Unit, Department of Economics and Statistics, National University of Singapore.

Alesina, Alberto and Lawrence H. Summers (1993), 'Central bank independence and macroeconomic performance', *Journal of Money, Credit and Banking*, May.

Amadeo, Edward J. (1989), *Keynes's Principle of Effective Demand*, Aldershot: Edward Elgar.

Ariff, M. (1994), 'Open regionalism a la ASEAN', *Journal of Asian Economics*, **5**(1).

Asher, Mukul G. (1994), 'An analysis of Singapore's 1994–1995 budget', in Anthony Chin and Ngiam Kee Jin (eds), *Outlook for the Singapore Economy*, Singapore: Trans Global Publishing.

Barro, Robert J. (1974), 'Are government bonds net wealth?', *Journal of Political Economy*, December.

—— (1990), *Macroeconomics*, 3rd edn, New York: Wiley.

—— (1991), 'Economic growth in a cross section of countries', *Quarterly Journal of Economics*, May.

—— (1994a), 'Democracy and Growth', paper presented at the Third Asian Development Bank Conference on Development Economics, Manila, 23–5 November 1994.

—— (1994b), 'Democracy: A recipe for growth?', *Asian Wall Street Journal*, 2–3 December 1994, p.6.

Bautista, Romeo M. (1992), *Development Policy in East Asia: Economic Growth and Poverty Alleviation*, Singapore: ASEAN Economic Research Unit, Institute of Southeast Asian Studies.

Bird, Graham (1987), *International Macroeconomics: Theory, Policy and Applications*, London: Macmillan.

Bodkin, Ronald G., Lawrence R. Klein and Kanta Marwah (1991) (eds), *A History of Macroeconometric Model-building*, Aldershot: Edward Elgar.

Bordo, Michael D. and Lars Jonung (1987), *The Long-run Behaviour of the Velocity of Circulation*, Cambridge: Cambridge University Press.

Brown, Adam (1992), *Making Sense of Singapore English*, Singapore, Kuala Lumpur and Hong Kong: Federal Publications.

Bryant, Ralph C. (1989), 'The evolution of Singapore as a financial centre', in Kernial Singh Sandhu and Paul Wheatley (eds), *Management of Success: The Moulding of Modern Singapore*, Singapore: Institute of Southeast Asian Studies.

Caves, Richard E., Jeffrey A. Frankel and Ronald W. Jones (1993), *World Trade and Payments: An Introduction*, 3rd edn, New York: Harper Collins.

Chan, Kenneth S. and Ngiam Kee Jin (1992a), 'Currency interchangeability arrangement between Brunei and Singapore: A cost–benefit analysis', *The Singapore Economic Review*, **37**(2), October.

—— (1992b), 'A tale of two currencies – Brunei and Singapore', in *Prudence at the Helm*: *Board of Commissioners of Currency, Singapore 1967–1992*, Singapore: Board of Commissioners of Currency.

Chan Kok Peng (1993), 'Effects of CPF liberalization and lower budget surplus', *Times Economic Link*, no. 1, July–September.

Chee Soon Juan (1994), *Dare to Change: An Alternative Vision for Singapore*, Singapore: Singapore Democratic Party.

Chen, Edward E.K.Y. (1979), *Hyper-growth in Asian Economies: A Comparative Study of Hong Kong, Japan, Singapore and Taiwan*, London: Macmillan.

Chen, Peter S.J. (ed.) (1983), *Singapore Development Policies and Trends*, Singapore: Oxford University Press.

Chenery, Hollis (1960), 'Patterns of industrial growth', *The Economic Journal*, 72.

—— , Sherman Robinson and Moshe Syrquin (1986), *Industrialization and Growth: A Comparative Study*, New York: Oxford University Press for the World Bank.

Chia Siow Yue (1985), 'The role of foreign trade and investment in the development of Singapore', in W. Galenson, (ed.), *Trade, Foreign Investment and Economic Growth in the Newly Industrializing Countries*, Madison: University of Wisconsin Press.

—— (1986a), 'The economic development of Singapore: A selective survey of the literature', in Basant K. Kapur (ed.), *Singapore Studies: Critical Surveys of the Humanities and Social Sciences*, Singapore: Singapore University Press.

—— (1986b) 'Direct foreign investment and the industrialization process in Singapore', in Lim Chong-Yah and Peter Lloyd (eds), *Resources and Growth in Singapore*, Singapore: Oxford University Press.

—— (1989), 'The character and progress of industrialization', in Kernial Singh Sandhu and Paul Wheatley (eds), *Management of Success: The Moulding of Modern Singapore*, Singapore: Institute of Southeast Asian Studies.

—— (1993), 'Foreign direct investment in ASEAN economies', *Asian Development Review*, **11**(1).

—— (ed.) (1994a), *APEC: Challenges and Opportunities*, Singapore: Institute of Southeast Asian Studies.

—— (1994b), 'ASEAN economic cooperation and external relations', in Sueo Sekiguchi and Noda (eds), *Economic Interactions and Interdependence in East Asia*, Japan: Ushilsa Memorial Foundation Study.

Chow Hwee Kwan (1993), 'Performance of the official composite leading index in monitoring the Singapore economy', *Asian Economic Journal*, **7**(1).

Chow Kit Boey (1988), 'Singapore business cycles', in *Business Cycles in Five ASEAN Countries, India and Korea*, vol. 1, Tokyo: Institute of Developing Economies.

—— (1992), 'Monitoring the Singapore business cycle', *Times Economic Link*, no. 2.

Chow, P., M. Kellman and Y. Shachmurove (1994), 'East Asian NIC manufactured intra-industry trade 1965–1990', *Journal of Asian Economics*, **5**(3).

Chowdhury, A. (1993), 'External shocks and structural adjustments in East Asian newly industrializing economies', *Journal of International Development*, **5**(1).

Clad, James (1989), *Behind the Myth: Business, Money and Power in Southeast Asia*, London: Unwin Hyman.

Cukierman, Alex (1992), *Central Bank Strategy, Credibility, and Independence: Theory and Evidence*, Cambridge, Mass./London: MIT Press.

Daquila, Teofilio, C. and Alan Phua Kia Fatt (1993), 'Demand for money in Singapore revisited', *Asian Economic Journal*, **7**(2), July.

Davidson, Paul (1992), 'Would Keynes be a New Keynesian?', *Eastern Economic Journal*, **18**(4), Fall.

—— (1994), *Post Keynesian Macroeconomic Theory: A Foundation for Successful Economic Policies for the Twenty-first Century*, Aldershot: Edward Elgar.

DBS Bank (1992), 'Singapore Briefing No. 29: Singapore's Export Competitiveness vis-à-vis other Dynamic Asian Economies', Economic Research Department, June.

De Long, J. Bradford and Lawrence H. Summers (1991), 'Equipment investment and economic growth', *Quarterly Journal of Economics*, **106**(2).

Deluty, Philip J. and Perry L. Wood (1986), *Singapore: The Dynamics of Free Trade Regime*, Indianapolis: Hudson Institute.

Dore, Mohammed H.I. (1993), *The Macrodynamics of Business Cycles: A Comparative Evaluation*, Cambridge, Mass./Oxford: Basil Blackwell.

Dornbusch, Rudiger and Stanley Fischer (1994), *Macroeconomics*, 6th edn, New York: McGraw-Hill.

Drake, P.J. (1981), 'The evolution of money in Singapore since 1819', in *Papers on Monetary Economics*, edited by the Economics Department, Monetary Authority of Singapore, Singapore University Press for the Monetary Authority of Singapore.

The East Asian Miracle: Economic Growth and Public Policy, (1993), Washington, D.C.: The World Bank.

The East Asian Miracle: Economic Growth and Public Policy, Summary (1993), Washington, D.C.: The World Bank.

Econometric Studies Unit (ESU) (1990), 'Report on the ESU macroeconometric model (version 3.0) for the Singapore economy', National University of Singapore, July.

Econometric Studies Unit (ESU) (1991a), 'Report on the ESU macroeconometric model (version 4.0) for the Singapore economy', National University of Singapore, July.

Econometric Studies Unit (ESU) (1991b), 'Singapore's economic outlook: Forecasts, some policy issues and simulation results', ESU Modelling Workshop on 'Monitoring the Singapore Economy', National University of Singapore, February.

Econometric Studies Unit (ESU) (1992), 'Singapore's economic outlook: Forecasts, some policy issues and simulation results', ESU Modelling Workshop on 'Monitoring the Singapore Economy', National University of Singapore, February.

Econometric Studies Unit (ESU) (1993), 'Report on the ESU macroeconometric model for the Singapore economy', National University of Singapore, July.

Econometric Studies Unit (ESU) (1995), 'Outlook for the Singapore economy', paper presented at the Workshop on 'Economic Outlook for Singapore and the Region', 24 February, Department of Economics and Statistics, National University of Singapore.

El-Agraa, Ali M. (ed.) (1988), *International Economic Integration*, London: Macmillan.

Ezaki, M. (1985), 'Singapore model', in S. Ichimura and M. Ezaki (eds) *Econometric Models of Asian Link*, Tokyo: Springer-Verlag.

The Financial Structure of Singapore (1989), Singapore: Monetary Authority of Singapore.

Findlay, Ronald (1989), 'Theoretical notes on Singapore as a development model', in Kernial Singh Sandhu and Paul Wheatley (eds), *Management of Success: The Moulding of Modern Singapore*, Singapore: Institute of Southeast Asian Studies.

—— and Basant Kapur (1992), 'An analytical growth model of the Singapore economy', *Asian Economic Journal*, **5**(1), March.

Fleming, J. (1962), 'Domestic financial policies under fixed and floating exchange rates', *International Monetary Fund Staff Papers*, November.

Friedman, Milton (1957), *A Theory of the Consumption Function*, Princeton: Princeton University Press.

―― (1968), 'The role of monetary policy', *American Economic Review*, 58, March.

―― (1976), 'Inflation and unemployment', in *Nobel Lectures: Economic Sciences 1969–1980*, Singapore: World Scientific (1992).

―― (1987), 'The quantity theory of money', in John Eatwell, Murray Milgate and Peter Newman (eds), *The New Palgrave: A Dictionary of Economics*, vol. 4, London: Macmillan.

―― and David Meiselman (1963), 'The relative stability of monetary velocity and the investment multiplier in the United States, 1897–1958', in *Commission on Money and Credit: Stabilization Policies*, Englewood Cliffs: Prentice-Hall.

―― and Anna Jacobson Schwartz (1963), *A Monetary History of the United States 1867–1960*, Princeton: Princeton University Press.

Froyen, Richard T. (1993), *Macroeconomics: Theories and Policies*, 3rd ed, New York: Macmillan.

Galenson, W. (ed.) (1985), *Trade, Foreign Investment and Economic Growth in the Newly Industrializing Countries*, Madison: Univerity of Wisconsin Press.

Garnaut, Ross (1994), *Asian Market Economies: Challenges of a Changing International Environment*, Singapore: ASEAN Economic Research Unit, Institute of Southeast Asian Studies.

Gayle, Dennis John (1988), 'Singaporean market socialism: Some implications for development theory', *International Journal of Social Economics*, **15**(7).

Geiger, Theodore and Frances M. Geiger (1973), *Tales of Two City-States: The Development Progress of Hong Kong and Singapore*, Washington, D.C.: National Planning Association.

―― (1975), *The Development Progress of Hong Kong and Singapore*, London: Macmillan.

George, F.J. (1985), *The Singapore Saga*, Singapore: Society of Singapore Writers.

George, T.J.S (1984), *Lee Kuan Yew's Singapore*, Singapore: Eastern Universities Press.

Goh Chok Tong (1969), 'Industrial growth', in Ooi Jim-Bee and Chiang Hai Ding (eds), *Modern Singapore*, Singapore: University of Singapore Press.

Goh Keng Swee (1977), *The Practice of Economic Growth*, Singapore: Federal Publications.

Gordon, Robert J. (1990), 'What is New-Keynesian Economics?', *Journal of Economic Literature*, 27, September.

―― (1993) *Macroeconomics*, 6th edn, New York: Harper Collins.

Greenaway, David (ed.) (1988), *Economic Development and International Trade*, Basingstoke: Macmillan.

—— and C. Milner (1986), *The Economics of Intraindustry Trade*, Oxford/New York: Basil Blackwell.

Grubel, Herbert G. (1989), 'Singapore's record of price stability, 1966–84', in Kernial Singh Sandhu and Paul Wheatley (eds), *Management of Success: The Moulding of Modern Singapore*, Singapore: Institute of Southeast Asian Studies.

Grubel, H. and P. Lloyd (1975), *Intra-industry trade: The Theory and Measurement of International Trade in Differentiated Products*, London: Macmillan.

Hall, Robert E. and John B. Taylor (1993), *Macroeconomics*, 4th edn, New York: W.W. Norton.

Hallwood, C. Paul and Ronald McDonald (1994), *International Money and Finance*, 2nd edn, Oxford/Cambridge, Mass.: Basil Blackwell.

Hanke, Steve H., Lars Jonung and Kurt Schuler (1993), *Russian Currency and Finance: A Currency Board Approach to Reform*, London/New York: Routledge.

Heller, R. (1978), 'Determination of exchange rate practices', *Journal of Money, Credit and Banking*, **10**(3).

Hickman, B. (1991), 'Project link and multicountry modelling', in Ronald G. Bodkin, Lawrence R. Klein and Kanta Marwah (eds), *A History of Macroeconometric Model-building*, Aldershot: Edward Elgar.

Hicks, George (1989), 'The four little dragons: An enthusiast's reading guide', *Asian-Pacific Economic Literature*, **3**(2), September.

Hill, Hal and Pang Eng Fang (1989), 'Technology exports from a small, very open NIC: The case of Singapore', Working Paper 89/6, National Centre for Development Studies, Australian National University, Canberra.

—— and Prue Phillips (1993), 'Patterns of import penetration in East Asian Industrialisation', *Asian Economic Journal*, **7**(1) March.

Holmes, Kim R. (1994), 'In search of free markets', *Asian Wall Street Journal*, 15 December.

Hoon Hian Teck and Ho Kong Weng (1992), 'A short macroeconomic account of the Singapore economy', *Times Economic Link*, no. 3, October–December.

—— and Teo Kai Lin (1992), 'A model of the link between the fiscal system and Singapore's Central Provident Fund in general equilibrium', *The Singapore Economic Review*, **37**(2), October.

Huff, W.G. (1994), *The Economic Growth of Singapore: Trade and Development in the Twentieth Century*, Cambridge: Cambridge University Press.

Hutchison, T.W. (1981), *The Politics and Philosophy of Economics: Marxians, Keynesians and Austrians*, Oxford: Basil Blackwell.

Ichimura, Shinichi and Mitsuo Ezaki (1985), *Econometric Models of Asian Link*, Tokyo: Springer-Verlag.

Ichimura, S. and Y. Matsumoto (eds) (1994), *Econometric Models of Asian–Pacific Countries*, Tokyo: Springer-Verlag.

Islam, Iyanatul and Colin Kirkpatrick (1986), 'Export-led development, labour-market conditions and the distribution of income: The case of Singapore', *Cambridge Journal of Economics*, 10.

Ito, Shoichi and Tay Boon Nga (1994), 'The impact of the oil shock on the Singaporean economy: Simulation results of a CGE model', *Asian Economic Journal*, **8**(1), March.

Jao, Y.C., Victor Mok and Ho Lok-sang (eds) (1989), *Economic Development in Chinese Societies: Models and Experiences*, Hong Kong: Hong Kong University Press.

Jenner, W.J.F. (1992), *The Tyranny of History: The Roots of China's Crisis*, London: Penguin.

Kaldor, Nicholas (1985), *The Scourge of Monetarism*, 2nd edn, Oxford: Oxford University Press.

Kalecki, Michal (1943), 'Political aspects of full employment', in Michal Kalecki (1971), *Selected Essays on the Dynamics of the Capitalist Economy*, Cambridge: Cambridge University Press.

Kapur, Basant K. (1981), 'Exchange rate flexibility and monetary policy', in *Papers on Monetary Economics*, edited by the Economics Department, Monetary Authority of Singapore, Singapore University Press for the Monetary Authority of Singapore.

—— (1983), 'A short-term analytical model of the Singapore economy', *Journal of Development Economics*, **12**(2), June.

—— (ed.) (1986), *Singapore Studies: Critical Surveys of the Humanities and Social Sciences*, Singapore: Singapore University Press.

Keuzenkamp, Hugo A. (1991), 'A precursor to Muth: Tinbergen's 1932 model of rational expectations', *Economic Journal*, 101, September.

Keynes, John Maynard (1936), *The General Theory of Employment, Interest and Money*, London: Macmillan.

—— (1973), *The Collected Writings of John Maynard Keynes: Volume XIV*, London: Macmillan for the Royal Economic Society.

Khan, H., C. Seng, and W. Cheong (1989), *The Sociological Impact of Tourism on the Singapore Economy*, National University of Singapore, Multidisciplinary Research on Tourism.

Khan, Habibullah (1988), 'Role of agriculture in a city-state economy', *ASEAN Economic Bulletin*, **5**(2), November.

Khan, Moshin S. (1981), 'The dynamics of money demand and monetary policy in Singapore', in *Papers on Monetary Economics*, edited by the Economics

Department, Monetary Authority of Singapore, Singapore University Press for the Monetary Authority of Singapore.

King, Philip (1995), *International Economics and International Economic Policy*, London: McGraw-Hill.

Klamer, Arjo (1989), 'An accountant among economists: Conversations with Sir John R. Hicks', *Journal of Economic Perspectives*, **3**(4), Fall.

Klein, Lawrence (1994), 'The treatment of Pacific basin economies in the Link system', *Journal of Asian Economics*, **5**(3).

Koh Ai Tee (1987), 'Saving, investment and entrepreneurship', in Lawrence B. Krause, Koh Ai Tee and Lee (Tsao) Yuan, *The Singapore Economy Reconsidered*, Singapore: Institute of Southeast Asian Studies.

—— (1989), 'Diversification of trade', in Kernial Singh Sandhu and Paul Wheatley (eds), *Management of Success: The Moulding of Modern Singapore*, Singapore: Institute of Southeast Asian Studies.

—— (1990), *Booms and Busts in Modern Societies*, Singapore: Longmans.

—— (1992a), 'Singapore: Monetary and Financial System', in Peter Newman, Murray Milgate and John Eatwell (eds), *The New Palgrave Dictionary of Money and Finance*, vol. 3, London: Macmillan.

—— (1992b), 'How much do we know about Singapore's business cycles?', *Times Economic Link*, no. 1, April–June.

Koh Seng Khon (1988), 'Demand for money in Singapore', academic exercise in part fulfilment for the Honours Bachelor of Social Science degree, Department of Economics and Statistics, National University of Singapore, academic year 1988/89.

Krause, Lawrence B., Koh Ai Tee and Lee (Tsao) Yuan (1987), *The Singapore Economy Reconsidered*, Singapore: Institute of Southeast Asian Studies.

Krugman, Paul (1994), *Peddling Prosperity: Economic Sense and Nonsense in the Age of Diminished Expectations*, New York/London: W.W. Norton.

Laidler, David (1991), *The Golden Age of the Quantity Theory: The Development of Neoclassical Monetary Economics 1870–1914*, Hemel Hempstead: Harvester Wheatsheaf.

Lau D.C. (1979), 'Introduction', in *Confucius: The Analects (Lun Yu)*, London: Penguin.

Lee, Sheng-yi (1984), 'The demand for money in Singapore, 1968–82', *ASEAN Economic Bulletin*, **1**(2), November.

—— (1985), *Demand for and Supply of Money in Singapore, 1968–1982*, Chung-Hua Institution for Economic Research Monograph Series no. 4, Taipei, Taiwan.

—— (1990), *The Monetary and Banking Development of Singapore and Malaysia*, 3rd edn, Singapore: Singapore University Press.

Lee, S.Y. and Y.C. Jao (1982), *Financial Structures and Monetary Policies in Southeast Asia*, London: Macmillan.

Lee, S.Y. and W.K. Li (1983), 'Money, income and prices and their lead–lag relationships in Singapore', *The Singapore Economic Review*, **28**(1) April.

Lee (Tsao) Yuan (1987a), 'The government in macroeconomic management', in Lawrence B. Krause, Koh Ai Tee and Lee (Tsao) Yuan, *The Singapore Economy Reconsidered*, Singapore: Institute of Southeast Asian Studies.

—— (1987b), 'The government in the labour market', in Lawrence B. Krause, Koh Ai Tee and Lee (Tsao) Yuan, *The Singapore Economy Reconsidered*, Singapore: Institute of Southeast Asian Studies.

—— (1994), *Overseas Investment: Experience of Singapore Manufacturing Companies*, Singapore: Institute of Policy Studies/McGraw-Hill.

Li Yeow Ju (1993), 'Domestic resource mobilization in Singapore', in Y.M.W.B. Weerasekera, *Domestic Resource Mobilization in the Seacen Countries*, Kuala Lumpur: The South East Asian Central Banks (SEACEN) Research and Training Centre.

Lim Chong-Yah (1980), *Economic Development in Singapore*, Singapore: Federal Publications.

—— (1986), 'Singapore: resources and growth – an introductory overview', in Lim Chong-Yah and Peter Lloyd (eds), *Resources and Growth in Singapore*, Singapore: Oxford University Press.

—— (1989), 'From high growth rates to recession', in Kernial Singh Sandhu and Paul Wheatley (eds), *Management of Success: The Moulding of Modern Singapore*, Singapore: Institute of Southeast Asian Studies.

—— and Peter Lloyd (eds) (1986), *Resources and Growth in Singapore*, Singapore: Oxford University Press.

—— and associates (1988), *Policy Options for the Singapore Economy*, Singapore: McGraw-Hill.

Lim, D. (1974), 'Export instability and economic development: the example of West Malaysia', *Oxford Economic Papers*, 26.

—— (1991), *Export Instability and Compensatory Financing*, London: Routledge.

Lindauer, John (ed.) (1968), *Macroeconomic Readings*, New York: The Free Press.

Liu Pak-wai (1992), 'Economic Development of the four little dragons: Lessons for LDCs and China', Hong Kong Institute of Asia-Pacific Affairs, Chinese University of Hong Kong, Occasional Paper No.12.

Lloyd, Peter J. and Roger J. Sandilands (1986), 'The trade sector in a very open re-export economy', in Lim Chong-Yah and Peter Lloyd (eds), *Resources and Growth in Singapore*, Singapore: Oxford University Press.

Love, J. (1987), 'Export instability in less developed countries: consequences and causes', *Journal of Economic Studies*, **14**(2).

Low, Linda (1991), *The Political Economy of Privatisation in Singapore: Analysis, Interpretation and Evaluation*, Singapore: McGraw-Hill.

—— (1993a), 'From entrepot to a newly industrialising economy', in Linda Low, Toh Mun Heng, Soon Teck Wong, Tan Kong Yam and Helen Hughes, *Challenges and Response: Twenty Five Years of the Economic Development Board*, Singapore: Times Academic Publishers.

—— (1993b), 'The Economic Development Board' in Linda Low, Toh Mun Heng, Soon Teck Wong, Tan Kong Yam and Helen Hughes, *Challenges and Response: Twenty Five Years of the Economic Development Board*, Singapore: Times Academic Publishers.

—— (1993c), 'Conclusion', in Linda Low, Toh Mun Heng, Soon Teck Wong, Tan Kong Yam and Helen Hughes, *Challenges and Response: Twenty Five Years of the Economic Development Board*, Singapore: Times Academic Publishers.

—— and Toh Mun Heng (1989), *The Elected Presidency as a Safeguard for Official Reserves: What is at Stake?*, Singapore: Institute of Policy Studies Occasional Paper No. 1, Times Academic Press.

—— and —— (eds) (1992), *Public Policies in Singapore: Changes in the 1980s and Future Signposts*, Singapore: Times Academic Press.

——, ——, Soon Teck Wong, Tan Kong Yam and Helen Hughes (1993), *Challenges and Response: Twenty Five Years of the Economic Development Board*, Singapore: Times Academic Publishers.

Low, Vincent (1994), 'The MAS model: Structure and some policy simulations', in Anthony Chin and Ngiam Kee Jin (eds), *Outlook for the Singapore Economy*, Singapore: Trans Global Publishing.

Lucas, Robert E. Jr. (1983), *Studies in Business-cycle Theory*, Cambridge, Mass./London: MIT Press.

—— (1987), *Models of Business Cycles*, Oxford: Basil Blackwell.

Luckett, Dudley G., David L. Schulze and Raymond W.Y. Wong (1994), *Banking, Finance and Monetary Policy in Singapore*, Singapore: McGraw-Hill.

MacBean, A. (1966), *Export Instability and Economic Development*, London: Allen and Unwin.

—— and D. Nguyen (1988), 'Export instability and growth performance', in David Greenaway (ed.), *Economic Development and International Trade*, Basingstoke: Macmillan.

—— and P. Snowdon (1987), *International Institutions in Trade and Finance*, London: Allen and Unwin.

Mankiw, N. Gregory (1989), 'Real business cycles: A new Keynesian perspective', *Journal of Economic Perspectives*, **3**(3) Summer.

Margolin, Jean-Louis (1988), *Singapour: Genèse d'un nouveau pays industriel*, Paris: Editions L'Harmattan.

McCrum, Robert, William Cran and Robert MacNeil (1986), *The Story of English*, London/Boston: Faber and Faber.

Medhi Krongkaew (1994), 'Income distribution in East Asian developing countries', *Asian-Pacific Economic Literature*, **8**(2), November.

Metzger, Tilman Alexander (1994), 'Singapore: A centre for financial services in south east Asia', visiting student's academic exercise, Department of Economics & Statistics, National University of Singapore.

Mill, John Stuart (1848/1987), *Principles of Political Economy with Some of their Applications to Social Philosophy*, new edition of 1909 edited by Sir William Ashley, Fairfield: Augustus M. Kelley.

Milne, R.S. and Diane K. Mauzy (1990), *Singapore: The Legacy of Lee Kuan Yew*, Boulder/San Francisco/Oxford: Westview Press.

Minchin, James (1990), *No Man is an Island: A Portrait of Singapore's Lee Kuan Yew*, 2nd edn, Sydney: Allen & Unwin.

Mirza, Hafiz (1986), *Multinationals and the Growth of the Singapore Economy*, New York: St Martin's Press.

Moore, Basil J. (1988), *Horizontalists or Verticalists: the Macroeconomics of Credit Money*, Cambridge: Cambridge University Press.

Moreno, Ramon (1989), 'Exchange rates and monetary policy in Singapore and Hong Kong', *Hong Kong Economic Papers*, no. 19.

Mori, Kazuo (1991), 'Business cycles in Asian countries', in Osada Hiroshi and Dasuke Hiratsuka (eds), *Business Cycles in Asia*, Tokyo: Institute of Developing Economies.

Mullineux, Andy, David G. Dickson and Peng Wensheng (1993), *Business Cycles: Theory and Evidence*, Oxford/Cambridge, Mass. Blackwell.

Mundell, R. (1963), 'Capital mobility and stabilization under fixed and flexible exchange rates', *Canadian Journal of Economics and Political Science*, 29, November.

Nair, C. V. Devan (1994), 'Foreword', in Francis T. Seow, *To Catch a Tartar: A Dissident in Lee Kuan Yew's Prison*, New Haven: Yale University South East Asia Studies.

Ng, Chee Yuen (1989), 'Privatization in Singapore: Divestment with control', *ASEAN Economic Bulletin*, **5**(3), March.

Nuaw Mee Kau (1979), *Export Expansion and Industrial Growth in Singapore*, Hong Kong: Kingsway International Publications.

Ooi Jim-Bee and Chiang Hai Ding (eds) (1969), *Modern Singapore*, Singapore: University of Singapore Press.

Osada, Hiroshi and Dasuke Hiratsuka (1991) (eds), *Business Cycles in Asia*, Tokyo: Institute of Developing Economies.

Ostby, I. (1977), 'Macroeconomic Relationships in Singapore: An Econometric Study', occasional paper, Singapore: Nanyang University Institute of Economics and Business School.

Ow Chin-Hock (1986), 'The role of government in economic development: The Singapore experience', in Lim Chong-Yah and Peter Lloyd (eds), *Resources and Growth in Singapore*, Singapore: Oxford University Press.

Parkin, Michael (1993), *Economics*, 2nd edn, New York: Addison-Wesley.

—— and Robin Bade (1986) *Modern Macroeconomics*, 2nd edn, Scarborough: Prentice-Hall.

——, —— (1992), *Macroeconomics*, 2nd edn, Englewood Cliffs: Prentice-Hall.

Peebles, Gavin (1988), *Hong Kong's Economy: An Introductory Analysis*, Hong Kong/New York: Oxford University Press.

—— (1991), *Money in the People's Republic of China: A Comparative Perspective*, Sydney/London/Wellington: Allen and Unwin.

—— (1993a), 'National income accounting and the case of Singapore', *Times Economic Link*, no. 6, July–September.

—— (1993b), 'Gross Domestic Product, Gross National Product and the case of Singapore', mimeo, Singapore.

—— (1994), 'Review of *Russian Currency and Finance: A Currency Board Approach to Reform* by Steve H. Hanke, Lars Jonung and Kurt Schuler', *Europe–Asia Studies*, **46**(6).

—— (1995), 'Money demand in Singapore revisited: A comment with implications', unpublished typescript, Singapore, January.

Phillips, A.W. (1958), 'The relation between unemployment and the rate of change of money wage rates in the United Kingdom, 1861–1957', *Economica*, 25, reprinted in John Lindauer (ed.) (1968), *Macroeconomic Readings*, New York: The Free Press.

Phua Kia Fatt, Alan (1989), 'Demand for money specifications and its stability in Singapore', academic exercise in part fulfilment for the Honours Bachelor of Social Science degree, Department of Economics and Statistics, National University of Singapore, academic year 1989/90.

Pindyck, R. and D. Rubinfield (1991), *Econometric Models and Economic Forecasts*, Singapore: McGraw-Hill.

Plosser, Charles I. (1989), 'Understanding real business cycles', *Journal of Economic Perspectives*, **3**(3) Summer.

Prest, A.R. and D.J. Coppock (1984), 10th edn, *The UK Economy*, London: Weidenfeld & Nicolson.

Prudence at the Helm: Board of Commissioners of Currency Singapore 1967–1992 (1992), Singapore: Board of Commissioners of Currency.

Przeworski, Adam and Fernando Limongi (1993), 'Political regimes and economic growth', *Journal of Economic Perspectives*, **7**(3).

Pugh, Cedric (1986), 'Housing in Singapore', *International Journal of Social Economics*, **13**(4/5).

Rachain Chintayarangsan, Nattapong Thongpakdee and Pruttipohn Nakornchai (1992), 'ASEAN Economics: Macro-Economic Perspective', *ASEAN Economic Bulletin*, **8**(3), March.

Rana, Pradumna B. (1984), 'Inflationary effects of exchange rate changes: The case of the ASEAN countries, 1973–1979', *ASEAN Economic Bulletin*, **1**(1), July.

Rao, V.V. Bhanoji (1988), 'Income distribution in East Asian developing countries', *Asian–Pacific Economic Literature*, **2**(1).

—— (1990), 'Income distribution in Singapore: Trends and issues', *The Singapore Economic Review*, **35**(1).

—— (1993), 'A primer on income inequality', *Times Economic Link*, no. 7, October–December.

—— and M.K. Ramakrishnan (1980), *Income Inequality in Singapore*, Singapore: Singapore University Press.

Report of the Public Sector Divestment Committee (1987), Singapore.

Reynolds, C. (1963), 'Domestic consequences of export instability', *American Economic Review*, 53.

Richardson, Graham (1994), *Singapore to 2003: Aspiring to the First Word*, London: The Economist Intelligence Unit.

Rivera-Batiz, Fransisco and Luis Rivera-Batiz (1985), *International Finance and Open Economy Macroeconomics*, New York: Macmillan.

Rodan, Garry (1989), *The Political Economy of Singapore's Industrialization: Nation State and International Capital*, London: Macmillan.

Rousseas, Stephen (1986), *Post Keynesian Monetary Economics*, New York: M.E. Sharpe.

Sachs, Jeffrey D. and Felipe Larrain B. (1993), *Macroeconomics in the Global Economy*, New York: Harvester Wheatsheaf.

Salvatore, Dominick (1995), *International Economics*, New York: Macmillan.

Samuelson, Paul A. and Robert M. Solow (1960), 'Analytical aspects of anti-inflation policy', *American Economic Review*, 50, reprinted in John Lindauer (ed.) (1968), *Macroeconomic Readings*, New York: The Free Press.

Sandhu, Kernial Singh and Paul Wheatley (eds) (1989), *Management of Success: The Moulding of Modern Singapore*, Singapore: Institute of Southeast Asian Studies.

Sandilands, Roger J. (1992), 'Savings, investment and housing in Singapore's growth, 1965–1990', *Savings and Development*, **15**(2).

—— and Tan Ling Hui (1986), 'Comparative advantage in a re-export economy: The case of Singapore', *The Singapore Economic Review*, 31, October.

Schulze, David L. (1986), 'Monetization in ASEAN: 1970–1984', *The Singapore Economic Review*, 31, October.

—— (1990), *Domestic Financial Institutions in Singapore: Public Sector Competition*, Centre for Advanced Studies, National University of Singapore, occasional paper, Singapore: Times Academic Press.

Seah, Linda (1983), 'Public enterprise and economic development', in Peter S.J. Chen (ed.), *Singapore Development Policies and Trends*, Singapore: Oxford University Press.

Sekiguchi, Sueo and Noda (eds) (1994), *Economic Interactions and Interdependence in East Asia*, Japan: Ushilsa Memorial Foundation Study.

Seow, Francis T. (1994), *To Catch a Tartar: A Dissident in Lee Kuan Yew's Prison*, New Haven: Yale University South East Asia Studies.

Simkin, Colin (1984), 'Does money matter in Singapore?', *The Singapore Economic Review*, **29**(1), April.

Sinclair, T. and A. Tsegaye (1988), 'International tourism and export instability', University of Kent Studies in Economics, 88/4.

Singapore 1,000 1993: Industrial (1993), Singapore: Datapool Ltd.

Singapore 1,000 1993: Services (1993), Singapore: Datapool Ltd.

Smith, Peter (1993), 'Measuring human development', *Asian Economic Journal*, **7**(1), March.

Snowdon, Brian, Howard Vane and Peter Wynarczyk (1994), *A Guide to Modern Macroeconomics: An Introduction to Competing Schools of Thought*, Aldershot: Edward Elgar.

Soesastro, Hadi (1994), 'Military expenditure and the arms trade in the Asian–Pacific region', *Asian–Pacific Economic Literature*, **8**(1), May.

Soh, Doreen (1990), *From Cowries to Credit Cards: Stories of Singapore's Money*, Singapore: Federal Publications.

Soon Teck Wong, Linda Low and Toh Mun Heng (1990), 'On using statistics in Singapore', *Singapore Journal of Statistics*, 1, October.

Sowell, Thomas (1974), *Classical Economics Reconsidered*, Princeton: Princeton University Press.

Stiglitz, Joseph E. (1993), *Economics*, New York/London: W.W. Norton.

Tan, A. (1984), 'Changing patterns of Singapore foreign trade and investment since 1960', in You Poh Seng and Lim Chong Yah (eds), *Twenty-five Years of Development*, Singapore: Nanyang Xingzhou Lianhe Zaobao.

—— and Ow Chin Hock (1982), 'Singapore', in Bela Balassa and associates, *Development Strategies in Semi-Industrial Economies*, Baltimore: The Johns Hopkins University Press for the World Bank.

Tan, Augustine H.H. and Basant Kapur (eds) (1986), *Pacific Growth and Financial Interdependence*, Sydney/Boston: Allen and Unwin in association with the Pacific Trade and Development Conference Secretariat, the Australian National University.

Tan Chwee Huat (1992), *Financial Markets and Institutions in Singapore*, 7th edn, Singapore: Singapore University Press.

Tan, Gerald (1992), *The Newly Industrializing Countries of Asia*, Singapore: Times Academic Press.

Tan Kong Yam (1993), 'Comparative development experience with the other NIEs', in Linda Low, Toh Mun Heng, Soon Teck Wong, Tan Kong Yam and Helen Hughes, *Challenges and Response: Twenty Five Years of the Economic Development Board*, Singapore: Times Academic Publishers.

Tan Teck Yoong (1995), 'An analysis of Singapore's external trade in the light of the new (1988) input–output tables', unpublished M.Soc. Science dissertation, Department of Economics and Statistics, National University of Singapore.

Tang, Siew Taeng (1985), 'Control Stabilisation for a Simple Macro Model of the Singapore economy', academic exercise in part fulfilment for the Honours Bachelor of Social Science degree, Department of Economics and Statistics, National University of Singapore, academic year 1984/85.

Tay Boon Nga (1992), 'The Central Provident Fund: Operation and schemes', in Linda Low and Toh Mun Heng (eds), *Public Policies in Singapore: Changes in the 1980s and Future Signposts*, Singapore: Times Academic Press.

Teh Kok Peng and Tharman Shanmugaratnam (1992), 'Exchange rate policy: Philosophy and conduct over the past decade', in Linda Low and Toh Mun Heng (eds), *Public Policies in Singapore: Changes in the 1980s and Future Signposts*, Singapore: Times Academic Press.

Thanisorn Dejthamrong (1993), *The Budget Deficit: Its Impact on Money Supply and Output in Selected Seacen Countries*, Kuala Lumpur: The South East Asian Central Banks (SEACEN) Research and Training Centre.

Theroux, Paul (1976), *Saint Jack*, London: Penguin.

Thornton, John (1993), 'A test of the rational expectations–permanent income hypothesis for Singapore', *Asian Economic Journal*, 7(1), March.

Tobin, James (1992), 'An old Keynesian counterattacks', *Eastern Economic Journal*, 18(4), Fall.

Toh Mun Heng (1984), 'Production, Growth and Input/Output Analysis: An Empirical Application to the Singapore Economy', unpublished PhD thesis, London School of Economics.

—— (1986), 'Income redistribution and trade policy effects on macroeconomic aggregates: A simulation study of the Singapore economy based on an extended input–output model', *Journal of Economic Development*, 11(1), July.

—— (1990), 'Developments in econometric modelling in Singapore' *Singapore Journal of Statistics*, 1, October.

—— (1993), 'Partnership with multinational corporations', chap. 4 in Linda Low, Toh Mun Heng, Soon Teck Wong, Tan Kong Yam and Helen Hughes, *Challenges and Response: Twenty Five Years of the Economic Development Board*, Singapore: Times Academic Publishers.

—— and Linda Low (1990a), 'An econometric model of the Singaporean economy: Modelling the trade sector', in Joseph T. Yap and Yoichi Nakamura (eds), *ASEAN Link: An Econometric Study*, Singapore: Longman.

——, —— (1990b), *An Economic Framework of Singapore*, Singapore: McGraw-Hill.

——, —— (1994), 'Capital stock, latent resource and total factor productivity in Singapore', paper presented at the workshop on 'Measuring Productivity and Technological Progress', Faculty of Business Administration, National University of Singapore, August.

—— and Eric D. Ramstetter (1994), 'A structural model of Singapore for Asian Link', in S. Ichimura and Y. Matsumoto (eds), *Econometric Models of Asian–Pacific Countries*, Tokyo: Springer-Verlag.

Toida, Mitsuru (1984), 'A small econometric model for Singapore 1971–1982', in *Preliminary Results of Econometric Models in the ELSA Project*, Tokyo: Institute of Developing Economies.

—— (1985), 'A monetarist small econometric model for Singapore', in *Econometric Link System for ASEAN*, ELSA Final Report, vol. 1, Tokyo: Institute of Developing Economies.

—— and D. Hiratsuka (1994), *Forecasts for Asian Industrializing Region*, PAIR Econometric Forecasting Report no. 2, Tokyo: Institute of Developing Economies.

Tremewan, Christopher (1994), *The Political Economy of Social Control in Singapore*, New York: St Martin's Press in association with St Antony's College, Oxford.

Tsao Yuan (1985), 'Growth without productivity: Singapore manufacturing in the 1970s', *Journal of Development Economics*, **19** (1/2), September–October.

—— (1986), 'Sources of growth accounting for the Singapore economy', in Lim Chong-Yah and Peter Lloyd (eds), *Resources and Growth in Singapore*, Singapore: Oxford University Press.

Tseng, Wanda and Robert Corker (1991), *Financial liberalization, money demand, and monetary policy in Asian countries*, Occasional Paper no. 84, July, Washington D.C.: International Monetary Fund.

Tumnong Dasri (1991), *Open Market Operations: Its Nature and Extent in the Seacen Countries*, Kuala Lumpur: The South East Asian Central Banks (SEACEN) Research and Training Centre.

Turnbull, C.M. (1969), 'Constitutional development 1819–1968', chap. 12 in Ooi Jim-Bee and Chiang Hai Ding (eds), *Modern Singapore*, Singapore: University of Singapore Press.

—— (1989), *A History of Singapore 1819–1988*, 2nd edn, Singapore: Oxford University Press

Tyson, Laura (1995), 'From MOSS to Motorola and Cray: Managing trade by rules and outcomes', in Philip King (ed.), *International Economics and International Economic Policy*, London: McGraw-Hill.

Vasil, Raj (1992), *Governing Singapore*, Singapore: Mandarin.

Walters, A.A. (1987), 'Currency boards', in Peter Newman, Murray Milgate and John Eatwell (eds), *The New Palgrave: A Dictionary of Economics*, vol. 1, London: Macmillan.

Weerasekera, Y.M.W.B. (1993), *Domestic Resource Mobilization in the Seacen Countries*, Kuala Lumpur: The South East Asian Central Banks (SEACEN) Research and Training Centre.

Whitley, John (1994), *A Course in Macroeconomic Modelling and Forecasting*, London: Harvester Wheatsheaf.

Wilson, Peter (1983), 'The consequences of export instability for developing countries', *Development and Change*, 14.

—— (1986), *International Economics: Theory, Evidence and Practice*, London: Wheatsheaf.

—— (1993), 'The transmission of export shocks to domestic economic variables in a very open re-export economy: the case of Singapore, 1970–1986', unpublished manuscript, National University of Singapore.

—— (1994a), 'Tourism earnings instability in Singapore, 1972–1988', *Journal of Economic Studies*, **21**(1).

—— (1994b), 'Is managed floating the best exchange rate policy for Singapore?', *Global Economic Digest*, **1**(2), July–August.

—— (1994c), 'Export earnings instability of Singapore, 1957–1988: A time series analysis', *Journal of Asian Economics*, **5**(3).

Wong Chung Ming (1984), 'Trends and patterns of Singapore's trade in manufactures', paper presented to a conference on the global implications of the trade pattern of East and Southeast Asia, Kuala Lumpur, Malaysia, January.

Wong Fot-chyi and Gan Wee-beng (1994), 'Total factor productivity growth in the Singapore manufacturing industries during the 1980s', *Journal of Asian Economics*, **5**(2).

Wong, John (1988), 'The Association of Southeast Asian Nations', in Ali M. El-Agraa, (ed.), *International Economic Integration*, London: Macmillan.

—— (1989), 'Singapore's recent economic set-back: Lessons for the NICS', in Y.C. Jao, Victor Mok and Ho Lok-sang (eds), *Economic Development in Chinese Societies: Models and Experiences*, Hong Kong: Hong Kong University Press.

Wong, K. (1974), 'A macroeconomic model of Singapore 1960–1969', *Malayan Economic Review*, **19**(2).

Wong Kum Poh (1986), 'Saving, capital inflow and capital formation', in Lim Chong Yah and Peter Lloyd (eds), *Resources and Growth in Singapore*, Singapore: Oxford University Press.

Woon Kin Chung (1991), 'Net exports and economic growth: An assessment of the applicability of the export-led growth hypothesis to Singapore', unpublished MSoc Science dissertation, Department of Economics and Statistics, National University of Singapore.

Yap, Joseph T. and Yoichi Nakamura (eds) (1990), *ASEAN Link: An Econometric Study*, Singapore: Longman.

Yip, P. (1994), 'The Singapore dollar: Where do we stand? An application of the relative PPP on the valuation of a currency', National University of Singapore, Department of Economics and Statistics, Staff Seminar Series no. 11.

You Poh Seng and Lim Chong Yah (eds) (1984), *Twenty-five Years of Development*, Singapore: Nanyang Xingzhou Lianhe Zaobao.

Young, Alwyn (1992), 'A tale of two cities: Factor accumulation and technical change in Hong Kong and Singapore', in *NBER Macroeconomics Annual 1992*, no. 7, edited by Stanley Fischer and Olivier Blanchard, Cambridge: MIT Press.

—— (1994a), 'The tyranny of numbers: Confronting the statistical realities of the East Asian growth experience', National Bureau of Economic Research Working Paper No. 4680, March.

—— (1994b), 'Lessons from the East Asian NICS: a contrarian view', *European Economic Review*, 38.

Youngson, A.J. (1982), *Hong Kong: Economic Growth and Policy*, Hong Kong: Oxford University Press.

NEWSPAPER REPORTS

'A tale of two cities revisited' (Koo Tsai Kee), *The Straits Times*, 20/1/93.

'American firms boast US$20b in S'pore, employ one in 16 locals', *Business Times*, 22/11/94, p.2

'An unspectacular but far-sighted budget' (Chuang Peck Ming and Patrick Daniel), *Business Times*, 2/3/95, p.1.

'Analysts divided over Telecom shares outlook' (Tammy Tan), *The Straits Times*, 5/1/95, p.40.

'Bangkok versus Singapore', *The Economist*, 9/7/94, pp.23–4.

'Bankers welcome big bang move but seek more details' (Quak Hiang Whai), *Business Times*, 27/9/94, p.1.

'Banks told to stop booking S$ deposits in foreign affiliates' (Conrad Raj), *Business Times*, 6/2/95, p.1.

'Barings buckles under billion-$ derivatives loss' (Catherine Ong, Conrad Raj and Neil Behrmann), *Business Times*, 27/2/95, p.1.

'Barings faces bankruptcy after $932m loss', *The Straits Times*, 27/2/95, p.1.

'Barings fiasco taints Singapore's stature; City-state took pride in highly regulated markets; limited damage seen' (Marcus W. Brauchli and Jeremy Mark), *Asian Wall Street Journal*, 1/3/95, p.7.

'Barings is bust, losses hit S$1.6b, but Simex is safe' (Catherine Ong), *Business Times*, 28/2/95, p.1.

'Barings teeters over huge losses by trader, sparking market fears', *Asian Wall Street Journal*, 27/2/95 pp.1,2.

'Benchmarks too high, say 13 professionals, businessmen' (Wang Hui Ling, Chung Tsung Mien and Jimmy Yap), *The Straits Times*, 26/10/94.

'BG Lee spells out three long-term issues', *The Straits Times: Weekly Edition*, 18 February 1995, p.1.

'Billions of CPF Funds could head for the region' (Quak Hiang Whai), *Business Times*, 26/9/94, p.2.

'Budget 95: A Straits Times Special', *The Straits Times*, 2/3/95.

'CAD launches fraud probe at Barings' (Conrad Raj), *Business Times*, 1/3/95, p.1.

'City-state loses its glitter' (Tony Shale), *Euromoney*, January 1993.

'COE prices hit new records as two categories breach $80,000' (Ramesh Divyanathan), *Business Times*, 17/8/94, p.2.

'Competition will help sharpen skills of economic forecasters' (Tan Kim Song), *The Straits Times*, 12/9/94.

'CPF interest rate goes up to 3.1% from January', *Business Times*, 12–13/11/94, p.1.

'Credit card business starts to slow after MAS curbs' (Shiv Taneja), *Business Times*, 2/12/94, p.1.

'Dealers criticize Manila's efforts to curb Peso's surge on dollar', *Asian Wall Street Journal*, 11/11/94.

'Dr Hu: curbs aimed at excessive consumption; inflation not a worry', *Business Times*, 10/2/95, p.3.

'Economists fear CPI figures understate Asia's inflation' (Dan Biers), *Asian Wall Street Journal*, 24/1/95, pp.1, 5.

'Economists project full-year growth at 9.4%', *Business Times*, 7/10/94.

'External economy takes on greater urgency' (Chan Hwa Loon), *The Straits Times*, 17/3/94, p.29.

'Foreign workforce needs to grow 11 pc a year to achieve 6pc GDP growth' (Anna Teo), *Business Times*, 3–4/7/93, p.2.

'Fraud probe into Barings' (Gerry de Silva and Chan Sue Meng), *The Straits Times*, 1/3/95, p.1.

'Fund managers, investment bankers set to get windfall' (S.N. Vasuki), *Business Times*, 26/9/94, p.2.

'GDP crystal ball – who's the most accurate of all?' (Anna Teo), *Business Times*, 8/2/93, p.2.

'GLCs could become US competitors or partners', *Business Times*, 27/1/94, p.2.

'Govt revises levies on foreign workers' (Dominic Nathan), *The Straits Times*, 30/11/94, p.1.

'Govt-linked firms that don't play fair: Govt again offers to probe', *The Straits Times*, 12/3/92, p.22.

'Grads must give back to society', *The New Paper*, 13/2/95, p.5.

'GST revenue for first 9 months up 16% on whole-year estimates' (Ven Sreeni-vasan), *Business Times*, 10/2/95, p.2.

'If I'm in trouble, I know my brothers and sisters will not let me down' (interview with Lee Kuan Yew), *The New Paper*, 1/2/95, pp.6–9.

'I'm not carrying the big stick any more' (interview with Lee Kuan Yew), *The New Paper*, 2/2/95, pp.6–9.

'Just how competitive are Singapore banks?' (Tan Kim Song), *The Straits Times*, 15/8/94.

'Long-term issues for Singapore' (speech by Deputy Prime Minister Lee Hsien Loong), *The Straits Times*, 14/2/95, pp.28–9.

'MAS acts to rein in car loans, unsecured personal finance' (Shiv Taneja), *Business Times*, 4–5/2/95, p.1.

'MAS again warns on credit card ads' (Catherine Ong), *Business Times*, 6/10/94, p.1.

'MAS chief fields questions on a debacle' (Catherine Ong), *The Straits Times*, 4/12/85.

'MAS gives no clues on outlook for Singapore dollar', *Business Times*, 15/7/93, p.2.

'MAS intervenes as S$ hits record high against US$'(Paul Leo), *Business Times*, 4/1/95, p.1.

'No additional credit curbs for now: BG Lee' (Lilian Ang), *Business Times*, 6/2/95, p.1.

'Now Asia's tiger economies are joining the first world', *Asian Wall Street Journal*, 23/2/95, pp.1,4.

'Of strategies, subsidies and spillovers', *The Economist*, 18 March 1995, p.90.

'Only 12pc of S'pore share owners trade actively' (Catherine Ong), *Business Times*, 3/10/94, p.1.

'Overseas stocks: CPF can be used from Jan.1', *The Sunday Times*, Singapore, 25/9/94.

'Pan-electric saga defies spirit and rules of disclosure', *The Straits Times*, 22/11/85, p.23.

'Pan-Electric shock sends market reeling' (Homer Chen), *Business Times*, 25/11/85, p.15.

'Peso continues to defy moves to stem its rise' (Reginald Chua), *Asian Wall Street Journal*, 14/11/94, p.1.

'PM Goh: S'pore to focus on financial services, IT' (Chuang Peck Ming), *Business Times*, 19/9/94, p.1.

'PM's fear: Siemens' move to China might be followed by other MNCs', *The Straits Times*, 9/11/94, p.1.

'Replace GDP with other yardsticks: NUS don', *The Straits Times*, 25/2/95, p.46.

'Rich housewives join the fray as forex trading gains favour' (Quak Hiang Whai), *Business Times*, 20/9/94, p.1

'Richard Hu's rearguard action', *Euromoney*, February 1995, pp.85–7.

'ROV collected record $3.4 billion revenue last year', *The Straits Times*, 5/8/94, p.1.

'Salaries of ministers, civil servants to go up on July 1' (Ven Sreenivasan), *Business Times*, 9/3/95, p.2.

'SES suspends all share trading', *Business Times*, 2/12/85.

'Sheer luck, says winner of economic forecast award' (Tan Kim Song), *The Straits Times*, 29/3/95, p.38.

'Siemens to spend $60m a year honing S'Pore plant' (Claire Low), *Business Times*, 10/11/94, p.1.

'Sing dollar, interest rates expected to rise this year' (Paul Leo), *Business Times*, 3/1/95, p.1.

'Sing dollar slips against greenback, dealers expect further softening' (Paul Leo), *Business Times*, 5/1/95, p.1.

'Sing dollar would have been stronger if not for MAS intervention: Dr Hu', *The Straits Times*, 9/11/92.

'Singapore' (*Financial Times* Survey), *Financial Times*, 1/6/92.

'Singapore' (*Financial Times* Survey), *Financial Times*, 24/2/95.

'Singapore aims to boost finance industry' (G. Pierre Goad), *Asian Wall Street Journal*, 28/9/94, pp.1, 27.

'Singapore dollar soars without hurting exports' (Jesse Wong), *The Asian Wall Street Journal*, 1/12/94, pp.1,24.

'Singapore dollar will extend rise next year, economists forecast' (Darren McDermott), *Asian Wall Street Journal*, 14/12/94, p.24.

'Singapore group plans to research digital media' (Reme Ahmad), *Asian Wall Street Journal*, 3/8/94, p.8.

'Singapore keeps tight hold on TV, radio' (G. Pierre Goad), *Asian Wall Street Journal*, 3/10/94, p.3.

'Singapore to grow its own multinationals, says PM Goh' (Chuang Peck Ming), *Business Times*, 25–6/3/95, p.1.

'Singapore unveils plans for performing arts centre' (G.Pierre Goad), *Asian Wall Street Journal*, 22/7/94, p.1.

'Singapore's big bang could unleash $80b of funds' (Catherine Ong), *Business Times*, 26/9/94, p.1.

'Singapore's Contradiction' (editorial), *Asian Wall Street Journal*, 2/3/95.

'Singapore's soldier scholars' (Tim Huxley), *Asian Wall Street Journal*, 24–5/2/95, p.6.

'Smuggling of cigarettes into S'Pore on the rise' (Dominic Nathan), *The Straits Times*, 29/7/91, p.1.

'Son of Lee Kuan Yew wins promotion' (G. Pierre Goad), *Asian Wall Street Journal*, 3/10/94, pp.1 and 4.

'S'pore economy to see slower growth, say NUS economists' (Tan Kim Song), *The Straits Times*, 25/2/95, p.48.

'S'pore first choice for US firms relocating from HK: Survey' (Lim Soon Neo), *Business Times*, 20/9/94, p. 2.

'S'pore govt takes 5.3% stake in US company', *The Straits Times*, 12/3/94, p.48.

'S'pore growth likely to slow to 7–8% next year: Dr Hu', *Business Times*, 22/11/94, p.1.

'S'pore investors sink $600m into unit trusts in 18 months' (Agnes Chen), *Business Times*, 22/7/94, p.1.

'S'pore is top Myanmar foreign investor with over 59 projects' (Abdul Hadhi), *Business Times*, 6/2/05, p.3.

'S'pore team in US to promote trade and investment' (Leon Hadar), *Business Times*, 2/3/95, p.9.

'Stat boards told to comply with new investment policy now' (Catherine Ong and Quak Hiang Whai), *Business Times*, 28/9/94, p.1.

'Survey: 44% of low-income workers have no savings', *The Straits Times*, 17/10/92.

'Switch to GNP to keep in touch with reality' (Chan Hwa Loon), *The Straits Times*, 14/2/94, p.32.

'The numbers game', *Business Times*, 14/7/93, p.25.

'Tough times rattle Singapore retailers' (Jeremy Mark), *Asian Wall Street Journal*, 20/2/95, pp.1,4.

'Two-thirds of US$1.1b earned pumped back into local operations' (Chuang Peck Ming), *Business Times*, 21/10/92, p.1.

'US firms to raise investment in S'pore to US$1.6b', *Business Times*, 3/11/94, p.1.

'US reaps US$1.7b profits from S'pore investments' (Chuang Peck Ming), *Business Times*, 10/10/94, p.1.

'What limits S'pore's growth?' (Warren Fernandez), *The Straits Times*, 4/3/95, p.34.

'*Wo guo haiwai zhijie touzi zongzhi zengzhi 130 yi yuan*', *Lianhe Zaobao*, 31/8/94, p.21.

ELECTRONIC INFORMATION AND DISCUSSION

We will refer to just two sites available on the world wide web at which one can find information about Singapore's economy. One is official and is known as *Singapore InfoMap* and is at http://www.sg. Information about many aspects of Singapore are there as well as reviews of various aspects of the economy and institutions. Its economic data do not seem to be updated very often. For instance, in mid-August 1995 the information about economic performance was still limited to what happened in 1993.

Another site is that of Singapore Press Holdings, the publisher of the main newspapers in Singapore (at http://www.asia1.com.sg). It allows one to see the *Business Times* on screen and apply to buy their company profiles on more than six hundred companies listed on the stock exchanges in Singapore and Malaysia, amongst other things.

Discussions about Singapore are to be found in the group: soc.culture.singapore, which covers all aspects of life in Singapore including the economic. BG (NS) George Yeo, Minister for Information and the Arts and Minister for Health, suggested that the youth wing of the PAP, Young PAP, start using this group to correct mistakes and express the Party's point of view. He referred to these people as 'our battalions' thus illustrating the PAP's way of thinking (*The Straits Times*, 27 February 1995, p.24). *The Straits Times* sometimes lifts parts of postings from threads it thinks will be of interest to its readers.

We hope that electronic forms of what is often called information will not replace books and newspapers. How could they?

Index

DATE DUE
